Case Studies
in
Christian Counseling

RESOURCES FOR
CHRISTIAN COUNSELING

RESOURCES FOR CHRISTIAN COUNSELING

1. Innovative Approaches to Counseling   *Gary R. Collins*
2. Counseling Christian Workers   *Louis McBurney*
3. Self-Talk, Imagery, and Prayer in Counseling
   H. Norman Wright
4. Counseling Those with Eating Disorders   *Raymond E. Vath*
5. Counseling the Depressed   *Archibald D. Hart*
6. Counseling for Family Violence and Abuse   *Grant L. Martin*
7. Counseling in Times of Crisis
   Judson J. Swihart and Gerald C. Richardson
8. Counseling and Guilt   *Earl D. Wilson*
9. Counseling and the Search for Meaning   *Paul R. Welter*
10. Counseling for Unplanned Pregnancy and Infertility
    Everett L. Worthington, Jr.
11. Counseling for Problems of Self-Control   *Richard P. Walters*
12. Counseling for Substance Abuse and Addiction
    Stephen Van Cleave, Walter Byrd, Kathy Revell
13. Counseling and Self-Esteem   *David E. Carlson*
14. Counseling Families   *George A. Rekers*
15. Counseling and Homosexuality   *Earl D. Wilson*
16. Counseling for Anger   *Mark P. Cosgrove*
17. Counseling and the Demonic   *Rodger K. Bufford*
18. Counseling and Divorce   *David A. Thompson*
19. Counseling and Marriage   *DeLoss D. and Ruby M. Friesen*
20. Counseling the Sick and Terminally Ill   *Gregg R. Albers*
21. Counseling Adult Children of Alcoholics   *Sandra D. Wilson*
22. Counseling and Children   *Warren Byrd and Paul Warren*
23. Counseling Before Marriage   *Everett L. Worthington, Jr.*
24. Counseling and AIDS   *Gregg R. Albers*
25. Counseling Families of Children with Disabilities
    Rosemarie S. Cook
26. Counseling for Sexual Disorders   *Joyce and Clifford Penner*
27. Cognitive Therapy Techniques in Christian Counseling
    Mark R. McMinn
28. Case Studies in Christian Counseling   *Gary R. Collins, editor*
29. Conflict Management and Counseling
    L. Randolph Lowry and Richard B. Meyers
30. Excellence and Ethics in Christian Counseling   *Gary R. Collins*

VOLUME TWENTY-EIGHT

Case Studies in Christian Counseling

GARY R. COLLINS, Ph.D., Editor

RESOURCES FOR CHRISTIAN COUNSELING

—————— General Editor ——————

Gary R. Collins, Ph.D.

WORD PUBLISHING

Dallas·London·Vancouver·Melbourne

Unless otherwise indicated, all Scripture quotations in this volume are from The New International Version, copyright © 1983 by the International Bible Society. Used by permission of Zondervan Bible Publishers.

Library of Congress Cataloging-in-Publication Data

Case studies in Christian counseling / Gary R. Collins, editor.
      p. cm. — (Resources for Christian counseling ; v. 28)
   Includes bibliographical references and index.
   ISBN 0-8499-0885-X
   1. Pastoral counseling. 2. Counseling. I. Collins, Gary R.
II. Series
BV4012.2.C29 1991
253.5—dc20
                                                  91-3643
                                                    CIP

Printed in the United States of America
1 2 3 4 5 6 7 8 9 AGF 9 8 7 6 5 4 3 2 1

CONTENTS

Editor's Preface   *vii*

1. What Is Christian Counseling? *Gary R. Collins*   1
2. A Case of Sexual Obsessions *Stanton L. Jones*   19
3. Cognitive Therapy with a Depressed Client
   Mark R. McMinn   45
4. Marriage Counseling with Christian Couples
   Everett L. Worthington, Jr.   72
5. Counseling Another Counselor *David E. Carlson*   100
6. The Use of Hypnotherapy in Counseling a Christian
   Robert R. King, Jr.   124
7. Counseling a Fundamentalist Family with a Son Who
   Has AIDS *James L. Powell*   164
8. An Inpatient Assessment with a Severely Depressed
   Hospitalized Patient *Robert S. McGee*   186
9. A Case of Ritualistic Abuse *Lois Motz*   209
10. Counseling for Panic Disorder with Agoraphobia
    Timothy E. Clinton   231

Epilogue   254
Bibliography   257
Notes   260
Index   269

EDITOR'S PREFACE

How did you get interested in counseling?

The answers to that question may be as varied as the readers of this book. Some of us may have started as counselees whose times of therapy encouraged us to become counselors ourselves. Others may have fallen into the field after our experiences as pastors, teachers, employers, parents, or friends found us face to face with people who were asking for help that we felt unqualified to give. Many of us began as students in high school or college who learned about counseling and selected this as a career. Probably there are some whose own unsolved problems have drawn them to this field where they seek to help others but, sometimes unconsciously, are looking for answers to the inner conflict in their own lives. A few, no doubt, have joined our ranks because some book or film has led them to conclude that counseling is a glamorous and lucrative profession. (In time, reality will hit and counseling will be seen as difficult and demanding work.) Others who read these words may be academics or curious readers who do little or no counseling but who sincerely want to understand this growing field. Probably most of us have a genuine concern for others and want to be compassionate people-helpers. For these and other reasons, we have become interested in counseling—a diverse, sometimes confusing but surprisingly effective conglomeration of theories, techniques, personalities, and problems.

Even professionals can read about counseling and become over-whelmed by the many approaches, seminars, journals, books, techniques, counseling goals, and guru leaders. For those of us who are Christians, understanding the field is even more challenging. In addition to the secular and professional complexities in counseling, we have our own Christian publications, training programs, theories, methodological approaches, trends, spokespersons, and differences of opinion. This has led our critics, many of whom are fellow believers, to criticize and condemn our efforts. The casual observer is left bewildered, floundering and wondering if there is any "right" or basic Christian approach to helping others.

The thirty volumes of Word's Resources for Christian Counseling series attempt to clarify issues and bring practical guidance, especially to those who identify as evangelical Christians. In this book and in the final volume of the series, *Excellence and Ethics in Christian Counseling*, we try to cut through some of the complexities, clarify the issues, and suggest directions for Christian counseling as we move toward the year 2000.

The following pages seek to answer the question, What is Christian counseling? In the first chapter, I discuss this directly; then we look at several examples of Christian people-helping, written by different practitioners who are counseling professionals. In the last chapter, I have attempted to pull together a brief concluding statement that I hope will launch you into reading the followup *Excellence and Ethics* book.

As many readers are aware, I have written an introduction to each of the Resources for Christian Counseling volumes. Many of us skip over introductions like this; so I have tried, each time, to write something unique and interesting. Even so, in all of the editor's prefaces, I have restated the purpose of this series of books.

From the beginning, we have tried to find authors who have a strong Christian commitment, impeccable counseling credentials, and extensive counseling experience. We have wanted each of the books to be practical and helpful examples of accurate psychology and careful use of Scripture. Each was intended to have a clear evangelical perspective, careful documentation, a strong practical orientation, and freedom from the sweeping statements that sometimes characterize writing in the counseling field. Our goal has been to provide books that would be clearly written, useful, up-to-date overviews of the issues faced by contemporary Christian counselors—including pastoral counselors. Our work on previous volumes has continued to be guided by these standards. As a result, we have seen the appearance of books that many counselors continue to consult on a regular basis. By now you are aware that all of the Resources for Christian Counseling books have similar bindings and together they comprise what we hope is a helpful encyclopedia of Christian counseling.

The following pages draw on the expertise of three RCC authors, David Carlson, Everett Worthington, and Mark McMinn; but we have gone beyond this and sought contributions from others who have not appeared before in this series. Some, like Stanton Jones and Robert McGee, are already established authors. Others are competent counselors whose first publication appears as a chapter in this book. I am excited about drawing both on established masters of the Christian counseling field and on newcomers whose names and contributions may become better known in the years ahead.

If you have not discovered this already, the following pages should convince you that ours is still a diverse and stimulating field. It pulsates with an excitement and challenge that will continue to attract and interest people of different backgrounds.

I hope this book will stimulate your thinking and sharpen your people-helping capabilities. Most important, I pray that these pages will give you a renewed awareness of the Christian counselor's responsibility to serve God and our fellow human beings, to help others in Christ-pleasing ways, to seek the daily guidance and wisdom that comes from the Holy Spirit, and ultimately to bring honor and glory to the Sovereign God of the universe.

Gary R. Collins, Ph.D.
Kildeer, Illinois

CHAPTER ONE

WHAT IS CHRISTIAN COUNSELING?

Gary R. Collins

THE CHAIRMAN OF A STATE PSYCHOLOGICAL association recently visited the campus of a Christian college and met with one of the psychology professors. Over lunch the visitor raised some pointed questions.

"What do you mean by Christian counseling?" he asked.

"Is this some type of one-to-one preaching that religious people call counseling?"

"Do these so-called Christian counselors have any training? Are they concerned about professional ethics? Do they know what they are doing? Is the term 'Christian counseling' really a cover for counselor incompetence?"

The questions were probing and at times tinged with a touch of anger. They were asked by a man who was committed to counseling excellence but suspicious about the capabilities of those who describe their counseling as Christian.

Most of us can understand the visitor's concerns. During its relatively short history, Christian counseling has grown into a diverse movement. Its numbers include highly skilled, professionally trained psychiatrists, psychologists, social workers, and others who seek to be competent practitioners committed to the highest ethical standards. But the words "Christian counseling" also describe the activities of well-meaning but untrained lay people, along with dedicated but struggling pastors who freely admit that their one seminary counseling course could never equip them to deal with the pressing problems in their congregations. In addition, Christian counselors include the self-appointed Christian critics of professional counseling who condemn others even as they flaunt their own untested brands of people-helping. Scattered throughout the country are a host of Christian counseling centers and treatment facilities with staff members who range from top-quality therapists to rank incompetents. Books, articles, and seminars related to Christian counseling show the same range in quality and expertise.

Of course it is true that an equal—perhaps even greater—diversity exists among secular counselors. There seem to be many ill-equipped, ineffective, sometimes marginally unstable individuals who practice as therapists, write books, and conduct seminars or radio talk shows. But the presence of these people in our communities does not excuse incompetence among Christian counselors; neither does it prevent us from defining and articulating what we seek to do that is unique.

A few counselors and writers have attempted to develop definitive, biblically based approaches to Christian counseling; others have started with secular theories and have proposed "Christianized versions" of psychoanalysis, behavior modification, cognitive therapy, transactional analysis, reality therapy, client-centered counseling, rational-emotive therapy, multimodal therapy, Egan's problem-management approach, and other therapeutic systems.[1] A few Christian counselors have attempted to validate their approaches with biblical and/or empirical research; most have relied on personal experiences to "prove" the effectiveness of their methods. It is sad that many have ignored or resisted any efforts to test the real value of their theories and techniques. Several Christian approaches and their developers have attracted bands of enthusiastic followers; most others have had little widespread acceptance or application.

In describing his own profession, William P. Wilson has written that "Christians in the field of psychiatry seem as fragmented in what we believe and practice as our non-Christian colleagues."[2] The field of

Christian counseling is diverse and complicated. It is populated by counselors and writers who may be sincere, compassionate people but whose personalities, theologies, psychological orientations, values, and personal experiences have led to a variety of sometimes-clashing counseling goals, assumptions, theories, and techniques, all of which are labeled "Christian."

It could be argued that such complexity is a sign of healthy debate in a growing field, but the diversity also has potential for distracting counselors, harming counselees, confusing onlookers, and fueling the minds of critics. It may be true that secular approaches to counseling are even more diversified and sometimes confused, but many of us would like to see greater unity and greater evidence of effectiveness among those who claim to be Christian people-helpers. Like the campus visitor mentioned earlier, we would like to have a working definition of Christian counseling and an awareness of its unique features.

A number of psychologists, counselors, and therapists[3] have attempted to define Christian counseling. Most of these definitions have come from evangelical Protestant Christians who hold traditional values, seek to live and counsel in ways that are consistent with biblical teachings, want to maintain professional competence and respect, and are deeply interested in the integration of psychology and Christian theology. This does not describe a small and scattered group. The integration movement among Christian counselors and other professionals is growing at a rapid rate, as evidenced by the professional organizations, training programs, publications, Christian residential treatment programs, and well-attended Christian counseling congresses that have sprung up within the past decade.[4] Books by Ray Anderson, David Benner, Roger Hurding, Georgina Rodiger, Darrell Smith, Samuel Southard, and Everett Worthington, among others,[5] all show that Christian counseling, despite its weaknesses, is emerging as a significant field with increasing numbers of capable, proficient, effective committed Christian practitioners.

DEFINING CHRISTIAN COUNSELING

Writing in the *Christian Medical Society Journal,* psychiatrist Alan Nelson maintained that "there is indeed such a thing as 'Christian psychiatry' and . . . it can represent a unique and satisfying method of practicing psychiatry."[6] Psychologist David Benner would agree. While recognizing differences in the field, including the "often unclear line of differentiation between pastoral counseling and other forms of Christian therapy," Benner concludes that Christian therapy is "an approach to therapy offered by a Christian who bases his or her understanding of persons on the Bible and allows this understanding to shape all aspects of therapy and practice. This suggests an ongoing process rather than a finished product." According to Benner, Christian therapists do not all practice the same brand of therapy, but they all see themselves in God's service. Their primary allegiance and accountability is to God, and only secondarily to their profession or discipline.[7]

Writing from a pastoral-care perspective, William Clebsch and Charles Jaekle give a more specific definition of Christian people-helping:

> The ministry of the cure of souls, or pastoral care, consists of helping acts, done by *representative* Christian *persons*, directed toward the *healing, sustaining, guiding,* and *reconciling of troubled persons* whose troubles arise *in the context of ultimate meanings and concerns.*[8]

Attempts to define or describe Christian counseling tend to emphasize the *person* who does the helping, the *techniques* or skills that are used, and the *goals* that counseling seeks to reach. From this perspective the Christian counselor is:

- a deeply committed, Spirit-guided (and Spirit-filled) servant of Jesus Christ
- who applies his or her God-given abilities, skills, training, knowledge, and insights
- to the task of helping others move to personal wholeness, interpersonal competence, mental stability, and spiritual maturity.

Christian counselors are committed believers, doing their best to help others, with the help of God. Such a definition includes believers who come from different theological perspectives, use different approaches to counseling, and have different levels of training and experience.

It is unlikely that we will ever have one "true" Christian approach to counseling, any more than we can hope for one generally accepted approach to homiletics, church government, evangelism, or eschatology. In fields such as evangelism, preaching, Christian education, and counseling, the diversity of opinions and approaches probably is good. People are different, and we reach and help them in different ways. No one approach to counseling speaks to every problem and benefits every person. Jesus used different approaches with different people; counselors today do the same. But no one of us can help everyone like Jesus could. Our unique personalities let each of us be helpful to some people but not to others. Therefore, Christian counseling will continue to be a diversified field with diverse viewpoints and a variety of practitioners and approaches. The following chapters illustrate this clearly.

For all of us, however, to be Christian counselors we must begin with a commitment to Jesus Christ and must build our theoretical approaches on solid biblical grounds. We must encourage and challenge each other to evaluate our methods, conclusions, and assumptions . We must maintain a firm commitment to the best levels of training and the use of time-tested, established counseling techniques. But we also must accept the fact of individual differences and avoid petty arguments and criticisms, especially those that are based on personal biases, the desire to build up one theorist or writer, and/or an apparent need to prove that someone else is wrong. We never build up the body of Christ by tearing down one another. Of all people, counselors should be most aware of this.

With this background, let us consider some distinctives of Christian counseling. We will begin with the assumptions or presuppositions that form the basis of our work. Then, in accordance with the definition, we will consider the individual counselor, the procedures used, and the purposes or goals that Christian counselors seek to accomplish.[9]

PRESUPPOSITIONS IN CHRISTIAN COUNSELING

For most of this century there has been debate about the role of values in counseling. It is well known that Freud opposed any imposition of therapist values or beliefs on the client. Later theorists and researchers argued, however, that value neutrality in counseling is impossible: Even if we try to remain unbiased, therapists will inadvertently communicate their values to clients who, in turn, will be influenced by the counselors' belief systems.[10] Some counselors have proposed that we cannot be totally fair and ethical unless we let counselees know our values and beliefs before therapy begins. By calling ourselves "Christian counselors" we signal something about our perspectives. Whether or not that makes a difference to perspective counselees is still debated.[11]

A number of Christian counselors go beyond this debate and propose that followers of Jesus Christ have a responsibility to share Christian values and truths with counselees. "It is impossible to dispel the despairs of meaning, morality, or death if we do not evangelize," writes psychiatrist William Wilson. "We as Christians have been deputized to pass on the forgiveness of God to repentant men and women. This is not something that secular psychiatrists can do. They do not have the authority. What a difference we can make in the lives of our patients by forgiving them and helping them forgive others."[12]

The sensitive therapist does not impose his or her beliefs and values on the counselee in an insensitive or bombastic manner—any more than one seeks to force another to become a Christian. Counselees, like potential converts, must be respected and allowed to make their own choices. But it is difficult to believe in the Great Commission (Matt. 28:16–20) and then forget or ignore scriptural directives when we enter the counseling room. As you will see in the chapters that follow, however, there are different levels of value-sharing even in Christian counseling as practiced by competent professionals.

In an earlier book it was argued that every psychological or counseling system begins with underlying presuppositions or assumptions.[13] These presuppositions influence counseling whether or not the counselor is aware of them. Evangelical Christians for example, generally accept the following presuppositions which influence our perceptions of people and our goals and methods.

Concerning *God*, Christians believe in his existence, sovereignty, omniscience, omnipresence, and omnipotence. He exists eternally, without beginning or end (Ps. 90:2) and as a unity of three separate but co-equal persons—Father, Son, and Holy Spirit. He is intimately acquainted with each person in the world. Secular counseling says little about God and usually assumes that he is nonexistent, uninvolved, and/ or unconcerned about human affairs.

Concerning *the universe*, Christians believe that God created the universe (including its human inhabitants) through the Son, holds it all together, and is aware of all events and human affairs (Heb. 1:2, 3; 4:13).

Concerning *humans*, Christians believe that we were created in the divine image, and endowed "in finite proportions, with his attributes of intelligence, power, volition, creativeness, nobility, dignity, freedom, immortality, capacity for transcendence, moral goodness, capacity for communion and fellowship, and personhood."[14] Humans were endowed with freedom of choice and the capacity to depart from God's will. We fell into rebelliousness and thus are sinners who need a Savior, Jesus Christ, God's son, who came to earth in the form of a man, died for sinful human beings, rose from the dead, and makes salvation (the new birth) available for all who believe in him. For such believers there is promise of life eternal after death. Secular counseling, in contrast, says nothing about salvation, our ultimate destiny, or our relationships with God. Christians believe that we are valuable creatures who are loved by the Creator. Most secular counselors also assume that humans have value, but many would agree with Fromm that we are "alone in a universe indifferent to our fate."

Concerning *epistemology*, Christians believe that the Holy Spirit teaches and guides, especially through the pages of God's Word, the Bible, our infallible guide of faith and conduct. We also learn through such means as intellectual activities, interaction between people, and empirical research, although all of this must be tested against the unchanging truths of Scripture. The secular counselor dismisses the Bible's supernatural relevance and proclaims the superiority of science; but he or she has no basis other than subjective experience for making ultimate decisions.

Concerning *death*, Christians believe that the human spirit or soul continues to exist, even after the physical body has disintegrated and "returned to dust." The Christian believes that accepting God's offer of salvation leads to eternal life in the presence of God. Those who ignore or reject God's salvation are destined to spend eternity in physical and spiritual separation from God. As Smith has noted, "death phenomena . . . have powerful relevance to counseling and psychotherapy. Few topics warrant as much attention as death and dying. Yet most systems of psychology and psychotherapy have tended to omit discussion of these issues."[15]

Concerning *pathology*, most evangelical Christians agree that problems arise ultimately from sin in the human race and at times from sin in the counselee's own life. Christian counselors differ, however, in the extent to which we believe that individual sin in the counselee's life may cause problems. We also differ in our views of the relative importance of individual responsibility and environmental influences as causes for problems. Non-Christian counselors often debate the "responsibility-environmental causation" issue, and occasionally the secular literature mentions sin; but almost no one accepts the concept of sin as rebellion against God and as an important cause of pathology.

7

Although these and other assumptions distinguish Christian counseling from non-Christian approaches, it should not be assumed that all Christians have similar beliefs about God, the universe, human nature, epistemology, death, or pathology. Among those who call themselves Christian, there are different viewpoints. Even as counseling theorists have different philosophical presuppositions about human nature and behavior change, so Christian counselors have differences that depend largely on their theological viewpoints. These theological differences may rarely be acknowledged, but they surely affect counseling. Several years ago, for example, when Jay Adams and Paul Tournier were both widely read writers in the field of counseling, it was clear that both were Christians and both were Calvinists. Both agreed that humans are sinful and that Jesus Christ alone is our Savior. Tournier, however, was a universalist who believed that everyone would be saved; Adams, in contrast, wrote that "as a reformed Christian, the writer believes that counselors must not tell any unsaved counselee that Christ died for him, for they cannot say that. No man knows except Christ himself who are his elect for whom he died."[16] Theological differences such as these surely influence what the counselor says or does in counseling and account for some of the differences that exist even among evangelical Christians.[17]

Persons in Christian Counseling

Several decades ago, psychologist Carl Rogers wrote that therapist genuineness, empathy, and unconditional positive regard for others are both necessary and sufficient conditions for effective counseling.[18] Empirical studies confirmed that personal traits such as these were necessary for therapeutic effectiveness; but few counselors today would agree that counselor characteristics alone are sufficient to bring change in counselees. Even Jay Adams, whose counseling perspective differs from that of many other Christians, writes that good intentions (and presumably good character) can be no substitute for skill, knowledge, and understanding of the counseling process.[19]

Most counselors understand the importance of therapeutic techniques, processes, and goals, but we also recognize that counseling, at its core, involves human beings. When counselors are struggling with their own anxieties, insecurities, or unresolved conflicts, it is unlikely that they can be of maximum effectiveness in helping others. This is one reason why many counselor-training programs require students to get counseling for themselves before they get their diplomas. When they are relatively free of debilitating problems and have "human qualities" such as sensitivity, honesty, patience, compassion, trustworthiness, and confidence in their own abilities, skilled counselors are more likely to be effective in their work. Following a review of recent research on therapist characteristics, one writer concluded:

> These findings suggest that the therapist most likely to achieve positive outcome is active, optimistic, expressive, straightforward yet supportive, involved, and in charge of the therapeutic process but also able to encourage client responsibility. Not surprisingly, research has also suggested that therapists who are themselves psychologically healthy are more likely to promote health in their clients.[20]

Writing about Christian counseling, Ray Anderson presents the thesis that "before there can be competence in counseling, we must understand competence in being human, in living humanly, openly, and lovingly with others and with God."[21] This competence in being human involves more than "getting our own act together." According to Anderson, the effective therapist needs to experience "effective living" in a number of areas. For example, he or she has good self-esteem, is comfortable with his or her sexuality, is "glad to be living in this world, even with all its limitations and frustrations," is trustworthy and able to express feelings and actions openly toward others while retaining a strong sense of personal identity. Effective living also involves a healthy orientation toward God. Life may involve loss, hurt, and tragedy, but effective people believe that God is faithful, loving, and forgiving, even when our minds don't understand.

Ultimately, according to Anderson, counselors should seek to develop these areas of competence in their counselees as well as in themselves. Certainly no counselor, Christian or nonbeliever, is perfect, totally stable, or completely free of insecurities and personal struggles. But the effective people-helper is not bogged down with debilitating personal, interpersonal, or spiritual burdens. In contrast, he or she is growing in all three areas and is committed to helping counselees grow as well.

Within recent years there has been renewed interest among therapists in the topic of spirituality.[22] "Spirituality," however, tends to be vaguely defined and seems to mean something similar to values, "ultimate questions," the meaning of existence, or "connecting with something beyond ourselves." Almost never do the standard counseling journals refer to one's relationship with Jesus Christ, to divine forgiveness, grace, or discipleship. These are topics that interest believers. They are spirituality issues that concern many counselees, that often help people cope with the pressures of life, and that frequently are brought into the counseling room.

The Christian counselor seeks to understand and help others deal with these spiritual-theological issues. To be ultimately effective, the Christian counselor must be a follower of Jesus Christ, who participates in corporate and personal worship, consistently spends time in prayer and other disciplines that contribute to spiritual growth, seeks to be guided by the Holy Spirit, and is committed to showing the love of Christ that is the mark of all genuine followers of Jesus (John 13:34, 35).

This is not a description of the typical Christian counselor; it is an ideal toward which we strive. This is not an exhaustive list of Christian counselor traits, and neither is it a list that all Christian therapists would feel comfortable accepting. But surely most would agree that to be effective as Christian people-helpers we must be sensitive to and personally growing in our relationships with Jesus Christ

THE PROCEDURES OF CHRISTIAN COUNSELING

Someone has suggested that all therapeutic techniques have at least four common attributes. They seek to arouse the belief that help is possible, to correct erroneous conclusions about the world, to develop competencies in dealing with interpersonal living, and to help counselees accept themselves as persons of worth. To accomplish these ends, counselors consistently use such basic techniques as listening, demonstrating interest, attempting to understand, and at least occasionally giving direction. Most Christian counselors would have no problem with these four "attributes," and most use the basic techniques that characterize all counseling. Probably most professional counselors also would agree with Nelson's strong statement about Christian psychiatry:

The therapist may use whatever technique or school of thought he or she is comfortable with (i.e., Gestalt, cognitive, behavioral, analytic, or as is more often the case, a combination of the above). Good psychiatry can make use of all of these . . . [but] it must be stressed that there is simply no substitute for excellent clinical skills. If one attempts to practice any form of psychiatry, including Christian psychiatry, and is a poor clinician, that person will not only be embarrassed, but also will be a poor witness to colleagues. Once a good working knowledge of the patient and understanding of the dynamics of the pathology has been gained, the psychotherapist seeks to alleviate the conflict in the system that needs restoration, whether this be in the biological, psychological, social, or spiritual realm.[23]

At present, we can only speculate why counselors choose and use some techniques rather than others. Probably our training, mentors, personalities, values, philosophical and theoretical orientations, and client needs all influence the methods we use. Sometimes we try out methods that are presented at seminars or described in counseling books and articles. At times we may be influenced by the enthusiastic rhetoric of those who advocate different school of therapy, but most counselors know that research does little to back the claims that any one system is superior over all others.[24] In practice most of us probably are guided by pragmatics: If a technique seems to "work" it is used, often repeatedly, providing that no one is harmed physically or in other ways.

With the availability of thousands of techniques, each of us is inclined to use the methods with which we feel most familiar and most comfortable. But this is no excuse for a sloppy, haphazard selection of techniques. The effective counselor, Christian and nonbeliever alike, seeks to select methods carefully and to use those means that advance his or her counseling goals. Random eclecticism—taking bits and pieces from here and there—is poor procedure both when we choose theory and when we select methods.

Like all counselors, the Christian uses techniques that are widely respected in the profession and known to be effective, but he or she also must be guided by an additional, higher standard. In our counseling work, as in our lives, we seek to follow these biblical words: "Whatever you do, work at it with all your heart, as working for the Lord, not for men . . . . It is the Lord Christ you are serving" (Col. 3:23, 24). In all we do, we seek to please and bring glory to God (1 Cor. 10:31). Many of us see counseling as our area of service, a field of service as valid, needed, and potentially Christ-honoring as any other type of ministry. Christian counselors are dedicated to excellence in this work. We seek to use methods that are consistent with the teachings of what we believe to be God's Word, the Bible. Many among us also seek to test our techniques against the centuries-old conclusions of Christian theology.

In practice, it probably is true that many Christian counselors give little thought to whether their techniques are consistent with biblical teachings. This reality in no way excuses or undermines the Christian counselor's obligation to do his or her work in ways that, so far as we can tell, are consistent with the will and Word of God. Whatever their work, dedicated Christians seek to bring pleasure and honor to God. In practice, the Christian people-helper: (a) accepts and uses many standard counseling techniques, (b) refuses on moral, biblical, and theological grounds to use some techniques that may be used by some secular counselors, and (c) may use some techniques that secular counselors would avoid. Since we have already acknowledged the first of these conclusions, let us consider the other two.

The Christian counselor cannot condone or use any methods that might be considered morally wrong and contrary to biblical values. Most of us would agree, for example, that we should avoid the use of sexual surrogate partners, the encouragement or endorsement of extramarital or premarital sexual intercourse, the use of pornographic materials in treatment, the use of abusive or vulgar language, the encouragement of genital homosexual behavior, or encouraging any other antibiblical activities, sinful behaviors, and values.[25] The Christian counselor must seek to be Christlike in his or her speech and actions, avoiding the appearance of impropriety or evil, even if the use of some theologically questionable techniques might seem likely to help the counselee. Like Timothy of old, Christian counselors must be exemplary believers in our "speech, in life, in love, in faith and in purity" (1 Tim. 4:12). One can never assume that the end justifies the means in counseling. The "means" or techniques must be consistent with biblical teaching.

Recently strong disagreements have arisen among Christians concerning whether certain techniques are consistent with biblical teaching. Some authors have written hard-hitting, anger-filled books condemning Christians who use such controversial techniques as hypnosis, visualization, self-talk, imagery, or even counseling. Many of the criticisms are valid, although few are as new as the book writers seem to imply. Sincere followers of Jesus Christ do want to exercise great care in the techniques that are used. We do seek to be guided by the Holy Spirit in our work, and we are sensitive to the issues that our critics have raised. We have chosen, however, to avoid public debates with these critics or to divide the church by destructive name calling. Many of us, critics as well as counselors, have met together and discussed our differences in the spirit of Matthew 18:15–17. When this kind of interaction occurs in place of personal attacks, we are able to understand and appreciate the perspectives of our fellow believers, even though we may choose to disagree—like sincere Christians have disagreed for centuries.[26]

In contrast to techniques that tend to be avoided by Christians, other methods are distinctively Christian and used in Christian counseling at least occasionally. Some of these techniques would raise little objection among secular counselors; others are more controversial, even among believers. In the following list, which is not meant to be complete, the more controversial techniques are cited toward the end, but all may be used by at least some Christian therapists. Religiously oriented techniques include:

- private prayer for counselees by the counselor, without the counselee present;
- encouraging counselees to become involved in a local church, in other supportive Christian groups (including Christian self-help and Christian therapy groups),[27] in reading helpful books by Christian writers and/or in reading the Bible;
- praying with patients;
- summarizing and/or reading Bible passages that pertain to the counselee's problems;
- sharing the biblical message of forgiveness, seeking to lead counselees to Christ and, eventually, to growth as disciples;
- the use of Christian inner-healing or the healing of memories;[28]
- healing, often in the spirit of James 5:16 and accompanied by group support and caring; and
- deliverance, exorcism, or other attempts to deal directly with satanic forces.

Like many specialized therapeutic techniques, any of these can be taken to the extreme. References to the Bible can be used to pressure and browbeat clients. The healing of memories can overemphasize the past but ignore pressing issues in the present. Healing and deliverance can be set in opposition to competent counseling and medical treatment. Counselees can be blamed for a "lack of faith" when the religious methods fail to work. Such extremes are considered unethical and are carefully avoided by competent Christian counselors.

When extremes are avoided, are Christian techniques superior to the methods used by our secular colleagues? It appears that many believers, both counselors and counselees, feel more at ease when such methods are used, but research evidence thus far (it is minimal) does not support the superiority of these techniques or more traditional methods. Following a significant review of the literature in Christian and other religious counseling, Everett Worthington (who is both a competent professional counselor-researcher and a committed evangelical Christian) concluded that religious counseling techniques "did not differ in effectiveness from the same techniques used without religious content. Comparisons on other dimensions such as client satisfaction, number of premature terminations, rapidity and depth of therapeutic alliance, and willingness to refer to the therapist have not been made."[29]

Conclusions such as these raise a dilemma for Christian counselors. Most of us recognize the value of research methods and are willing to submit our work to empirical investigation. At the same time, we realize that empiricism is not the only way and often is not the best way to determine what is true. The effectiveness of prayer, the guidance of the Holy Spirit, the inner peace that comes from Christ (John 14:27; Phil. 4:6, 7), the sense of hope and freedom that come from accepting God's grace and forgiveness, the power of the Scriptures to guide—these are among those issues that are difficult, if not impossible, to investigate scientifically.[30] Christian counselors value the scientific method, but most of us recognize that God's truth as found in the Bible often cannot be made to fit into the scientific method or validated empirically. This does not give us an excuse to ignore research reports, especially when they do not support our beliefs. But we recognize that empirical outcome is not the only measure of a technique's validity.

THE PURPOSE OF CHRISTIAN COUNSELING

Counseling books often include similar lists of counseling goals: to help counselees change behavior, attitudes, values, and/or perceptions; to teach skills, including social, interpersonal and communication skills; to encourage the recognition and expression of emotion; to give support in times of need; to teach responsibility; to instill insights; to face emotional trauma and scars from the past; to guide as decisions are made; to clear away misconceptions about oneself, other people, therapy, Christianity or any additional area of misperception; to help counselees mobilize inner and environmental resources in times of crisis; to teach problem-solving methods; and to increase counselee competence and self-awareness . . . among others.

Christian counselors might be involved in helping counselees pursue any of these goals, but do we also have unique purposes because we are followers of Jesus Christ? Does the Christian counselor seek to:

- present the gospel message and encourage counselees to commit their lives to Jesus Christ?
- stimulate spiritual growth?
- encourage counselees to confess sin and to experience divine forgiveness?
- model Christian standards, attitudes, and lifestyle?
- stimulate counselees to develop values and to live lives that are based on biblical teaching, instead of living in accordance with relativistic humanistic standards?

The Christian who makes these issues a part of counseling is in danger of being criticized for not respecting counselee values, violating ethical principles, or bringing religion into counseling. These can be valid criticisms, especially when the Christian works with nonbelievers. Clients have come for therapy and not for evangelism. Both avoiding manipulation and treating others with respect are foundational to effective counseling. Apparently many Christian counselors choose to keep their beliefs hidden behind a professional facade, choosing to say nothing about religion unless the client raises the issue.[31]

If Christians ignore such theological issues, however, they build counseling on the religion of humanistic naturalism, stifle their own beliefs, and compartmentalize life into the sacred and secular. If we are convinced that belief in Jesus Christ makes a difference both now and for eternity, is it right, before God, to withhold such information? If we see counselees engaging in immoral behavior or reaching conclusions that are clearly inconsistent with biblical teaching aren't we being hypocritical, harmful, and cowardly if we watch the struggles and say nothing about Christ? If we claim to be Christian counselors are we being unethical (and perhaps cowardly) if we never mention Christ or

Christian issues during our counseling? Albert Ellis has no hesitation proclaiming his brand of humanism. Professional conventions and journals are increasingly introducing new age and eastern religious concepts into therapy. Do we watch these developments in silence and say nothing about Christian teachings—primarily because our professions are so intolerant of anything Christian?

Much depends on how Christian concepts are introduced in therapy. Nobody would propose that we pressure, indoctrinate, or intimidate clients into considering Christian teachings and values. But Christian counselors have every right to present the Word of God, gently and lovingly spoken, guided by the Holy Spirit in his timing, and by therapists whose lives reflect the indwelling presence of Christ. Like the rich young ruler who walked away from Jesus (Matt. 19:16–30), our clients may reject the message and we should not force them to do otherwise. But neither does the committed Christian counselor keep his or her beliefs hidden under a bushel where they are never seen and never allowed to make an impact.

In their standard textbook of counseling ethics, Gerald Corey and his colleagues conclude that it is "neither possible nor desirable for counselors to be scrupulously neutral with respect to values in the counseling relationship." Counseling is not indoctrination, according to these authors; but since counselor values do influence therapy, "it is important for counselors to be willing to express their values openly when they are relevant to the questions that come up in their sessions with clients."[32] Committed people, including those who are not believers, have values that are unlikely to remain hidden. Our most cherished values permeate our lives and influence almost everything we do.

Christian counselors recognize the importance of Christian values and of a personal and growing relationship with Jesus Christ. No person is forced to accept Christian ways of thinking, but the counselor is constantly aware of the spiritual needs of his or her counselees. One purpose of Christian counseling is to deal, at least briefly, with these spiritual issues.

DIVERSITY IN CHRISTIAN COUNSELING

It will not take long for you to discover that the following chapters are diverse. In part this is by design; in part the diversity came about spontaneously.

To assemble the following chapters, I wrote a letter of invitation to about twenty professional counselors. I tried to find people from different theological and professional backgrounds. I wanted people who clearly identified themselves as evangelical Christians, who were experienced counselors, and who were trained at a professional level. I approached both men and women, psychologists and non-psychologists, those who had written about counseling and those who had not. I did not try to find counselors to fit previously specified theoretical orientations, and I allowed each contributor to choose his or her case and type of problem. About half of the people I approached were unable to complete a chapter by the deadline, and in a couple of cases I gently said no to prospective writers whose cases tended to show overlap with what follows. The chapters are listed in no particular order of importance, value, or interest and they need not be read in sequence. Each begins with an introduction about the case and the counselor.

To guide your reading you might want to consider questions such as the following as you go through each chapter. Consider discussing these and similar issues with your counseling or student colleagues.

- What qualifies this case to be known as an example of Christian counseling?
- In what ways is this case uniquely Christian? In what ways is it no different from more secular counseling?
- Does the counselor use any methods that you would consider to be unethical, of questionable validity or inconsistent with biblical and/ or theological teaching?
- If you were the therapist, in what ways would you have approached the case differently?
- In what ways, if any, have you learned to be a more effective Christian counselor as a result of having read this case?
- How has this case encouraged (or discouraged) you in your own growth as a Christian counselor?

Whether or not you decide to read the following chapters in sequence, it may be helpful to have an overview of the cases to be presented. As you no doubt will expect, all of the names and details in these cases have been changed to maintain confidentiality, although the counselees themselves have given permission to have their cases included in the book. The therapists' names, of course, are the real thing!

The first case to be presented, in chapter 2, involves a professional man in his mid-thirties who has problems with sexual obsessions. The counselor, Dr. Stanton L. Jones, is on the faculty of the Wheaton College Graduate School in Illinois.

Dr. Mark McMinn, who teaches at George Fox College in Oregon, illustrates a Christian approach to cognitive therapy in his case study of therapy with a twenty-four-year-old depressed youth pastor.

Dr. Everett L. Worthington, Jr., teaches at Virginia Commonwealth University and has authored several books on marriage and the family. He presents a Christian approach to marriage counseling in a case that appears as chapter 4.

David Carlson, who is director of Arlington Counseling Associates in Illinois and whose training includes advanced study in theology, social work, and marriage-family therapy, presents a study of infidelity. The case, in chapter 5, has an interesting twist in that the counselee also is trained and employed as a professional therapist.

Chapter 6 is written by Dr. Robert R. King, Jr., executive director of CAPS, the Christian Association for Psychological Studies. Dr. King lives in California and has presented a case in which hypnotherapy is used, among other techniques, in treating a deeply depressed woman who appeared to have multiple problems.

Dr. James L. Powell is director of the Psychological Studies Institute in Atlanta. His case, presented in chapter 7, deals with a fundamentalist family whose son has AIDS.

Dr. Robert McGee, president of Rapha, an organization with headquarters in Houston, gives an example—in chapter 8—of inpatient treatment with a resident of a psychiatric hospital unit.

In chapter 9, Lois Motz, who counsels in Illinois and has training in both nursing and professional psychology, describes a case of Christian counseling with a young man who, many years prior to therapy, had been ritualistically abused by Satan worshipers.

The last case deals with a male who has a panic disorder. This is presented by Dr. Timothy E. Clinton, who works at Light Associates Counseling Center in Virginia and is associate dean and chairman of the counseling program at Liberty University School of Life Long Learning.

CHAPTER TWO

A CASE OF SEXUAL OBSESSIONS

Stanton L. Jones

Editor's note: *Christian counseling may be long term or very brief, depending in part on the therapist and on the client's problem. In this case, Dr. Jones worked with his client for many months and used a variety of techniques. As so often happens, the counselor and counselee both learned about counseling as they met together. Because of its length, much of the case is summarized instead of being presented in dialogue form.*

Stanton L. Jones is a native of Texas whose B.A. degree is from Texas A & M University. He earned his Ph.D. from Arizona State University and took his psychological internship at University of Mississippi Medical Center in Jackson. Currently he is associate professor of psychology and chairman of the psychology department at Wheaton College in Illinois. He is a registered clinical psychologist who organized and chaired

19

the 1990 Rech Conference on Christian Graduate Training in Psychology. He has edited Psychology and the Christian Faith: An Introductory Reader *(published by Baker) and with Dr. Richard Butman has co-authored* Modern Psychotherapies: A Comprehensive Christian Appraisal *(published in 1991 by InterVarsity).*

───────────

*An evil thought is made weak at the very second
it is manifested to another person;
Evil thoughts can dominate us only as long
as they are hidden in our hearts.*
—John Cassian,
quoted in a paper by T. Oden[1]

"I LIVE WITH CONSTANT FEAR. When will I lose control and do what I am terrified of and repulsed by? I worry that I will be lured into homosexual sin. I worry that I might assault a woman at work. I even worry that I will try to have sex with an animal! I am afraid that my wife will get pregnant because I have no assurance that I won't do something horrible to her or sexually molest my own child! I love my wife, I am able to function at work, and I enjoy my friends; but this constant fear is destroying me! I'm rarely free of any fear; usually it is there in the background like a headache, but sometimes it overwhelms me. Nights are the worst—I often sleep only three or four hours because I agonize over when it will happen, when I will lose control and do something repulsive and disgusting, and thus ruin my life and the life of my wife, and disgrace God as well. I am terrified to sleep because I might dream, and my dreams might show just how sick I truly am."[2]

When he came to see me, Carl was in his mid-twenties and receiving excellent feedback in his functioning as a young manager in a professional organization. He had been married for four years when he was referred to me. He was a young man whose faith in Christ was quite evident. Yet he was in agony about the fears and uncertainties of his life.

Carl was referred to me by a psychoanalytically oriented practitioner who had supervised fifteen sessions of prior therapy with Carl; that therapy was conducted by an associate therapist working with the analytic practitioner. Therapy had seemed to provide some temporary relief for Carl, but no basic change had occurred. The temporary relief seemed to have been effected by the reassurance given by the therapist and the relief engendered by Carl's confession of his fears and unacceptable impulses to another person. The analytic practitioner spoke of Carl's insecurity about his sexual identity and his difficulties with impulse control. The referral was apparently made because the associate therapist felt she did not possess the critical skills for helping Carl progress further. Carl had previously seen two other psychotherapists; those earlier experiences had also provided temporary relief but with little lasting change.

Summary of the Approach to Counseling

Integration of Christian faith with a discipline such as clinical psychology begins with a fundamental commitment to the Christian faith as the foundation for all understanding and living.[3] Contrary to the opinions of the Christian "psychology-bashers" today, it seems clear that neither Scripture nor the Christian pastoral tradition tells us all that can or needs to be known to understand and heal the incredible diversity of human problems in living. Christian faith informs, anchors, and undergirds all of our thinking, but does not exhaust it. Thus it is valid to draw upon systems of psychological thought to broaden our understanding. In doing so, we have a responsibility both to reflect upon and correct these secular systems of thought wherever they conflict with clear Christian belief. Carl's concerns are a good case example where the person suffering has already done what the Scriptures clearly suggest, but to no avail.

I use the cognitive-behavioral (CB) approach as my primary psychological orientation because it was the model I was trained in and because of its strengths. I recognize the many conceptual and practical limitations of the approach from a Christian as well as nonsectarian perspective, as I will summarize below. I have come to utilize psychological methods other than the traditional cognitive-behavioral and do not view my clients strictly from within this view. In my work with Carl, elements of the person-centered, existential, and even psychodynamic traditions can be detected. Further, with a client's consent I draw explicitly upon my understanding of the Scriptures, pastoral care, and my own faith experience to guide the process of therapy. These guide me even in working with a non-Christian, though I may not be free to be as explicit about this. I would thus consider myself a "theoretical integrationist" in my commitment to starting with a Christian foundation and willingness to move beyond the CB model to use other methods.[4]

As the reader will see below, Carl's concerns pushed me well beyond the comfortable confines of the CB model, toward treatment I would truly characterize as eclectic. Carl came to me when I was a fairly young practitioner, and he taught me much about my own limitations as well as those of the CB model. At the time I worked with him, 1 did not feel truly comfortable with any approach other than that of CB therapy, so I began my work viewing Carl's concerns in an almost exclusively CB fashion. Responding to his concerns, however, I was pushed further and further beyond that model. I will report the case in this fashion; thus the report will read more "behaviorally" at the first than at the last.

The CB tradition of psychotherapy sees problems of living as being the result of unfortunate learning experiences which result in the pain and suffering of the client. It is an approach which attempts to draw upon scientific psychology to inform its conceptualizations of client problems. For instance, many of the techniques for therapy are grounded conceptually in such basic psychological processes as operant conditioning (from the work of Thorndike and Skinner), classical conditioning (Pavlov), and modeling (from the work of Bandura). Any introductory psychology textbook can serve to refresh the reader on these matters.

CB interventions tend to be directed toward the direct alleviation of the problems the client presents. For example, in helping an obese person, other approaches might see the overeating as indicative of low self-esteem or self-punitive tendencies, or as a way to avoid intimacy with persons of the opposite sex. They might then try to work with the "depth" cause of the problem with little or no direct attention to the problematic pattern, itself. CB therapy, on the other hand, would directly target overeating behavior for change. In contemporary CB therapy, this attention to the problem itself does not result in the kind of superficiality for which behavior modification has been criticized. For instance, problematic thoughts and feelings are often a part of the focus of therapy. A person's low self-esteem can be part of the problem, but it is not always presumed to be *the* core of the problem.

From a Christian perspective, CB therapy has a number of important strengths.[5] CB embodies the kind of active attitude toward the change process the Scriptures so often illustrate. In Ephesians 4, for instance, we are told to put off the old self and put on the new, and in the process to stop engaging in sinful behaviors and replace them with righteous behaviors. The attitude in this and many other passages is unequivocally active—regardless of the reasons, start changing deliberately! CB therapy shares this orientation. It also recognizes the importance of habit in human life; extra exertions are necessary to dislodge us from ingrained patterns of behaving. Adams has developed this theme well from a Christian perspective.[6]

Further, we can say that CB therapy, with its secularized, exclusively human-oriented understanding of persons, serves to remind Christians of our *creatureliness*, the degree to which we are inevitably conditioned by our finite natures and the world about us. CB therapy values the rational aspect of human life, and sees rationality as a resource for change. Christianity is, in part, a rational religion which emphasizes belief, doctrine, and similar issues. "Think on these things" or "believe this" is a frequent emphasis in scripture. Finally, CB therapy has a high view of the scientific method, with the result that empirical evaluation of the effectiveness of therapy is stressed. This fits well with a Christian insistence upon stewardship—we should know whether the time, energy, and resources invested in the counseling process are producing the results desired.

CB therapy also has many limitations from a Christian perspective. Its implicit or explicit embracing of materialism and determinism is unacceptable. Humans are viewed as part of an exclusively physical reality, with the result that we are viewed as acting in accord with universal causal laws, not having the capacity to transcend our "programming" in any way whatsoever. People are viewed as collections of learned habits and behavioral/cognitive tendencies so that any understanding of the person as a *self*, as an agent who can make choices and be held morally accountable, disappears.

In contrast, Christianity demands that we see persons as more than programmed robots. Because of its scientific emphasis, CB cannot incorporate any of the immeasurable, spiritual realities of human life that Christianity demands we recognize. Also because of the commitment to science, to the study of *what is*, this approach has no articulated vision of what it means to be a healthy, well-functioning human being. CB textbooks and articles are generally focused upon the alleviation of pain and suffering, but seem to have little or no vision for taking the person beyond the absence of pain to growth. Christianity, on the other hand, has a compelling vision of true health in the person of Jesus Christ. While the prizing of rationality is a positive for this approach, rationality is clearly overly prized. There is little celebration of the affective or emotional aspects of life in the CB understanding of personality. Emotions are clearly not seen as important to wholeness or a means of growth. Mystery and the nonrational sides of human personality are given short shrift in the model.

INITIAL CONCEPTUALIZATION

I began therapy with only skeletal information from the referring therapist. I entered the first session with Carl wanting to understand the nature of his obsessive thought pattern, the events that tended to trigger the obsessive thoughts, the nature of the anxiety and other discomfort he experienced in response to them, and how he tended to respond to the obsessive thoughts.

In the first session, Carl described his fear much like the opening paragraph of this chapter. He was deeply worried about this life being controlled by fears of impulses to engage in homosexual action, bestiality, pedophilia, and sadomasochism, as well as the fear of insanity. Early in the first session he gave clear witness to a personal faith in Christ, and this resulted in a high level of commitment to overcoming this problem. I trusted him as a brother in Christ, and felt challenged throughout our work by the depth and sincerity of his Christian faith.

I asked Carl to describe his developmental history, emphasizing the area of sexuality. He grew up in a conservative Christian home where sexuality was never discussed, where affection was minimal, and modesty was the rule. He had no significant sexual experiences before puberty; the only sexual event he could remember was being "mooned" by a girl when he was about age six. He began masturbating at a somewhat early age, initially using both female and male images (as best he could remember as an adult). By age twelve or thirteen he used just female images. He read about homosexuality in an Ann Landers column at age thirteen and became immediately concerned that he might "be one." This may have been the starting point for his obsessive pattern.

He had only one date with a woman other than his wife, Barbara, whom he began dating his sophomore year of high school. Their sexual relationship gradually progressed over three years of dating to "very heavy petting" involving mutual orgasm. It was mainly fear of pregnancy

24

that prevented them from engaging in intercourse. They exerted more control over their sexual relationship over the next two years when Carl was away at college, and they married after Carl's second year of college.

Carl described his sexual relationship with Barbara as somewhat "rocky," especially in the early years of their marriage. Carl's developing fears made it hard for him to ever relax in their sexual relationship. He felt constantly on his guard against "deviant or perverse" thoughts. He felt tremendous pressure to guard against his "natural tendencies"; letting his guard down, he felt, could result in disaster. He was always vigilant, watching for signs of his perverseness to come out. This kind of hypervigilance is very disruptive of sexual pleasure and sexual adjustment. Carl reported that Barbara also experienced difficulty adjusting sexually in marriage; he felt that she vacillated in her interest in sex, was overly modest, still felt residual guilt over the extent of their sexual exploration while dating, and was not confident that she was sexually attractive to Carl.

I ended our first session with a discussion of just how common it is for most developing men to experience at least some thoughts of homosexual arousal, and that such thoughts do not make one a homosexual. Similarly, the occurrence of "deviant" sexual thoughts did not make one a deviant; the way that one responded to or acted upon those thoughts was the critical factor. Since he had never acted upon any of his unacceptable impulses, I was able to affirm his basic integrity and self-control. What did distinguish him from other people, I argued, was his extreme response of self-reproach when he experienced his unacceptable feelings, and his feeling that he must go to extreme lengths of self-vigilance to prevent himself from engaging in deviant activity. Perhaps we would be able to decrease the occurrence of the sexual thoughts, I said, but our main goal would be to work not on the thoughts, themselves, but on his extreme reaction to them. It was already my belief that if we could diminish his extreme reaction to these worries, his thoughts of the impulses would go away without direct intervention.

In the second session, I gathered more detail about the nature of the intrusive thoughts and his typical response to them. The thoughts were typically *not* actual impulses to engage in deviant behaviors, but rather thoughts such as *What if I have that impulse? How can I be sure that I won't have it? That I won't be overwhelmed by it? That I won't engage in that behavior?* For instance, he talked about seeing a young boy and being consumed with worry that he might feel a sexual impulse toward him. Carl did *not* have impulses toward deviant sexual behavior, such as having an immediate impulse to molest the boy. Rather, he was consumed with anxiety about *possibly* having such thoughts or impulses.

To complicate matters substantially, Carl, like many men, had found to his horror that if he entertained a thought long enough he might experience some sexual arousal to the thought. For example, if he worried that he might molest a boy, he would think about sexual acts such as the boy performing oral sex on him. He would think about the act to challenge himself to show that he was *not* a "deviant," which he hoped to prove by *not* having any sexual response to the image. He would always have some emotional reaction to these images and then would worry that that response was sexual: *I think that was revulsion, but what if I am a sadist, and that is what sadistic response feels like?* But on some occasions, the thoughts of sexual stimulation in the images were enough to produce some sexual response in Carl, in response to which he would feel greater doubts about his basic normalcy. Thus, the pattern fed itself: He felt compelled to check that he was not a "pervert," but the manner in which he checked himself added to his own doubts.

Carl reported two main methods for trying to control or deal with his recurrent thoughts. Most frequently he attempted to divert his attention by throwing himself into thinking different thoughts or getting involved in some other action. A typical sequence might be that he would begin to feel some vague sense of disquiet, and in response would begin to feel fear about impending impulses. To try and head off those thoughts about impulses, he would then try to throw himself into his work, concentrating more than ever. This renewed concentration was almost always a fragile one, as the possibility of unwanted thoughts always loomed over his shoulder. The other strategy he tried for control was to feel no emotions whatsoever. Perhaps, he had reasoned, if he felt nothing at least the fears would be deadened. So he had attempted to narrow himself to the thinking and acting domains of life only. He felt he had been partially successful at this.

From the information of these first two sessions, I tried to forge a working conceptualization to guide the early stages of therapy. In CB therapy, the initial conceptualization is always revised as new information on the client comes in, so this early conceptualization is held quite tentatively. The CB conceptualization of obsessions is grounded in a broader approach to understanding anxiety.[7] Anxiety is viewed as an acquired fear that is somehow not extinguished in the normal course of life. If, for example, a child is bitten by a dog, or is exposed to frightening stories of maulings by dogs, she can develop initial fears of dogs. If that child is then brought into contact with dogs that are harmless, those initial fears will extinguish naturally. But if the child is able to avoid contact with all dogs, a well-established phobia may result, since the child needs exposure to dogs to cause the fear to diminish. In some persons, even thoughts of dogs may be frightening. If these thoughts are dealt with directly, as when a parent talks with the child about the fear, the fear of the thoughts will also diminish. But if the child develops patterns of avoiding the feared thoughts by some form of distraction, the fear may never go away. Behavioral forms of avoidance or distraction can become compulsions—behavioral rituals that serve to diminish the anxiety-evoking thoughts. Forms of distraction that are cognitive can become obsessions—cognitive rituals that serve to defend the person against unwanted fears.

The paradox in the CB conceptualization of obsessions is that the cognitive ritual that is presumed to serve the function of anxiety reduction is itself anxiety provoking. How can it make sense to argue that anxiety-producing thoughts, thoughts that the person finds distressing and obnoxious (like Carl's worries about deviant sexual impulses), help to defend the person against anxiety? There is no conclusive answer to this dilemma, but there are at least three possibilities. One is that as distressing as the client may find the obsessive thoughts, there may be a set of *deeper* anxiety-provoking thoughts that are even more frightening. Second, it can also be true that a cognitive ritual can start because one set of unpleasant thoughts helps to repress another set of more unpleasant thoughts. Over time, however, the previously more frightening thoughts can diminish in their capacity to provoke fear, while the previously less frightening thoughts become more and more aversive and intrusive. Finally, the cognitive ritual may lend itself to the person doing something to defend against this anxiety. Fears of what we cannot control are probably more frightening than fears of what we can control.

At his early stage of therapy, I conceptualized Carl's problem in the general manner of the model above. It seemed that a great deal of anxiety was associated with the possibility of having sexual thoughts of an unacceptable nature. Carl never confronted these fears for a sufficient period of time to allow the anxiety to diminish. As a Christian, he felt it was his duty to resist any such thoughts. Thus, it seemed that Carl's tendency to try to avoid these feelings was actually serving to maintain

27

them. The sequence might go as follows: With some overpowering fear in place, anything could trigger a round of anxiety. Once something triggered the sequence, Carl would erroneously identify the discomfort as being due to an impending deviant sexual impulse. This identification led him to try desperately to contain the anxiety and to distract himself. Thus his avoidance was partially successful, but ultimately self-destructive because he never came face-to-face with what he feared. The anxiety would typically run its course, continuing until Carl was emotionally exhausted.

I decided to pursue two main initial strategies in counseling. First, I decided to focus for several sessions on Carl's marital relationship with Barbara, particularly their sexual relationship. My reasoning for doing this was that if Carl was going to confront his worst fears, he would do so most comfortably and confidently if he were assured of the basic integrity, including the sexual integrity, of his marital relationship, and of the basic acceptability of his sexual feelings toward and enjoyment of his wife. To do this, I would follow a basic strategy common to many approaches to sexual counseling of encouraging active dialogue in a married couple and "assigning" the kind of sexual communication exercises developed by Masters and Johnson[8] and discussed in a Christian context by Wheat,[9] and Penner and Penner.[10]

Second, I intended to pursue *exposure* to the fear-inducing thoughts. Exposure-based treatments, as developed by Marks[11] and others, have been prominently used in recent treatment methods developed for all anxiety-based disorders, but especially those which seem to be sustained by avoidance. For example, agoraphobia, obsessive-compulsive disorder, post-traumatic stress disorders, and to a certain extent panic disorder have all emphasized exposure methods.[12] To use some examples from Marks, an obsessive-compulsive who fears contamination by dirt and germs might be treated by the carefully controlled exposure to the very things that are feared. For example, a female inpatient might be led to "contaminate" herself with "filth" and then to restrain from engaging in the cleansing ritual that has been her pattern for fifteen years. Similarly, the combat veteran who has been desperately avoiding all thought of his horrible experiences in Vietnam might be asked to reexperience those memories in his imagination.[13] In this way, the client is helped to get over his or her catastrophic reaction to the feared stimulus. Unfortunately, such treatments have been thoroughly researched with persons showing overt avoidance behavior (such as agoraphobics and obsessive-compulsives), but have not been well researched with persons who are experiencing purely cognitive obsessions. Wegner has recently published a popular treatment of how confrontation with the feared or undesired thoughts can bring substantive relief from obsessive problems.[14] The John Cassian quote at the beginning of this chapter may indicate that this is not a totally new methodology for dealing with this kind of problem.

THE PROCESS OF PSYCHOTHERAPY

Sessions 3–5: Couple Therapy

Treatment began in the third session when I saw Carl and Barbara for their first couple session. Barbara confirmed the basic accuracy of Carl's description of their dating and marital relationship, including their sexual relationship. The bulk of session 3 was spent discussing a Christian view of sexuality as God's good gift to us[15] and explaining the Masters and Johnson pleasuring exercises that help couples to overcome sexual inhibitions and increase sexual communication. These exercises basically call for couples to engage in alternate nude whole-body touching without the goal of sexual arousal and with sexual activity during or after the exercises forbidden.[16]

In sessions 4 and 5, Carl and Barbara reported that these assignments went extremely well. Like most couples, they found these activities increased their comfort with each other, broke down some of their residual inappropriate modesty with each other, increased their awareness of the goodness of their physical relationship beyond "mere sex," and aided them in talking more directly with each other about their sexual likes and dislikes. Carl reported several moments of "breakthrough" when he felt genuinely fully aware of and comfortable with his sexuality. Given his hypervigilance, this was truly a breakthrough. Barbara felt that the two of them were enabled to communicate better and that they both felt freer to enjoy each other. She hoped she would continue to grow in her appreciation of her and Carl's sexuality, but she suspected that she still had residual guilt and shame to work through.

The sexual assignments precipitated several insights for Carl. Even in the midst of enjoying Barbara, he found himself struggling with vague feelings of anger—anger toward Barbara for not always meeting his needs or being excited about sex when he was, anger at himself for not "having it together," and more diffuse anger that felt like it could be directed at anything. After one of their pleasuring sessions, they had talked openly about Carl's struggle (Barbara was already quite aware of it). Carl had seemed relieved at first that Barbara could accept him even though he worried that he could be sexually aroused by so many stimuli; but this relief had faded when he began to wonder just how frequent normal sexual arousal was and just how broad the field was of stimuli which "normal" men could be aroused by.

Sessions 6–10: Preparation for Exposure Treatment

I had expected to go right into exposing Carl to the crucial thoughts immediately. A bright and thoughtful person, Carl asked so many questions about the procedure that my intended brief explanation turned into a whole session of describing how the procedure should work and the rationale for it. Carl had now been relatively free of the anxiety that had brought him to therapy for some weeks, but was still highly motivated for therapy. Two other things prevented us from jumping right into the exposure. The first was that Carl's father had just been diagnosed as having a terminal illness. Carl's concerns about his impending death were substantial, and we spent important time discussing the issues the illness raised for him and his anticipatory grief about his father's impending death.

Second, Carl's concern for the death of his father brought into focus the core of my own unease with going into the exposure—I still did not know if there was a deeper, core fear his obsessions were protecting him from. In discussing his father's illness, I began to explore more of Carl's recollections about his childhood. He did not have many strong recollections of his mother, but he had very clear memories of his father. He described his father as critical and demeaning; Carl remembered being called a "houseplant" by his father. Whether from specific words or general impression, Carl said he believed his father had viewed him as lazy and awkward. He felt that he had never been able to satisfy either of his parents, especially his father. This sense of rejection had led him to constantly question his basic acceptability and worth. This line of inquiry led to my belief that it was core fears surrounding fundamental acceptability and worth issues that were more basic than fears of possible sexual impulses. As I look back on our work, I see this time of discussing his father and his family history as crucial both for the information it provided and for the impact it had upon our relationship.

Sessions 11–25: The Exposure Treatment

One Christian concern about a cognitive exposure treatment is that the therapist is asking the client to intentionally focus on and *not resist* thoughts that the client and the therapist at least find extremely discomforting and often regard to be repulsive. These thoughts may depict behavior that is immoral, as shown in the following "transcript." Is such therapeutic strategy equivalent to encouraging mental immoral behavior? In this case involving both homicidal and sexually immoral behavior, was I encouraging the client to both lust and harbor hate in his heart? Such was clearly not my intent. Certainly, I am not suggesting that the way to get over lust is to lust more, or to get over it by "really getting into it."

This exposure methodology, however, calls for clients to directly confront that which they fear. That is the core distinction: The issue for Carl was not that he secretly enjoyed these thoughts, but that he abhorred and feared them but had no freedom over them. He had tried and tried to suppress these thoughts as directive "biblical" counseling methods would urge, and in doing so had never confronted what it was he really feared. We had to go into the dark valley of the fears to find out what he was really afraid of. Then, if there was a problem for which Carl was morally accountable, he would be more fully able to confess what was sinful in his thought life. In his current state, he did not fully know what he needed to confess or confront. I saw this process as akin to confession, that Carl needed help to confront and come to grips with his real nature. In that way he could confess it and deal with it with God's help and find out he was still acceptable to God.

The material for our first exposure session was supplied from Carl's current concerns. He came to the next session reporting significant anxieties at his work. Part of the session went approximately as follows:

T:* How did you come to feel this tremendous anxiety?

C: I was in the lunch room eating with several women from the office. One woman, Donna, had a paring knife that she was slicing an apple with. I became fixated on that knife. I began to worry that I might feel an impulse to pick it up and hurt her with it.

T: How do you feel about Donna?

---

* In dialogue throughout the book **T** represents the therapist's remarks, while **C** indicates the client's words.

C: She's attractive, pleasant. I don't feel anything in particular toward her.

T: What did you do?

C: Nothing. I excused myself as soon as I could, and then I obsessed the rest of the day about whether I might ever have an impulse to hurt or kill a co-worker. I spent the day, last night, and ever since trying to fight off those thoughts and images, but they won't go away. I'm such a mess, such a pervert. . . .

T: Let's wait and see on that. You did not act on it? [Carl shakes his head.] Perverts act on their impulses. In any case, you didn't really have an impulse but a fear that you might have an impulse, right?

C: What's the difference? Only a pervert would worry about such things, have to watch himself all the time over such things.

T: The difference is substantial, Carl. We've talked about that, and we will come back to it later. Now I would like to move intentionally into the exposure thing we talked about. Would you be willing to work with me on this? [Carl mutters "yeah," unenthused.] Good. I want you to close your eyes and picture the scene of you at lunch with Donna and the two other women. Look at the knife in your mind. Talk to me out loud about your thoughts, feelings, and impulses.

C: I'm looking at the knife. *What if I pick it up and do something with it? Why would I have this thought at all? Am I dangerous?*

T: Carl, look at Donna in your mind. You are not in that room now; you are here with me. If you let your mind run wild, if you were to turn loose of all control over your imagination, what happens next in this scene?

C: You want me to let all that out? It is so ugly!

T: I want you to let it out. Don't hold back. The whole problem may be that you have never faced the reality of what you really think and feel.

C: [long silence] I casually pick up the knife and feel it for a minute. I feel empty, afraid, angry, confused. [long silence] I get up behind her and hold the knife against her neck and stick my hands down her blouse to feel her breasts. I'm sick. . . .

T: Look at her in your mind; look at her face.

C: She looks petrified. She looks rigid, terrified; she's crying. [Opens his eyes and looks at me in agitation.] Do I have to do this? Do I?

T: Carl, I can't know for sure that this will work, but I think it will. You are sharing your thoughts. God knows them already; they come from your heart. I'm no better than you. I have my own problems. You may shock me, but we are not fundamentally different, you and I. I'm willing to hear what is in your mind. Please go on. Look down at her. . . .

As I pressed him, Carl went on to describe quite vividly how he imagined that he forced Donna to perform oral sex on him there in the lunch room with a knife to her throat and all his co-workers watching. In his horrified imagination he continued masturbating while he cut, tormented, and then killed Donna. The process of going through the scene was excruciating to Carl and to me, taking over forty-five minutes. There were long silences as I waited for Carl to form his words and as I left him to fully confront personally the horror of his thoughts. My own reactions were profound hurt and sadness that he had to go through this and guilt that I was leading him through it. While I detested the thoughts, themselves, I never had sustained feelings of rejection of him, as by that time I knew him well enough to know that these thoughts were not reflective of Carl's inner being. Much like Paul's struggle with sin in Romans 7, these thoughts were—and yet were not—the real Carl.

I expected Carl to spontaneously bring God into the picture, but that did not happen. I suppose in response to the picture that had evolved in Carl's mind during the exposure session, Carl had pushed away any thought of God. At the end of that session, Carl felt utterly empty and drained. The scene ended with everyone looking at Carl in the midst of the carnage he had committed, and his feelings were of utter abandonment, revulsion, despair, and loneliness. He described having felt some passing sexual arousal during his initial descriptions of the scene, but that had quickly faded. We finished the session in a somber mood, reflecting upon the experience. I commented upon the profound feelings of rejection he felt. I intentionally did not try to offer quick reassurances about his not being rejected by God or by me, as I believed that he needed to confront and more fully understand these feelings of rejection. This was very difficult for me, as I longed to comfort him. The session ended with my urging him to reflect upon the feelings of rejection and abandonment. I asked him to go over the scene again in his mind before the next session. I challenged him to face these fears of rejection directly, as they may have been the true culprit behind his suffering.

During the next session, Carl reported having had a difficult week. He had struggled with anxiety often, and had endured three horrible nightmares. One had pictured him being held by enormous, monstrous claws which came out of the floor. His own interpretation of this dream was that he was terrified that he would never be able to escape this problem that held him in its clutches. We talked about his reflections on the previous exposure session. Carl reported almost totally blocking it out. He did report that his feelings of rejection and abandonment at the end of the session—of being on the outside of the human race—were absolutely terrifying.

We proceeded into the next exposure scene, again building upon a fear that had gripped Carl in the last week. He said his boss had invited him to play racquetball and he had accepted. But now, with the date coming up, he was very frightened. He feared that he might experience homosexual arousal in the locker room of the racquetball club. How would he ever know for sure that would not happen? I set up the exposure process as before, asking him to imagine the scene and share with me whatever might unfold. He took me through his thoughts of going to the court, playing several games, and going into the locker room. He was quite agitated at that point as he described what he imagined. He reported imagining having intruding thoughts of an unknown man performing oral sex on him while he stood there in the locker room, with the result that he imagined having an uncontrollable and blatantly obvious erection in the locker room. The other men in the room began laughing at him, calling him a "queer," and/or expressing utter contempt and revulsion at him. He reported feeling a whirl of feelings to this, including resignation (*I deserve to be rejected because I am a pervert*), despair, isolation, and the desire to beg for their acceptance (*I want to plead "It is not my fault! I don't want to have these feelings!"*).

He reported one emotion in response to the imagined scene that was absent from the first—anger. His anger came out of the feeling *I don't deserve to be rejected, no matter what I have done.* Building upon this last feeling, I moved to more expressly draw his faith into our focus while he was struggling with these depths of despair. I helped him sustain his focus upon this dark, imagined experience until his emotional agitation had

34

substantially waned; this is what the CB methodology of exposure demanded. I was not content, this time, to let it stop there; I wanted to explore this experience spiritually and draw Carl's own faith into the experience.

T: Carl, you are still imagining the locker room; you are still there. You are being utterly rejected by all around you. You feel despairing. What do you imagine of God's response to you?

C: God is nowhere to be found.

T: Do you want him there?

C: Are you kidding? Yes, I want to be loved, to be cared for, but I'm despised and despicable.

T: You are utterly worthy of rejection?

C: I feel utterly alone.

T: Is it God's face, Christ's face, on those who are scorning you? Look at them in your imagination. Your boss, those anonymous men in the locker room—do they speak for God?

C: I feel as deserted by God as by them.

T: But that isn't what I asked. Look at any of them, all of them. Are their faces the face of Christ?

C: [long silence] No. [long silence] No.

T: Why not?

C: I feel rejected; I feel God's absence, but I don't see his rejection on the faces around me.

T: You feel God's absence, but you can't be sure he has rejected you?

C: I don't know.

T: I wonder why you feel God's absence. I wonder if God is really absent. [long silence] Talk to me.

C: My mind, my faith tells me that God is never absent, that he never utterly deserts anyone. But I feel so alone.

T: You did not in fact do what you imagined. You had never really even taken your thoughts as far as you took them just now. If you had, if what you described to me had actually happened, what would have been God's response? Would God despise you, abandon you, reject you, for having an erection as a thought popped into your head?

C: God certainly wouldn't be tickled pink that I thought of and got turned on thinking about another man giving me a blow job!

T: That's true, but how does God respond when he is not tickled pink? God is not tickled pink by a lot of things that you, I, and every other Christian does. How does God respond?

C: He stays faithful in his love.

T: Go on.

C: He doesn't abandon; he somehow loves through whatever a person does.

T: I believe that, too. I am here listening to you and sharing your experiences with you in part because of the small bit of God's love he has been able to give me to share with others. I don't feel like kicking you out of this office for what you have shared; I think that is partly because Christ wouldn't do that. You don't exhibit a callous heart toward God or toward these thoughts; instead you exhibit a heart breaking to be accepted by God and to be rid of these thoughts you hate. The other reason I wouldn't reject you is because I see you as a human being just like me—full of unspeakable things. I am amazed God, my wife, or anyone can love me in spite of these things. How could I reject you without also rejecting myself?

I remember at the time thinking that the preceding dialogue would have to be a pivotal turning point for Carl. Perhaps this would be the dramatic moment one hears about in psychotherapy when it all comes together (God's acceptance, my acceptance, and the client's own self-acceptance) and Carl would make a dramatic breakthrough! But it was not. Carl continued to struggle, and he did not experience a dramatic moment of healing. But it *was* a turning point of sorts. Carl was now willing to confront the rest of his struggles with me, though with great pain and considerable hesitation.

Over the following ten or so therapy sessions, I took Carl through imaginal exposures to abducting and sexually molesting a boy of about the age of eight, being sexually attracted to his adolescent female cousin, being unexplainably sexually aroused at his own father's funeral ("What if when my father dies I am so sick that even a dead body, the body of my own father for God's sake, turns me on?"), and several other scenes.

Remember for each of these that Carl did not experience the actual impulse itself, the desire to molest a child or the desire to be sexually aroused by a dead body. Rather, he was struggling with fear that he would have those impulses. Each of these exposure scenes was exhausting and stressful; neither Carl nor I looked forward to them. My commitment to continue was based on the fact that he was genuinely experiencing more freedom from his fears than he had in months. He was still struggling with the fear; but his "free" periods were potent times when he felt greater acceptance of and comfort with his own sexuality and indeed his entire character than he had experienced in the six or seven years prior to our therapy.

These sessions were not just mechanical exposure periods. We discussed other matters, including his father's illness and his relationship with Barbara. I continued to encourage their sexual intimacy and greater general communication. He also came to more personally "own" parts of the CB hypothesis about obsessions. Specifically, he began to see that the obsessive thoughts did serve several purposes. One he could see most clearly was that there was a payoff in worrying that he might be a pervert and then being tremendously relieved when he could convince himself he was not. The problem was that sometimes he could not convince himself. Second, given his doubts about who he really was, worrying about the "worst-case scenarios" might help to prevent at least the worst cases from becoming reality in the future. Maybe worrying now would prevent later incidents.

Sessions 25–55: Broader Issues and Resolution

As we hit about the twenty-fifth session, I approached a bit of a personal/professional crisis. Exposure treatment had worked, and yet it had not worked. He was experiencing more freedom. Carl reported that his "good" days were times of great joy and comfort in being who he really was. The specific worries did not seem to terrify or dominate him as much. But the periods of oppression were still substantial. Further, we had applied the exposure treatment to a substantial number of specific scenes, but Carl still had general concerns about his sexuality that were not well suited to exposure treatment. I had wanted Carl to be a text-book case that was improved and content after fifteen sessions, but he was not. Carl was better. But he did not want to stop therapy. We actually had one session where I essentially told him that I did not know what to do next, but he felt that progress was occurring and did not jump at the chance to terminate therapy. It was in the final half of therapy with Carl that I was the most stretched beyond my preconceived notions as a CB therapist and beyond my simplistic notions of what it means to be a Christian "caregiver."

Rather than go through a chronological summary of what transpired in our remaining sessions, I will try to summarize it thematically. First, I should say that the desired dramatic breakthrough never occurred. Rather, Carl began slowly to experience greater and greater freedom from his obsessive concerns. He demonstrated tremendous courage and maturity in facing the struggles that had oppressed him for so long.

Carl's father died before the twenty-seventh session, and his death clearly had been approaching for several months. A theme had come up repeatedly in our discussions and in response to the exposure sessions—the theme of acceptance. Carl had never felt accepted by his father. I began to realize that this need for acceptance may have been the fuel for Carl's obsessions, as he had developed a pattern of hyper–self-vigilance as a way of insuring that he always measured up in some form. On this basis, I encouraged him to talk with his father before he died to ask how his father felt about him. Carl courageously did this, though the periods when his father was lucid were brief. He returned from that experience deeply moved with grief over his father's death, but also deeply affected by his father's assurance that he was proud of Carl, and that he did love him. Carl, in turn, had felt greater freedom to feel his own love for his father, and to grieve effectively for his loss.

A significant event in our work was Carl's insight that he could not put off living his life until the problem disappeared. The problem could not be his handicap that kept him out of the game of life. In his own words, he increasingly saw that the residual of the problem might be "something to be lived with and in spite of, like a thorn in the flesh, rather than something to be gotten rid of."

Carl's defense strategy (mentioned earlier) of shutting himself off from all feelings loomed larger and larger as a problem. We began to see a pattern where he would do well for a period, then slowly begin to feel a vague discomfort. He would then try to cut out all feeling whatsoever, and this defensive move would soon be followed by a plunge into the pits of depression. Thus a major emphasis in our work became encouraging him to "embrace the ambiguity of his experience." In Alfred Adler's term, he had to have the "courage to be imperfect." In Christian terms, we talked about his responsibility not to deny who he was and what he felt, but rather to choose to live rightly in full knowledge of himself with all his faults and and all his strengths ("Now all has been heard; here is the conclusion of the matter: Fear God and keep his commandments, for this is the whole duty of man," Eccles. 12:13). This went quite counter to all of Carl's instincts. In the later sessions, he again talked about "building fences" around his fears; in other words, he was talking about a return to trying to defend against his impulses. I saw this as extremely dangerous in that it was precisely the unwillingness to confront his fears that was the core of his problem. We talked earnestly about living as if his fears were *irrelevant*. In other words, he was to fully enjoy the good experiences God gave him, including his sexual feelings toward and interactions with his wife, his interactions with friends, his work, and so forth. When he experienced negative feelings, he was to face them, probe their depths, and act responsibly in the face of them, including confessing them to God and continuing to choose not to act on them.

This strand of our work was summarized well by Carl at the end of our therapy. He stated that in therapy he had been forced to confront the truth that the barrier between goodness and acceptability and depravity, abnormality, and evil was not and could never be an impassable one. To feel good about himself, he had been prone previously to demand that he be without fault, that he was not capable of the heinous acts he feared. He described every bout with the fear as a "High-Noon" experience (in the sense of a "shootout" in a vintage western movie) in which he was to find out or prove this time whether or not he was ultimately a "pervert." He began to recognize this dysfunctional nature of this dichotomous, black-or-white, "pervert-or-normal" thinking. Now, he had to confront the truths we all must face, namely that we all have evil within us, that any of us is capable of acts of great depravity. What distinguishes the virtuous person from the depraved is not that the virtuous one is pure, but that he or she knows what is inside, can come to terms with it, and can choose to live as God would wish in spite of his or her depravity.

In response to these insights, Carl began to change his manner of responding to initial anxiety. Previously, discomfort (which could be caused by almost anything including fatigue, tension with his wife or others, physical illness, or job stress) would inevitably result in Carl's becoming increasingly panic-stricken because his "deviant impulses" were surely just around the corner. Carl worked hard to change this approach to one which could be summarized by the following thoughts: *I am a complex person with some aspects that bring glory to God and other aspects that are shameful. I am just like other people. My task is not to run from life, but to live it fully through my relationship with Christ. I don't have to run from any evil within me; I will be better able to make the right choices if I confront what is inside myself and not let it intimidate me. I don't have to run from fully experiencing "external" life either; I don't have to run from my God, my wife, my friends, my work, or anything. I will face the truth in myself and outside of myself, and live my life rightly in the face of it.*

Carl was greatly helped late in our therapeutic work by reading several of the psychological works of Søren Kierkegaard during the period of therapy. The most powerful element of Kierkegaard's ideas for Carl was the very notion of forming a self. To be a human is to be a composite being with the potential to *become*. The true self, the fully developed person, makes conscious choices of who he or she will be in full knowledge of the nature of the choices and in the context of a personal relationship with God. Carl identified deeply with Kierkegaard's analysis of the desperate search by many for some way out of the human responsibility of choosing; he felt this was precisely what he had been doing. He did not want to choose; rather, he wanted total reassurance that he simply was not evil, was not a "pervert." He was coming to realize that no one had that assurance, and that he had to make choices anyway.[17]

In later sessions, we spent substantial time talking about acceptance and self-worth. I challenged Carl to formulate a coherent groundwork for acceptance of himself, one which he could defend practically, philosophically, and theologically. He took on this task with some enthusiasm, and surprised himself at how effectively he was able to do it. In working at this, we returned several times to a discussion of his feelings of having to work to prove his acceptability in childhood.

Carl continued to experience substantial and discouraging setbacks. There were times as late as the forty-fifth session when he was truly struggling and I wondered if we had really made any progress. Yet Carl was sure progress had occurred, and could feel the differences in his struggles. The worst times seemed to occur when he put himself on trial again, demanding that he somehow prove he was not abnormal, and especially when he began to take his obsessive ruminations as signs of a deep disturbance of his whole character that proved he was unacceptable. Thankfully, these times became briefer and less disrupting.

Our last six sessions were held once per month. During this time, we saw the true stability of the changes in Carl. The periods of anxiety were minimally intrusive, and he reported vibrant times of joyful experience. I have had periodic contacts with Carl since the termination of formal therapy. Life has not been universally wonderful. But he has felt a greater freedom in his relationship with God, greater love for and comfort with Barbara, has enjoyed the birth and nurturance of their two children, and has experienced a burst of productivity in his career. As he said to me after reading a draft of this chapter, "I still have obsessional tendencies. But enough healing has occurred in my life so I can experience my real emotional reactions to things, anxiety or depression or anger or joy, without experiencing profound doubts about whether the feelings are really sexual and whether they are a prelude to some sort of deviancy. I struggle, but my struggles are the normal struggles of an aware, feeling person in a complex world." He certainly does not struggle with the obsessions as he used to.

CONCLUDING COMMENTS

At the end of the psychotherapy, I asked Carl what he felt made our work successful. His answer surprised me back then, though it would not now. I had expected him to point to a particular technique I had used or a particular experience he had had as a turning point, but he did not do this. Instead, he paused thoughtfully, and said, "I think what made the difference was that you were a person I got to know well. You have a sincere faith in Christ and are basically a normal person. Yet when I spewed out all of the filth inside me that so terrified me, you didn't despise me. You witnessed it all, down to the bottom of the barrel. Yet I did not sense that you were disgusted by me or ever lost faith in me or the fact that God had his hand on me. That was healing."

As I reflect upon my work as a therapist, several things stand out. The first is how much I learned from Carl, particularly from his inner integrity in the face of worries and concerns that would daunt anyone.

Second, my work with Carl was a vibrant testimony to the usefulness and the limitations of traditional cognitive-behavioral methods. But other psychological approaches are evident in this case, though undoubtedly in somewhat adulterated forms.[18] I attempted to embody the person-centered therapeutic attitudes, and found it instructive to have the Rogerian patience and trust of Carl rather than the impatient attitude of the cognitive therapist who is always ready to change the client's thinking. There were strong Christian existential themes[19] operative in my encouraging Carl to make his choices well in full awareness of the ambiguity of those choices. Indeed, the standard existential themes of death, meaning, aloneness, choice, and virtue came up even more than my description may indicate. Finally, I am sure that a psychodynamic practitioner would emphasize the way our work was a corrective emotional experience of some sort for Carl, that we were working out the parental acceptance issues from the past and working on reintegrating the splits within his character whereby harsh distinctions had emerged between the good, acceptable Carl and the bad, unacceptable Carl.

Throughout our work, our common bond in the Christian faith was critical. Carl worked on these concerns in a spiritual manner, praying, studying the Scriptures, and seeking God directly for help, comfort, and healing. I found it pivotal that I could trust the integrity of his love for God, his commitment to obedience, and the ultimate meaning of his struggles. I sensed that Carl was a man who was clinging to God, and upon whom God's hand rested. I had a strong sense of communicating God's love and acceptance to Carl as we worked together. In sharing his burden, one which had been so dominant in his life, we were able with God's help to put it in its proper place.

EDITOR'S COMMENTS

This case illustrates a number of Christian counseling principles that need to be remembered by all counselors regardless of our level of experience.

First, Carl's comments about the therapist express the essence of Christian counseling. His words are worth repeating. "I think what made the difference," he said, "was that you were a person I got to know well. You have a sincere faith in Christ and are basically a normal person. Yet when I spewed out all of the filth inside me that so terrified me, you didn't despise me. You witnessed it all, down at the bottom of the barrel, and I did not sense that you were disgusted by me or ever lost faith in me or the fact that God had his hand on me. That was healing."

Some might question whether the counselor needs to be somebody else's "garbage pail," but Carl clearly needed to feel accepted even as he "spewed out" evidences of his distorted sexuality. The therapist demonstrated the love of Christ and "never lost faith" in the client; but there was never any condoning of immorality or even a hint that one could ignore or overlook biblical standards of purity and morality. In this case, the therapist stayed with the client, despite the difficulties and "filth."

Second, the counselor was willing to be flexible. He started with the cognitive-behavioral approach, but he was not afraid to move to other methods. Carl may have pushed his therapist beyond the comfortable confines of one theoretical model, but the therapist selected his other methods carefully—based on prior awareness of techniques that are likely to be effective. When issues like the death of Carl's father arose, there was no attempt to avoid the stress involved, even though this was not the presenting problem. Dr. Jones clearly was aware of the client's needs and of other techniques that were available for use when earlier methods were not working.

Was it appropriate for Dr. Jones to say he was stuck at one point? With some counselees this might be threatening, but with Carl, a good rapport had been built and probably he appreciated the honesty. It is interesting to note that this counselor mentions his responsibility to be a good steward of one's God-given time, energy, and resources. Here is an example of Christian values that surface, almost automatically, as counseling progresses.

Third, the counselor was well aware of the client's uniqueness. Carl was intelligent and the counselor respected this. The counselor recommended that Carl read several works by Søren Kierkegaard. With most clients we might select something a little simpler, but for Carl this book choice was a good adjunct to therapy. When the counselee asked about procedures, the counselor took an entire session to explain the methods that were being used. Is this a waste of time? It is not if the resulting explanation puts the client at ease and helps move along the therapeutic process.

Fourth, the counselor was aware of his own feelings. He mentions his "profound hurt and sadness" in watching the client's pain, his longing to reach out and give comfort, his discomfort with some of the sexually explicit issues, and his feelings of guilt as he led Carl through some needed but painful discussions. On occasion, the counselor shared his own feelings, but these were not allowed to interfere with the therapy. Clients need to know both that we have feelings and that we are handling them without expecting our clients to be our therapists.

In his analysis, Dr. Jones comments about his frustration when the case did not have a dramatic breakthrough or significant turning point. That is reality. Most counseling, including long-term counseling, is hard work; dramatic turn-arounds are rare.

Fifth, the counselor and counselee talked directly about God, his love, acceptance, and forgiveness. There can be no rules concerning what is said about theological issues or when. Remember that Carl was a committed Christian, so talk about God was a natural part of the counseling. As part of his lifestyle, Carl spent time praying, seeking God's help, reading the Bible, and looking for guidance and meaning in his struggles. Even so, the counselor was careful not to slip in "proof-text" Bible verses or "God-talk" when there was a need to honestly talk about the counselee's specific fears and obsessions.

Stan Jones noted that this was one of his earlier cases. This chapter is an example of a committed Christian therapist who was growing in his knowledge and expertise as a counselor. He still is growing—and that is the sign of a good counselor.

CHAPTER THREE

COGNITIVE THERAPY WITH A DEPRESSED CLIENT

Mark R. McMinn

Editor's note: *Counseling experts tend to agree that counseling is likely to be more effective if the process is guided by a theory. Over the years, from Freud to the present, a variety of theories have been proposed, used, and evaluated. Some of these—transactional analysis, reality therapy, and many of the psychodynamic therapies, for example—subsequently have faded in popularity, but others have persisted. Cognitive therapy is an approach to people-helping that currently is popular, often effective, and consistent with many of the tenets of basic Christianity.*

In the field of Christian counseling, Dr. Mark McMinn is recognized as an expert in cognitive therapy. His book Cognitive Therapy Techniques in Christian Counseling *(Word, 1991) is a definitive statement of this approach. The chapter that follows illustrates cognitive therapy by presenting the case of a twenty-four-year-old youth pastor.*

Mark McMinn is a native Oregonian whose B.S. degree is from Lewis and Clark College and who has a Ph.D. (in clinical psychology with a biochemistry minor) from Vanderbilt University. He is a licensed psychologist who is associate professor of psychology at George Fox College and in private practice with Valley Psychological Associates in Newberg, Oregon. He has authored a number of professional scientific papers and written several books, including Your Hidden Half *(Baker, 1988) and* Christians in the Crossfire, *co-authored with James Foster (Barclay, 1990).*

———————————

"WHEN I IMAGINE GOD, I SEE HIM standing before me with his arms crossed. The look on his face scares me. He looks upset, like I've done so much to displease him. He doesn't say anything; he just stares at me and I feel uncomfortable and judged."

These were Jeff's words early in the counseling process. *How could God love me?* was a question reverberating in Jeff's mind when he first came for counseling. Despite his burgeoning career in Christian ministry, he felt distant from God and unloved. Jeff also displayed symptoms of mild depression, feeling discouraged about the future, guilty about the past, and like a failure in the present. He reported being irritable, apathetic, and disappointed with himself. He was experiencing frequent headaches and difficulty concentrating.

Others looked at Jeff with respect and admiration. He was a twenty-four-year-old youth pastor who was well liked by parishioners and others in the community. His background in athletics helped give him rapport with high-school and college students. Because of his success and gregarious nature, those around him would not have guessed that Jeff felt unloved by God and others. He had recently been married to Sarah, but at times felt unloved by her as well.

Jeff was the youngest of three children reared in a home where time together was emphasized. "My dad was always my hero," Jeff reported during our first session. They went fishing and hunting together, played catch in the back yard, and enjoyed chatting whenever they could. Once his dad went with Jeff and his friends to toilet paper another friend's house. Jeff's dad was his biggest fan throughout his years in junior-high and high-school football.

Jeff and his sisters were model kids: popular, bright, sociable, and motivated. Life seemed smooth and predictable until junior high school when Jeff became aware of his parents' marital stress.

"Do you love Dad, Mom?"

"How can I, Jeff? We're only staying together for you." These words were exchanged after Jeff's dad had left for the night following what Jeff labeled a "huge fight." Jeff recalled that he was never close to his mother after that conversation.

Jeff began to recall more painful experiences as our counseling continued. During the third session, he recalled visiting Europe with his parents, stopping to look in a store window and not being able to find his parents for several minutes on a crowded London street. He also recalled falling down the stairs as a child, feeling hurt, and having no one respond with care. Most significantly, he recalled being taken to a pastoral counselor in seventh grade to talk about his parents' marital problems. What happened in that session is hard to know, but Jeff left feeling blamed for his parents' problems.

As we pieced together Jeff's memories of these experiences and analyzed his feelings of being unloved, we uncovered deep fears of abandonment. Feeling lost on the streets of London was a symbol of Jeff's deepest fear—a symbol we used frequently as we discussed his fear of abandonment.

Because Jeff feared rejection from others, he felt he needed to please them, and frequently wondered if he was succeeding. When interpersonal tension occurred, he assumed it was his fault, just as he had assumed his parents' marital problems were his fault. His need to please others kept Jeff from authentically expressing himself. He functioned as a social chameleon, expecting himself to be what others wanted him to be. Yet little he did seemed good enough because he looked for cues of rejection and ignored indications of success.

Initial psychological testing indicated that Jeff was mildly depressed and anxious, and that he depended a great deal on others. He happily submitted to the desires of others in order to please them, but often felt anger and resentment because he had not adequately expressed his own feelings and desires.

In many ways, Jeff was an ideal candidate for cognitive therapy. He was uncomfortable enough to be motivated for treatment, but showed no indication of personality disorder or longstanding mental illness. He was bright and had good awareness of his feelings and thoughts. Jeff was committed to high moral standards and a consistent Christian testimony even when he didn't feel close to God. And Jeff lived in the midst of close friends and had the social support he needed to feel loved and accepted once he was able to shed his unrealistic demands of pleasing others all the time.

BASICS OF COGNITIVE THERAPY

Cognitive therapists assume that faulty thinking patterns cause emotional disturbance. As the thinking patterns are revised, the troubling emotions dissipate. Although it is a crude division, one can distinguish between *automatic thoughts* and *core beliefs* .

Automatic thoughts, also called dysfunctional automatic thoughts, are those that occur in response to specific situations on a daily basis. Clients are often aware of their automatic thoughts. Core beliefs are those consistent ways of viewing the world that are formed in childhood. Core beliefs cause us to selectively attend to certain parts of our experiences and ignore others, so that our experiences are as much a result of what we perceive as they are of what happens to us. Clients are usually unaware of their core beliefs when they start therapy.

Jeff called me at home one afternoon and described how he had just finished meeting with another pastor who was critical of his leadership techniques. Jeff had listened politely and nondefensively, but felt crushed and hopeless by the time the meeting was over. On the phone, as we had done previously in our sessions, we worked on identifying the automatic thoughts that were occurring. We found several:

I'll never be a good pastor.
I never do things right.
I'm going to lose my job.
The kids I work with think I'm doing a terrible job.

Predictably, these automatic thoughts led Jeff to feelings of depression and hopelessness.

After identifying automatic thoughts, cognitive therapists work with their clients to assess the accuracy of their thoughts. On the phone that afternoon, I asked Jeff what evidence he had that he never does things right. We discussed the things he does well and eventually Jeff concluded he does most things well, but it is impossible to please everyone all the time. We did the same with his other automatic thoughts.

AUTOMATIC THOUGHT: *I'll never be a good pastor.*
REVISION: *I'm doing all right now, and I'll get better with experience. But I will never please everyone.*

AUTOMATIC THOUGHT: *I never do things right.*
REVISION: *I do most things well, but it is impossible to please everyone all the time.*

AUTOMATIC THOUGHT: *I'm going to lose my job.*
REVISION: *I'm doing a fine job and I have no evidence that I may lose my job.*

AUTOMATIC THOUGHT: *The kids I work with think I'm doing a terrible job.*
REVISION: *Most of the kids respond well to me. I can't please everyone.*

Of course, it takes good clinical judgment to change surface thoughts. The counselor needs to listen carefully and sensitively to the surface thoughts before trying to change them. And the counselor needs to collaborate with the client in obtaining the revised thought. It is not enough for the counselor to tell the client how he or she ought to think.

As the automatic thoughts are confronted over the course of several sessions, a pattern begins to emerge. This is because automatic thoughts emerge from deeper core beliefs. In Jeff's case, his automatic thoughts centered around the need to please others, reflecting his core belief that others are likely to reject him.

Core beliefs also affect the ways we experience God. One person views God as angry and judgmental and another views God as caring and loving. These different theologies flow from different core beliefs about oneself, others, and the world. Because Jeff believed he needed to please others to avoid rejection, he viewed God as punitive and distant. He created an image of God that required him to be perfect to obtain God's love. Since Jeff was not perfect, he felt unloved by God.

Core beliefs are changed by recognizing their existence and then rehearsing new ways of believing. Just as an actor rehearses lines over and over before a performance, one trying to change core beliefs needs to repeatedly rehearse new ways of thinking. Jeff and I used Scripture, contemplative prayer, and logical thinking to create more productive core beliefs.

REVISED CORE BELIEFS:
*God loves me because of God's character, not because of my perfor-
    mance.*
God loves me even when I don't feel his love.
Others love me and it is not likely that they will reject me.
It is nice to please others, but not essential.

Over a period of several sessions, Jeff and I worked on identifying and
revising his core beliefs. As sometimes happens, his change occurred suddenly. After our sixth session, he wrote me a letter explaining that his
rehearsal work was starting to influence the way he was thinking. It was
hard work, he said, but it was worth the work in order to feel better. It
was a turning point for Jeff. The session dialogue below came two sessions later, our eighth.

Session Dialogue

T: How did your week go?(1)*

C: It went well. The interesting thing is that it wasn't like it was just a
fantastic, on-top-of-the-world type of week, but it was good. Some
difficulties came up, but I was really able to calm down and think
through them. Let me see if I can think of a couple of situations.
One was I started feeling really down and kind of depressed because my job isn't structured—it's really flexible, especially in the
summertime.(2)

T: When the students aren't. . . .(3)

C: Right. You know, it's more of just general planning and being with
people. It's all so new to me that I had a hard time for a while
adjusting before I was able to walk through it and just say its not
me, I'm not failing, it's just a part of the job, and as time goes on
I'll get used to it. I was able to tell myself that, and I really believe
it, and I've heard that from folks who have been around. You know,
my superintendent tells me that all the time. He asks me how I'm
handling the ambiguity of the whole thing. So I was really happy
about that.

—————————
* Parenthetical numbers at the end of each paragraph are used to identify the comments in the discussion that follows the session dialogue.

And then yesterday, which I took as a real major kind of victory, Sarah and I went out to dinner and we were talking and I was asking her that question that you told me to ask her. Our time was really light and kind of friendly. This is a serious thing for me and I got serious and she didn't see that and she made a joke. You know, I asked her, "How do you feel about me when I make mistakes or hurt you and stuff?" and she laughed and said, "Oh, I hate you." It was really funny, but as I sat there I thought, *Wait a minute. I am trying to be serious here and she's laughing.* And to tell the truth, I had a hard time not cracking up, too; but for some reason, I don't know, I wanted it to be serious and just kind of get it over so we could get on with the rest of the evening.

But I told her that that hurt a little, that this is a sensitive area, and I'm trying to be serious. But I didn't lose my temper and usually when that kind of thing happens, usually I feel that's a rejection and it's somebody not being consistent with me anymore. You know that the whole image of my folks leaving me in the streets of London and the whole thing. I'd turn around and they'd be gone, and it came back to me, and I sat there and was anxious to share this with her. Maybe it wasn't good timing and I understand, "I don't want you to feel bad, it's just the way I feel, and I want to tell you that."(4)

T: This is my response to what was just said [clarifying client's comments].(5)

C: Yeah. It was just matter-of-factly speaking and it just hurt. Then I got quiet, and she started feeling bad, which is kind of the normal thing, and she says, "Well, what's wrong?" Well, I just wanted to be quiet for a little bit and just kind of work it through and continue to talk, myself. I know this is the kind of situation where normally I would get upset and really hurt if I were not to stop right away so I could look at the situation. I mean it was really rough for me, but I was able to do that and then something else came up after that that I was really happy about. It was just a sure sign to me that I am getting somewhere, because I asked her, "Well, are you okay? What's the matter?"(6)

T: I was going to say, her quietness would probably add some pressure to you in not responding.(7)

51

C: Yeah. And she said, "I feel really bad for hurting you." And it is— we've talked about this—hard for me to deal with when I let somebody down and they feel bad. I said, "Well, that's okay, I didn't intend for you to feel bad. Please, I really don't want you to feel bad." I told her that; but immediately started feeling all this guilt on me to make myself try to take it off her and crucify myself, or whatever and. . . (8)

T: So she would feel better?(9)

C: Yeah. And I was able to say, "No, it was her response and in time she'll feel all right and I'll just show her that I'm okay, which I really was."(10)

T: Yeah, that's a really good example. One of the things I was thinking is that essentially you had a choice as to how you responded when Sarah said what she did to you and you felt rejected. Even as you were talking you were describing how you felt rejected—you talked about your parents leaving you in London and these things—it was essentially your choice to respond that way. You handled it well. You expressed your feelings very well, and you didn't blame Sarah for your feelings. You didn't say, "You made me feel this way." In that same sense as you took responsibility for how you feel, it was appropriate and it seems good that you let Sarah take the responsibility for how she was feeling. You didn't make her feel bad for what she had said—that was her feeling. Just as you had your own feelings.(11)

C: Yeah. And I kept telling myself that. That's one of those self-talk things that I am having a hard time dealing with, that I'm not responsible for her feelings. It's hard, because sometimes—I know it's not intended—but it sounds so cold and irresponsible. So sometimes I struggle with that. But I know when it comes down to the brass tacks and the bottom line. . . . (12)

T: That's a good point, and let's face it, it's not a simple matter. I mean, I've said it, but it's not entirely true that we're each responsible for our own feelings, because we all live in a system where you say something and it will have some impact on me and vice versa. But I think it's a useful thing to think, *I am primarily responsible for my feelings, and Sarah is primarily responsible for her feelings.*(13)

C: I was able to think about that, and I had a great piece of advice from a friend of mine when we were at camp. He was excited that we were married and he said, "Hey, just don't get upset at the little things." He gave me an example: you know, if you come home and your wife is in a bad mood just let her be in a bad mood and when she's ready to come and talk to you, she will. I mean, don't take that personally. There's so much wisdom in that little thing and so I was able to do that. As the night wore on she ended up even crying when we got to the car. That would normally just make me feel horrible. I felt upset that she was upset, naturally, but I didn't feel the guilt I normally feel. I think that for the first time in my life I am becoming free. I'm obviously not there yet, but I am becoming free from a lot of the things. . . . (14)

T: That's a good feeling.(15)

C: It's a great feeling! She couldn't appreciate it as much as I could, you know. She's pretty good at letting things go, but because it's me I was really appreciative.(16)

T: You know, your friend's advice is interesting. If you come home and your wife is upset and you let her come to you, you essentially give her responsibility for her feelings and you don't feel like you have to fish it out. Now there would probably be some marriages where those things would never get resolved if you didn't talk to each other; but assuming she *will* come and talk to you, it is a much better way to do it.(17)

C: Yeah. I imagine there has to be give and take on that. Maybe sometimes someone does need a little push to open up.(18)

T: That's wonderful, Jeff—both of those examples. My guess is that there is an initial reaction, for example you felt guilty about not doing more on the job, and there were probably the automatic thoughts that always come. But very quickly then you responded with more reasonable words.(19)

C: Yeah. I tend to feel that and again I was talking to Sarah and I was feeling kind of down because of the job, feeling like I haven't done anything. Those feelings usually come when I do the most, and she pointed that out. She said, "Jeff you feel that way when you work eighteen hours a day." I guess there's something to that. It was good again to stop and say, "Okay, what is this thinking that is going on?" and I was able to cut it off. It doesn't mean I haven't felt that way again today. But I understand it's normal when you don't have a structured environment like I am used to.(20)

T: The automatic thought says, *I'm not doing enough*.(21)

C: Yeah.(22)

T: And as you think about it, the more reasoned response says, *This is the summer time, I don't have a lot of structure in my job, but I am still working hard*.(23)

C: Yeah. Exactly. Right. I go on doing what I am supposed to be doing. And as far as I know my boss hasn't been complaining about what I'm doing, so I must be on the right track.(24)

T: Good. Just keep saying those things.(25)

C: Yeah. It's still a struggle. I'm really finding out the benefits of that are just great. I mean today, something happened that's totally uncharacteristic and is something I've always wanted to be able to do, and now I'm finally experiencing it. This dives into a bigger thing, but there's another youth pastor in town that I work pretty closely with and we're good friends and I really consider him a brother. He came to me Monday and he was excited that we had a great week at camp. He wanted to start figuring out some way to get some of these kids involved in his church. I was all for that, but he made one comment that really scared me to death. He mentioned a guy's name. Well, it was the man I mentioned that one night when I had that really bad day. . . .(26)

T: Oh yeah.(27)

C: . . . and I had that confrontation with him—that's the man. We've had a rotten year together, that's a whole other topic that I hope we can talk about today. But he mentioned him and he said something about the kids coming back from camp and we don't really do anything for them and I got really scared. My thought was, *Oh, no, I'm going to lose this brother because this guy is telling him all these things about me and really poisoning the well*.

So after he was getting up to leave, I said, "Hey, can we get together this week to talk?" We got together today and I was scared. I thought I was going to throw up, but I was able to really share. I said, "Hey, this is my fear: I'm not discounting your motivation for coming to me at all, I just fear that I'm going to lose you as a friend because of what you're hearing from this guy." It took so much courage for me to say that. It was really hard, because normally I would just, you know, just hold it in and just try to tough it out with these things going on. But instead I was just able to share that with Eric. And he accepted it like the brother I knew he was. He said, "Don't worry about it. He may have mentioned a few things, but I know you better." So it was good.(28)

T: That's a powerful example of how, as the fears of rejection lessen, you can take more risks. And that was a risk you took today. You essentially walked into a situation saying, "I don't want him to reject me but I want to put something on the line and let him know I really want to be close to him," and it worked out. But you could probably do that because you didn't fear the rejection. It seems like you kind of turned a corner a couple of weeks ago.(29)

C: Yeah.(30)

T: Since then, you have really been working and thinking in ways that avoid that rejection mindset.(31)

C: Yeah. I thought about a whole bunch of different scenarios on how to do it. You know, I could talk about things with the guy who has it in for me and blame all this stuff on him; but I knew that the deeper thing for me was that I didn't want to lose or doubt Eric's friendship. And to be assertive I said, "Hey, I just need to get this out; so take it for what it's worth. Now you know where I'm at."(32)

T: That sounds really good. You had these images in the past about God, as you've approached God in prayer. You imagined him not catching you when you jumped into his arms. Have you thought any more about that during these past couple weeks?(33)

C: I haven't done that image exercise, but this thought came to my mind: I feel like for the first time I'm just really living. I'm stepping out, you know, and really experiencing what it means to be a Christian. And (knock on wood), I say this because in the last few weeks I've been able to be more of who I am, and just let it go. My picture of God has turned—not so much an image, but ideas maybe—of understanding, compassionate, patient, which are all new things. And when I blow it and make bad choices that we make throughout the day and sin, normally the guilt would build and build and build. The guilt has still been there, but not to the degree it has been before. And it does something I think it's supposed to do, showing us we made a mistake.(34)

T: It points out problems.(35)

C: And I see God and I confess that to him and I see him saying, "You're going to make these mistakes. It's not that I like you doing them. It hurts both of us, but you're human." And I think lately I've given myself the freedom to make those mistakes. And I almost laugh at them because, like Paul says, I do what I don't want to do, and I don't want to do what I do. But then he says that God's grace is sufficient. I think for the first time, without any kind of weekend camp high or spiritual revelation or anything, I'm really discovering the grace that is there. And I think it's just starting. And I'm learning to give myself the freedom to be who I am and not to have any excuses for that.(36)

T: I'm glad to hear you say that last part. You said, "knock on wood" a few minutes ago when you were talking about how your views of God have changed. I'm quite convinced, too, that it's just starting. This is a giant step you've made in the process that will continue on. And that, in fact, you will have times when you feel bad again. As all change occurs, you get better—take two steps forward and one step back. Who knows? Maybe next week or a few weeks from now, you'll find that there is a tough week again. But the thing that's important is realizing that you're moving in the direction you want to move and you're seeing yourself and you are seeing God's view of you in more accurate ways. And you're not plagued as much by him as a judging God who is always disappointed in who you are—which is a really good thing to see.(37)

C: It's still hard and I think maybe I haven't really thought specifically about this. I haven't sat down and said, "What do I think about God? What are my images of him now?" It's been more like this is it. And it wasn't a big revelation. Slowly, through the process I've been through, I realize now that I can feel bad, I can feel guilty, I can feel angry, but it doesn't matter because God's still going to love me.(38)

T: In fact, God gave you those feelings.(39)

C: Yeah.(40)

T: Well, let's tie this in with what you were saying a minute ago about this other person who was critical of your work. I know that was a really tough thing for you.(41)

C: For me, right now, that is the hardest thing to deal with. I find that I get the anxiety, and I feel it physically in my muscles. Whenever I think about this man, I have a hard time finding the right things to say to myself to really believe. I've tried. God, I'm sure, is really softening a lot of bitterness in my heart toward him. He hurt me pretty deeply. And I'm sure that will take time and I've given myself the freedom to let that take time and let God do that. But, you know, in terms of right now and how the ways that he treats me affects me, I don't know how. It's hard. And I don't understand why yet.(42)

T: Okay. Well, let's work on that some. It's a good thing to focus on. Jeff, let's find a time in the last twenty-four hours—it sounds like this has been a recent thing—when you remember noticing this physical anxiety. Maybe driving in the car. . . . (43)

C: Yeah. Driving, my shoulders get really tight. I know when I'm under a lot of stress—my shoulders get really tight.(44)

T: You've been driving recently when you're thinking about this situation?(45)

C: Yeah. Well, I drove down to Salem and talked with my superintendent about it.(46)

T: Was that today?(47)

C: Yeah.(48)

T: So you were driving to Salem today. What were you feeling on the way?(49)

C: Tense, anxious, angry, resentful, and bitter—and another thing, trapped. I think that's why I feel so anxious, because I feel so defenseless and trapped.(50)

T: That's a particularly troubling feeling, like there's no way out of the situation.(51)

C: Yeah.(52)

T: All right. Well, that's quite a list of unpleasant feelings. Let's try now to go back and recapture the thoughts if you can remember what thoughts were going through your mind.(53)

C: I picture him saying things to other people about me.(54)

T: Okay, so there are conversations in your head that he's having with others.(55)

C: Yeah, or just jokes maybe. And then I think about the kids at the high school. I took two years to build some really positive relationships with them and I think about how he indirectly turned them against me. That hurts pretty deep.(56)

T: Now, this is more than a fear; this is something you have some evidence for.(57)

C: Yeah. I mean, it may or may not be true, but they look at me a lot differently than they did before. You know, they look at me as a bumbling idiot who makes all these mistakes, who's unorganized, and tries too hard to be with people. And I guess I feel trapped because I know there's nothing I can do to change their minds, or the people that he's talking to.(58)

T: Let me see if I've got this right. One of the things you were saying to yourself on the trip down to Salem today was, *He's talking to other people about me, saying negative things about me.*(59)

C: Yeah.(60)

T: And then you were also saying, *These kids at the high school liked me before and now they look at me as a disorganized idiot.*(61)

C: Yeah, like I'm just kind of a joke.(62)

T: They see you as a joke?(63)

C: Yeah.(64)

T: Other things you were telling yourself on your trip down there?(65)

C: What was I telling myself? Well, that there is really nothing I can do about it.(66)

T: That's feeling trapped, feeling *I'm helpless.*(67)

C: Another one was, *He's just a jerk. Don't even listen to him.* But I think my main feeling was that I wanted to stand up for myself and not be defensive, but say, "Hey, you're saying some things about me that aren't true." But the trapped part comes in there, too, because it's hard to do that. He's such a great manipulator that he will turn it against me.(68)

T: So you've tried that in the past.(69)

C: Yeah. It's really a one-sided . . . it turns into, you know, all of the sudden here I am saying things and he's turning this into another rip session. So that doesn't work and it's kind of hopeless.(70)

T: Well, it sure sounds like an unpleasant kind of thing to have to deal with. Let's look at some of the things you were saying. There are times when unpleasant things happen and there are not good alternatives, but let's just see what we can find out. The thought *He's talking to other people about me*—what evidence do you have for that?(71)

C: Oh, I thought that was the case with Eric and I found out it wasn't. Even if it was, Eric told me, "I support you 100 percent and he knows that." A little evidence I have is when I'm with the kids. Just some things, you know, they don't call me anymore or come over. They usually go to his house. And things come out. Some kids have kind of alluded to some things a few times that he has mentioned.(72)

T: How would it be to say to yourself, *He's probably not talking to as many people as I think, but he may be talking to some people.* You mentioned that he hadn't talked to Eric, even though you thought that he had. Would that be a fair conclusion?(73)

C: I think that's accurate. I feel he's talking to the whole world.(74)

T: Which, of course, would be quite unpleasant since he doesn't have a high opinion of you—if he were out talking to everyone.(75)

C: Yeah.(76)

T: So he's probably talking to some people but not as many you feel. It's still unpleasant. I'm not trying to turn it into a good situation.(77)

C: I think it's the fact that it's these kids and I really did invest my life in them. It makes it pretty hard on me.(78)

T: Yeah, that's the one that was real strong as I was noticing what you were saying to yourself. "Before they liked me; now they look at me as a disorganized idiot. They see me as a joke." Is there evidence for that, Jeff?(79)

C: Well, they've been pretty critical of me, you know. I started noticing that at camp last year. He went as a junior counselor to me (even though he's ten years older than I am), and it was an awful situation. It ended up that he and I played a mental tug-of-war over right and wrong. I felt he definitely crossed some boundaries and I tried to call him on that a few times and he just didn't respond. The kids picked up on that. I usually talked to him in private, but I made a couple of statements in front of kids, thinking since I had tried talking in private it might work better in front of kids. Then he would just rip on me. And the kids would join in. And pretty soon they were all hanging with him because he would let them do whatever, let them get away with anything whereas I was a little more firm and required a little more discipline. Any kid, given a pick between the two, is more likely to turn to the one who's a lot easier. I realize that. Still, that didn't make it much easier.(80)

T: That's a tough situation.(81)

C: And there was a situation where we couldn't go with the rest of the camp on our way back—and you have to take a big packing trip for seven hours. It wasn't my choosing and I tried to get out of it for us, but the camp said, "No way. You've got to do it." So I was determined to make the best of it. He got pretty upset and flew off the handle. It was kind of embarrassing. It was okay to be upset, I can understand that; but he was upset for the kids that they weren't getting the whole camping experience. I figured I didn't like it either, but the kids were going to follow our lead. If we play it up like it's the biggest deal in the world, they'll think it's the biggest deal in the world.(82)

T: Sure.(83)

C: And it just turned out rotten because they saw how upset he was. It was kind of a bitter deal. And then somehow he took that whole situation and he turned it. I mean, he needed someone to blame. He put the blame on me, not that I was defensive or anything. I didn't find this out until a few months ago that he did this. He turned the blame on me because of a lack of organization. And I had nothing to do with it, because—that's not even important. He put the blame on me for lack of organization. And when we were leaving for camp this year, one of the kids was there from last year because his girlfriend was going. And he looked at me and said, "How are you getting home this time?"(84)

T: So you took that to mean, "You blew it last time."(85)

C: Yeah. And I talked to his girlfriend and she told me that he thinks it's my fault. That's hard.(86)

T: That's where you get the word *disorganized* in the statement, "They see me as a disorganized idiot."(87)

C: Yeah. And he's told me before, you know, to my face, that he thinks I'm disorganized.(88)

T: It's an unpleasant kind of thought. There are a few things we might revise a little bit. Now, "They look at me as a disorganized idiot," implies that all of these high-school students do. Is that reasonable?(89)

C: As I started thinking more and more about the situation, I remember telling Sarah, "I feel like I'm not cut out for this job." But I think I did generalize a little, "kids just don't like me."(90)

T: Which probably is inconsistent with other evidence—the kids who do respond well to you.(91)

C: Right. Exactly. It was just that day that I had breakfast with a kid who was thanking me a hundred times for all I've done for him. Wait a minute here.(92)

T: It is interesting, isn't it, how we can selectively look at the negative evidence and ignore the positive? Do we need to have that word idiot there? "Some of them look at me as disorganized." Or do we have to keep the word idiot there? "They look at me as a disorganized idiot."(93)

C: I feel like . . . I don't know if it's true. I'm sure disorganized is true, but I don't know if idiot is true.(94)

T: Would there be any way to find that out?(95)

C: I don't know. They treat me pretty harsh and pretty cold. And I have . . . I'm really quitting investing my time with them at this point. They've shut me out and not responded to me. I still talk to them and things like that.(96)

T: That seems reasonable. I suppose one of the ways, then, you can talk to yourself about this is, *It stings. It stings that I spent my time and tried to help these kids and essentially I don't have much rapport with them right now. But there are other people I can reach and I can focus on those people.* There's no need to make a bad situation good here with your self-talk, and I know this is a bad situation.(97)

C: Yeah. I don't want to try to kid myself. I know it's hard.(98)

T: Let's focus, though, on this statement: "I'm helpless; there's nothing I can do." Are there things you can do?(99)

C: Yeah. Like talk to my superintendent. We're going to move my office. My office is where he's at. I'm getting away from him. I'm hoping the old out-of-sight, out-of-mind principle will come back.(100)

T: Another advantage to that—it sounds like from what you've said somehow you've pushed one another's competitive buttons. If you're out of sight, maybe that's not going to be as much of a problem.(101)

C: Yeah, that could be. He is interesting. I don't want to focus on him, but he thinks the whole situation is bad because he thinks that I think of him as a threat.(102)

T: Oh, I see.(103)

C: And so that could be, you know, one way of saying . . . that's a whole other thing. I know I need just to be away from him. I recognize that I'm through feeling bad about not being able to get along with everybody.(104)

T: Yeah, that's excellent.(105)

C: There are going to be people like that that I just don't get along with. Fortunately, in my life there have been very few people I have not been able to get along with.(106)

T: It seems like a very limited number from what you've said in the past.(107)

C: Yeah. And this is one of them, and it is difficult for me.(108)

T: Okay. So one of the things you can do is move the office. That's a good suggestion. You and your superintendent came up with that?(109)

C: Yeah.(110)

T: Another possibility came to my mind, Jeff . One of the things you can do is continue doing what you do well. That doesn't seem like it's directly addressing the problem. But as you continue to do your work with the other kids that you do have contact with and continue to feel that you are serving God and using your talents well, then you defend yourself in the best way possible by being productive and by being a servant of other people. It doesn't necessarily protect you from him saying other things to other people; but at least it keeps you doing what you're called to do, instead of focusing on this one problem area.(111)

C: The battle for me is to always focus on just this one instance. And to try to make it right where I can. I try, you know, to focus my energies into what I do well. It's hard.(112)

T: Yeah, it's hard, but it is certainly well worth it. If the belief, the self-statement, is, *I can't be rejected by even one person,* then every one of us is destined to feel miserable in life. But if the belief is, *I'm going to live my life obediently and faithfully before God as much as I'm able, and along the way probably some people won't like me,* then these things are still tough but they are things we can cope with. And you know we've talked a lot about rejection. The fact that you can even cope with this as well as you have (which, really, has not been too bad. I mean, it's been unpleasant for you, but you've coped with it really well compared to the incident a couple months ago) is evidence of the fact that you're giving up this belief that rejection by one person would be an awful thing.(113)

C: This is just a harder belief to give up than some of the other ones.(114)

T: Like you say, this is one of the few times in your life when you really have been vocally rejected. Is that too strong, to say rejected?(115)

C: Yeah. I think so . He wouldn't say rejected, but I would.(116)

T: It feels like rejection.(117)

C: Yeah.(118)

T: And so that's why it's hard. It's getting you right in the Achilles heel, that part of you that says, *I'm worth being rejected.* Now you're starting to fight back.(119)

C: Yeah. And I remember as I was driving down the road, it really hit me that I can start standing up for myself. I think I realize now what that really means. Inside, I say, *Hey, I'm okay. I'm loved by God even though this guy doesn't think the world of me.*(120)

T: That's right. And that's not a selfish perspective, it's an accurate perspective: *God loves me, others love me, Sarah loves me, even if one other person doesn't. It doesn't make me a bad person if one person doesn't like me.*(121)

C: I guess I realize again that I overlook the core of that—this whole thing that if I'm rejected then I'm unworthy. I remember we talked about that. I guess I just haven't really narrowed it down to that.(122)

T: Well, it's not something to feel bad about.(123)

C: No, I don't.(124)

T: But, that's right. That is, as I see it, what we're doing. We're finding the common source of lots of the pain you used to experience, and still experience. We're just going to chip away at that until it's gone. You've done a whole lot of the work on that already, but we need to keep chipping away—keep tying things back in. I'd guess— this is speculation, but I'd guess—that if you took the next week and tried to figure out every time you feel bad about something, that it would either directly or indirectly tie into this feeling of being rejected or unloved. It would be an interesting experiment to try. Just follow it for a week and see if you can tie in those bad feelings with fearing rejection or abandonment or unlovability.(125)

C: Yeah.(126)

T: And I thought it was fascinating that you mentioned in your conversation with Sarah this picture of your parents—being lost on the streets of London—which came back to you at that very moment. Do you see how it ties in?(127)

C: Yeah.(128)

T: It's very directly related to those early experiences, as we've talked about before.(129)

C: Yeah, I hadn't thought about that for a while.(130)

T: You were going to also look for some Scripture, you said, to kind of help you.(131)

C: Yeah, I decided to not reinvent the wheel and just do the ones I knew. Romans 5:8 is, "But God demonstrates his own love for us in this: While we were still sinners, Christ died for us." Titus 3:5 is a great one: "He saved us, not because of righteous things we had done, but because of his mercy. He saved us through the washing of rebirth and renewal by the Holy Spirit." And 1 Peter 3:18 is, "For Christ died for sins once for all, the righteous for the unrighteous, to bring you to God." And those are ones that, even on the way up here I was saying to myself and I had this little battle going on: *Yeah, you could quote Scripture, but there are other verses, you know.*(132)

T: That's true, there are.(133)

C: Yeah, like, "all have sinned. . ." But then I think, *Well, Satan quoted verses.*(134)

T: That's right. That's a really good point. So what we need to do is look for common themes. So, for example, you mentioned that Romans 3:23 says, ". . . all have sinned and fall short of the glory of God," which is true. But the interesting theme there is the next verse: " . . . and are justified freely by his grace through the redemption that came by Christ Jesus." So we need to keep the themes and the whole picture of Scripture in perspective.(135)

C: That was verse 24?(136)

T: Yeah. We say 23 and we forget the next one sometimes.(137)

C: Or you just never even think about it. You read 23 and that's it.(138)

T: Yeah, it's not even the end of the sentence in the New International Version. Well, I sure feel good about how you're doing, Jeff. Like I say, I think you turned a corner a couple weeks ago and we just need to keep doing what we're doing. It's great to see your enthusiasm.(139)

C: Yeah, I'm having fun. It's still not easy, but what I'm experiencing is great.(140)

T: Yeah.(141)

C: I feel free in a lot of ways. I think it's good for me to hear you say we keep chipping away at the core of all this, because sometimes I think it's easy for me not to see that. I don't want to forget we're dealing with something inside of me, deep down. I feel confident that you're directing this in that way.(142)

T: I may be directing, but you're doing most of the work; so feel good about that.(143)

Comments about the Session

This session can be roughly divided into three distinct sections. In the first section, comments 1 to 40, Jeff described in detail the progress he felt he was making. He realistically pointed out that he was having to work hard to keep control over his negative thoughts, but seemed enthusiastic about feeling better.

In addition to reviewing his progress, this first part of the session allowed Jeff to articulate his healthy patterns of coping. Despite my impulses to move on to another topic to make the most of our session, it was good to let Jeff talk about his progress. We believe things more strongly after we say them; saying is believing. So as Jeff described how well he was coping with life stresses, he was building confidence in himself and strengthening the very skills he was discussing.

In looking for progress, it is wise to be skeptical of change that occurs too quickly or too easily. So as Jeff began the session (comment 2), it was affirming to hear that his feelings had been under control but that his week had brought some trials. I would have been skeptical if Jeff would have started with, "My week went great, and there were no difficult times. Everything is fantastic!"

During this first part of the session, most of my comments were reflective (designed to keep Jeff talking about his progress) and affirming (to help him feel confident about the changes he was making). Later in the session I became more confrontive, but my goal at first was to reinforce his sense of progress.

In response to Jeff's comment 36, one could fear he was getting an unbalanced view of God's grace. Rather than confronting Jeff on his perspective, I assumed he was using some exaggeration in his light-heartedness toward sin. This assumption seemed natural because of our earlier sessions. Jeff had very high standards of morality and I saw no risk that his standards would crumble. The greater risk for Jeff was that he would become so overwhelmed by guilt that he would feel unloved by God. So, despite his exaggeration, I saw this comment as an indication of progress.

The second division of the session can be seen in comments 41 to 110. In these comments, our attention is focused on recognizing and changing automatic thoughts. Jeff is obviously familiar with this procedure from earlier sessions and is quite willing to revise his thoughts to be more rational than they were when he originally experienced them.

To evaluate automatic thoughts, it is useful for the counselor to follow a five-step process. First, the counselor helps the client identify a specific situation. Second, the client identifies feelings that occurred during the situation. Third, the thoughts that accompanied the feelings are described. Fourth, the counselor helps the client evaluate the truthfulness of the thoughts. Fifth, more accurate alternative thoughts are created. When Jeff reported anxiety in comment 42, my job was to find a recent, specific episode in which he could remember some precise thoughts. The episode we identified was driving in the car to Salem earlier that morning.

After identifying a specific situation, I helped Jeff articulate the feelings he had experienced. He had felt anxious, angry, and trapped (comment 50). Then we looked for the thoughts that led to those feelings. His automatic thoughts were:

This man is talking to other people about me, saying negative things. (comment 59)

The high school kids liked me before and now they look at me as a disorganized idiot. (comment 61)

67

I'm helpless. (comment 67)

Next, I prompted Jeff to provide evidence for the thoughts he was having. It was clear to me, but not to Jeff, that his thoughts were exaggerated and excessively negative. As he discussed evidence and realized he had overstated things to himself, he was willing to consider rational revisions to his thoughts. Eventually, he revised his automatic thoughts to:

He's probably not talking to as many people as I think, but he may be talking to some people about me. (comments 73–77)

Some of the high school kids think I'm disorganized. (comments 89–94)

I'm not helpless. There are things I can do. (comments 99–100)

Early on in therapy this process of identifying and revising automatic thoughts takes much longer. Each step requires coaching and careful collaboration. Because Jeff was used to the process by the eighth session, he was able to quickly correct his dysfunctional automatic thoughts.

The final division of the session, comments 111–143, focused on Jeff's core belief that he will be rejected. Although we had talked about core beliefs previously, he had not yet learned to connect his automatic thoughts with underlying fears of rejection. During this session, he began to understand the connection.

In the final part of the session, both Jeff and I verbalized alternatives to his core belief that the rejection of one person would be terrible and awful. Some of the alternatives were:

I'm going to live my life obediently and faithfully before God as much as I'm able, and along the way probably some people won't like me. (comment 113)

Hey, I'm okay. I'm loved by God even though this guy doesn't think the world of me. (comment 120)

God loves me, others love me, Sarah loves me, even if one other person doesn't. (comment 121)

Dealing with core beliefs is an essential part of effective cognitive therapy. A superficial understanding of cognitive therapy sometimes results in counselors teaching clients to effectively deal with automatic thoughts, but not to understand or deal with core beliefs. The result is short-term symptom relief without substantive underlying change. Effective cognitive therapy requires the counselor to look for deeper issues, usually fears that come from early life experiences, and to help the client develop an understanding of how those fears relate to everyday experiences. My goal for Jeff was not primarily symptom relief—all of us experience anxiety and discouragement—but that he would learn to be his own therapist by understanding how his past memories generate fears of rejection, the need to please others, and feelings of irrational guilt. Effective cognitive therapy gives clients the skills to regain control over their thoughts and feelings.

Cognitive therapy with Christian clients is not substantially different than cognitive therapy with others; but Christians may have some benefits that others do not have. Christian clients have a broader data base for evaluating their automatic thoughts and core beliefs. For example, Christians recognize the authority of Scripture and are usually willing to evaluate their beliefs by considering Bible passages. At the end of the seventh session, I assigned Jeff the job of finding Scripture passages that addressed his core belief that he was bound to be rejected. Because Jeff participated in a disciplined program of Scripture memory, I thought this would be a valuable assignment for him. As I hoped, Jeff came back with several passages emphasizing the grace of God. But he discounted the credibility of those passages by noting that other passages emphasize the justice of God (comment 134).

Fortunately, the passage he used to discount his memorized verses about God's grace was one that I had read just a few days before, and I remembered it was actually a passage about God's mercy (comments 135–141). There are many passages about God's justice in Scripture, but when the Bible is viewed as a whole, God's justice does not contradict God's mercy. God's justice points to God's mercy.

A second benefit Christian clients have in cognitive therapy is the experience of unconditional love. Humans can approximate unconditional love, but the only love that is truly unconditional is God's love for humankind (see Romans 8:31–39). If one of the deepest human needs is to feel loved, then Christians have an added resource in coping with life's stress because they are loved unconditionally by God. Both Jeff and I emphasized this as we discussed his core belief of rejection (comments 120–121). God's unconditional love is relevant to the variety of maladaptive core beliefs cognitive therapists address with their clients.

Follow-up

Jeff and I had one more weekly session, for a total of nine, before changing to a less frequent schedule. We met biweekly for two sessions and continued to chip away at his core belief. A month separated our eleventh and twelfth sessions. In each of the maintenance sessions, he continued to feel positive about his progress and to fight his fears of rejection. At the end of the twelfth session, I retested Jeff on the anxiety and depression scales that he had completed after his first session. His anxiety and depression symptoms had completely dissipated, and he felt confident about his future. Jeff has occasional recurrences of depression, so we have not stopped meeting altogether. We continue to meet every month or two. I provide Jeff with reinforcement for his healthy self-talk as he continues to battle his core belief. He is winning the battle and is, for the most part, his own therapist. I am his coach.

The normal course of cognitive therapy is twelve to twenty sessions, but some take longer. Many clients, like Jeff who is motivated and insightful, are able to progress rapidly as they experience greater emotional and spiritual health.

"When I imagine God, I see him as strong and powerful. But he looks kind and I can tell he loves me. I want to obey him, but I don't fear his rejection." Jeff's image of God changed as he better understood himself.

EDITOR'S COMMENTS

Every counselor knows that past experiences can have an influence on present thinking and behavior. Some theories, like psychoanalysis, focus on the past. Others, such as cognitive therapy, put more emphasis on the present; but the past is not ignored. This case shows how parental conflict and child-rearing practices can make a lasting impression. Jeff felt abandoned, unloved, rejected, and insecure as a child. This influenced his adult self-perceptions and his views of God. He was surrounded by supportive friends and involved in a ministry, but prior to therapy he was unable to shed the unrealistic demands (based in his childhood) that he had to be pleasing others and seeking God's approval all the time.

In describing his client, Dr. McMinn notes that Jeff was "an ideal candidate for cognitive therapy." He was uncomfortable enough to want treatment but showed no indication of personality disorder, long-standing mental illness, or inability to think clearly. It is unlikely that any one theoretical approach can be effective with all clients. Christian counselors need to recognize that some counselees will respond best to an approach like cognitive therapy; others will not. As I recall, it was Thorndike who many years ago advised psychologists to hold their theories lightly and not get so entrenched in any one way of thinking that they lose flexibility.

Dr. McMinn shows flexibility in this case as he illustrates a variety of cognitive therapy methods. The therapist points to the importance of self-talk, but helps the counselee say things to himself that are realistic. Statements, especially sweeping statements, are challenged in ways that are likely to bring change but not defensive reactions.

Clients are prodded to provide the evidence for their thoughts and conclusions. When evidence cannot be found, the statements tend to get modified into more healthy and realistic ways of thinking. As part of therapy, the Scriptures are used to counteract some of the client's faulty thinking, but the therapist involves Jeff in this. He doesn't just hear Bible verses cited; he is encouraged to look them up for himself. Many of these techniques have relevance for our personal lives as counselors, just as they can be useful for our counselees.

As you read through the dialogue did you find it consistently interesting and exciting? Probably not. Straight dialogue tends to be boring, in part because the "nitty-gritty" of counseling involves hard work and piece-by-piece discussion of details. But this careful analysis of the client's specific actions and thoughts is part of what makes counseling effective.

In his comments on the case, Dr. McMinn expresses his skepticism about fast cures and quick changes. He notes that "effective cognitive therapy gives clients the skills to regain control over their thoughts and feelings." Such a process takes time. It need not take years, as this case shows, but skills need to be cultivated and practiced. If one of your clients claims to be free of the presenting problem after one or two sessions, be skeptical. Sometimes this happens, but more often these claims of quick cure indicate there has been either temporary relief until the problem resurfaces, or the counselee could be avoiding some painful issues that counseling might be starting to uncover. When we feel threatened, it is common to smile and retreat.

If you have a further interest in cognitive therapy, you are encouraged to read Dr. McMinn's book that was mentioned earlier, *Cognitive Therapy Techniques in Christian Counseling*. It is volume 27 in the Resources for Christian Counseling series.

CHAPTER FOUR

MARRIAGE COUNSELING WITH CHRISTIAN COUPLES

Everett L. Worthington, Jr.

Editor's note: *Several surveys have shown that marriage problems rank at or near the top of the list of issues people bring to counselors. While most therapists deal at times with troubled marriages, some professionals are specialists in this area. Among Christian marriage counselors, nobody is more of a leader than the author of this chapter. Everett Worthington's* Marriage Counseling: A Christian Approach to Counseling Couples *(InterVarsity, 1989) has already become a standard textbook.*

Everett L. Worthington, Jr., is associate professor of psychology at Virginia Commonwealth University in Richmond, but his career began with a B.S. in nuclear engineering from the University of Tennessee and an M.S. from the Massachusetts Institute of Technology. Following his time in the United States Navy, where he served as an instructor in the

Naval Nuclear Power School, Dr. Worthington changed careers and enrolled at the University of Missouri, where he earned both an M.A. and a Ph.D. degree in counseling psychology.

Author of numerous professional and scientific papers dealing with counseling, Dr. Worthington has also written several books related to Christian counseling, especially in the marriage and family area. In addition to his marriage-counseling text, other publications include two earlier volumes in the Word Resources for Christian Counseling series: Counseling for Unplanned Pregnancy and Infertility, *and* Counseling Before Marriage.

As you read this chapter you will discover that it differs from all of the others in at least two ways. First, the case study is available on video tape. Portions of that tape transcript are included in this chapter. Second, to protect the identities of the couple involved, the video tape and dialogue in this chapter are "acted out" by advanced graduate students. The students did not follow a script, but they studied the case and acted "as if" they were the couple involved. The author's commentary deals with the real case, but the verbatim material is not the real clients'. As you read, however, you will discover a freshness in the dialogue that illustrates many of the counselor's marriage counseling interventions.

THIS APPROACH TO MARRIAGE COUNSELING GREW from my research and therapy with married couples.[1] Although most couples I have seen are committed Christians and have been referred to me by their pastors, former clients, friends, or professionals who know I am a Christian, some of the couples have not been committed to Christianity. My approach has had to deal with both Christians and non-Christians.

My approach to Christian counseling is derived mainly from clinical or counseling psychology, but I address religious topics and use pastoral methods where clinically appropriate. Counseling principles and techniques should be *consistent* with Scripture but need not be derived explicitly from Scripture.

My approach is eclectic. Techniques are drawn from almost any school of marital therapy; however, techniques are generally explained to couples in light of the conceptualization of their case, which may not follow the rationale or explanation used by the developer of the technique.

Despite my eclecticism, there are five major influences on my theory. Of most import is my reliance on Christian values of love, marital commitment, forgiveness, respect for individual beliefs and values, and Christian growth. Dealing with Christian beliefs and values is not always appropriate. Troubled couples attend marital counseling primarily to improve their marriage rather than for spiritual growth. Spiritual issues are addressed only when clients are amenable, when clients bring up spiritual concerns, or when spiritual issues clearly need to be addressed for effective therapy. Fortunately, much of contemporary United States culture shares implicit Christian values on love, commitment, forgiveness, and respect for individual beliefs and values—even if individuals do not adhere to Christian beliefs.

The second major influence is strategic family therapy, which advocates planned, active intervention.

Third, structural family therapy has influenced my approach. Structural family therapy uses metaphorical communication, especially use of physical space as a metaphor for psychological intimacy. Structural family therapy also attends to how couples organize their behavior into hierarchies to accomplish different functions within the marriage and how couples enact patterned communications that reveal those hierarchies.

Fourth, behavioral marital therapies have influenced my approach by emphasizing the necessity of a structured initial assessment prior to attempting to help couples modify their marital interactions. From the careful assessment, plans can be constructed that will tailor interventions to couples' weak points. In addition, behavioral therapies emphasize cooperation rather than resistance and paradox. I find straightforward attempts to induce partners to cooperate more useful than more devious methods of counseling, except under dire circumstances.

Fifth, cognitive therapies have influenced me by suggesting that partners perceive their marriage differently and attribute the cause of their difficulties to different sources. In addition, partners hold different ideals for marriage, trying to conform themselves and their spouses to their vision of marriage, which often forces the marriage into a painful Procrustean bed.

Because of the five major influences on this theory of marital therapy and because many techniques from a variety of schools of therapy may be used with any couple, the therapist must know when and how to make particular interventions. This implies that the therapist must be able to assess the couple's problems accurately to match interventions to couples.

ASSESSMENT PROCEDURES

Initially, I have couples attend three sessions for assessment. I tell them that by agreeing to assessment, they have *not* committed for counseling because it would be premature to counsel them before I knew the severity and description of their problems.

The first session begins with a social greeting. Partners introduce themselves and may ask me about my approach to counseling and even about my religious beliefs. Committed Christians who have been referred to me *because* I share their Christian values often want to check out my beliefs prior to beginning the assessment. Rather than view this as abnormal, as resistance, or as a challenge to my authority, I expect it.

Once assessment begins, I ask each partner briefly to describe the problem *"from your point of view."* I try to establish from the beginning (without saying so explicitly) that problems are understood from a particular perception, which implicitly is open to change. After the problem is described, I say, *"You* understand how your problems developed, but *I* know only the current state of the problem. It would help me if you described a history of your relationship from its beginning to the present." This directive helps me understand a larger context to the problem, and it makes the couple recall some pleasant memories. Often, this is therapeutic, helping the couple regain a sense that they share positive memories and have much to lose if the relationship dissolves.

At the end of the first assessment session, I direct the couple to complete two inventories prior to attending the second session. I use the Personal Assessment of Intimacy in Relationships[2] and the Couples Precounseling Inventory.[3]

At the beginning of the second assessment session, I collect the completed instruments. I usually begin the interview by having the couple discuss a topic about which they habitually disagree. The discussion is audiotaped (with their permission) while I leave the room and peruse the completed PAIR and Couples Pre-counseling Inventory. After seven minutes, I return and ask the couple to describe a typical weekday and weekend. Knowing the couple's schedules helps assess their intimacy and provides information about whether they have time to complete homework assignments that I might make later in therapy.

I usually ask directly about their conflict and their sexual relationship. I also determine whether individual psychological difficulties or problems with children might interfere with marital therapy.

During the third assessment session, I provide feedback to the couple about their relationship. I compile the information into a written report to the couple, which they read and we discuss. We determine whether the couple agrees to attend marital therapy for the number of sessions I have recommended. At the end of the feedback session, I give couples a brochure about how they can benefit from their counseling with me. (This is printed in my book *Marriage Counseling: A Christian Approach to Counseling Couples.*) Therapy begins during the following session.

The written report summarizes the salient facts about the relationship—ages, years married, and children. I then describe the relationship history and the development of the problem. I describe the couple's *strengths* and *weaknesses* in both marital satisfaction and commitment. Under marital satisfaction, I comment on five areas: closeness, communication, conflict resolution, cognition, and confession/forgiveness. Under commitment, I comment on three areas: their alternatives to marriage, investments in the marriage, and overall level of marital satisfaction. Finally, I assess complicating factors.

Understanding the Areas to Assess and Treat

The five elements of marriage satisfaction are used to structure my thinking and later my interventions toward helping the couple have a more satisfying marriage.

Closeness involves how the couple meets their needs for intimacy, distance, and co-action through arranging their daily activities. Closeness also concerns satisfaction with their emotional, sexual, social, recreational, and intellectual intimacy.

Communication includes how partners exchange information, self-disclose (especially negative and positive emotions), and meta-communicate (i.e., communicate about their communication). Further, communication involves whether each partner can communicate in ways that allow clear understanding or whether each one's communication has unintended impacts on the spouse.

Conflict resolution concerns topics about which partners disagree and the ways they try to resolve disagreements. I particularly look for power struggles in which couples care more about winning arguments than about resolving their differences.

Cognitions include differences in perceptions of the problems, misconceptions, negative expectations about the relationship and its future, attributions of causality that blame the spouse and refuse personal responsibility for one's part in the difficulties, and unrealistic assumptions about the marriage.

Confession/forgiveness is the willingness of the partners to admit their own failings and to be truly sorry about the pain each has caused the spouse. It is the openness to try to repair their damaged marriage and the ability and willingness to put hurts and anger behind and forgive the spouse for inflicting pain. Signs of difficulty include focus on the self, bitterness, abiding anger, and unforgiveness.

Under marital *commitment,* the second major topic (after marital satisfaction), I look for (a) level of satisfaction with the relationship—as distinct from the five elements of satisfaction evaluated earlier—(b) investments in the marriage (such as children, common friends, joint ownership of property, a perception by the community that the partners form an established couple, or a strong faith that discourages or prohibits divorce), and (c) alternatives that may threaten the marriage (such as competing friends, other sexual partners, alcoholism, workaholism, or overinvolvement in the community).

Complicating factors, the third main area of assessment, are factors that may make a couple difficult to help successfully. In particular, individual psychopathology in either or both partners can impair treatment. Most couples who attend marital therapy are depressed and worried about the future of their relationship.[4] Often marital therapy is a treatment of choice for that depression. However, if the depression or anxiety is severe, chronic, or biologically based (such as bipolar depression), then marital therapy may be postponed until the severely depressed partner has individual therapy. I usually do not do individual therapy with a partner of a couple that I intend to counsel or am counseling for marital problems. Individual therapy provides too much emotional contact between myself and one partner for the other partner thereafter to feel confident in my impartiality.

Other complicating factors may involve an important outsider of the marriage. Often partners' parents or siblings may interfere with a marriage. Sometimes a child will develop psychological problems as a response to parents' marital troubles. Family therapy might be necessary prior to marital therapy if a child is having substantial psychological or conduct problems. Sometimes one partner will be receiving individual therapy from another therapist or pastor, who usually empowers that person and complicates marital therapy. Alcohol or drug abuse or sexual affairs can also complicate or render impossible effective marital therapy.

ASSESSMENT OF WILLIAM AND NICKI

In the sections that follow, I discuss my assessment and four major interventions I made with William and Nicki. William and Nicki are, of course, pseudonyms for the partners. Personal information has been changed to protect their identities. In addition, the transcripts are not those of actual sessions with the couple. Rather, two graduate students role played the couple during videotaped demonstrations of a few of my interventions.[5]

In this chapter I discuss three interventions. One involves training in conflict management. The second deals with closeness and intimacy. The third attempts to promote a forgiving spirit. With each intervention, I discuss my rationale, give excerpts from the role play, and discuss what actually happened (in the case on which the role play is based) within the interaction and between sessions. Finally, I discuss what became of my actual clients.

Although the interventions are role plays, they are not scripted. Thus, they are quite realistic. The graduate students were instructed about the general personalities and presenting difficulties of the clients, but were told to be as difficult as real clients in their response to counseling.

Presenting Information

William and Nicki had been married thirteen years prior to their initiation of marital therapy. They were referred to me by their pastor, who led a theologically conservative Protestant congregation. Both husband and wife were professionals. William was a business manager, and Nicki worked about twenty-five hours each week, mostly before noon or at night. They considered it important for Nicki to be at home with their children during the before-school hours and when the children arrived home. Whenever Nicki worked at night, William cared for the children.

Three Assessment Sessions

Both partners completed the PAIR, which measured their ideal and perceived intimacy. Both wanted almost perfect intimacy, but they rated actual emotional and sexual intimacy at rock bottom and intellectual and recreational intimacy as very low.

On the Couples Pre-counseling Inventory, both partners repeatedly named emotional and sexual differences as important. Communication about conflictual topics was seen as particularly weak. Both partners identified Nicki's propensity to lose her temper as needing attention.

Within the assessment interviews, both partners referred to their loss of romance and desire to reestablish a romantic, loving, and sexual relationship. Both pointed to a need to communicate better on the issues about which they disagreed. Nicki wanted reassurance that she could trust William though she admitted to no reason to distrust him. Both partners felt "overextended" by their time commitments. They felt their overcommitments were causing strains in their marriage. Both professed to be committed to their marriage, but William was strongly considering a separation.

At the feedback session, I described their commitment to each other as a strength of their marriage, and I commended them on their attempt to seek help before the problems became worse. Together we prioritized the main goals for their marital therapy.

1. They wanted to rebuild love, romance, and a vibrant sexual relationship, which they thought would increase their warmth toward each other and would calm Nicki's jealousy and fears that William would leave her for another woman.

2. They wanted to learn better communication and conflict-management methods, especially what both partners could do to avert violence whenever Nicki began to lose her temper. They also wanted to resolve some of their differences, notably over how much William should support Nicki emotionally and how much Nicki should trust William.

3. They wanted to relinquish the hurt and anger each felt in response to the past year of conflict.

Both partners firmly maintained the children were uninvolved in the marital troubles. Though both expressed sadness and concern over the poor quality of their marriage, especially in recent months, neither partner showed signs of clinical depression or other diagnosable psychopathological difficulty. Nicki was diagnosed as Adjustment Disorder with Mixed Emotional Features,[6] showing anxiety and depression due to marital stress.

We agreed to meet weekly for ten hourly sessions over four months to work toward those three main goals. The tenth session was scheduled as an evaluation.

AN INTERVENTION TO DEAL WITH CONFLICT MANAGEMENT

Rationale

William and Nicki were experiencing substantial conflict that had arisen only within the last year. I thought the conflict might interfere with their establishing a more intimate relationship, so I proposed that we tackle communication and conflict management before trying to discuss intimacy.

Importantly, when I conduct a session on either conflict management or general communication, my main goal is almost always different from any couple's main goal. Generally, couples want to resolve the immediate issue, and when power struggles exist (as in the present case), the couples may want to "win" by convincing each other to accept their own position. As their counselor, I don't believe that they can solve longstanding problems problems in one, two, or three thirty-minute sessions. Rather, I want to help the couple develop a different *method* of resolving differences, so they can resolve the present and other future differences at home (without my presence). Because we may be working at some cross-purposes, I must continually keep my goals before the couple to prevent them from becoming bogged down in trying only to solve a specific problem.

In the first counseling interview after the three assessment sessions were complete, I began to teach the couple a language of communication—that their *intent* did not always perfectly produce the expected *impact* of the communication. I thought the first session was only moderately successful at accomplishing this, which is normal for counseling couples in conflict. Only through repetition will couples learn effectively to change their communication.

In the second counseling session, I wanted them to learn a new method of conflict resolution. I always use the method developed by Roger Fisher and William Ury and described in their best-selling book *Getting to Yes: Negotiating Agreement Without Giving In.*[7] Their premise is that chronic conflict occurs because people establish "positions" they assume to be the only ones able to meet their interests. The positions are often incompatible. This incompatibility is sensed as an insoluble difference and the partners feel that no solution is possible except (as a minimum) compromise, which both partners feel is an abandonment of their position and thus as "losing" the conflict. Ury and Fisher maintain that the partners have lost sight of their true objective, which is to *satisfy*

their interests. Many solutions to their differences will allow them to satisfy both sets of interests simultaneously once the couple is persuaded
that they really want to meet their interests more than to "win."

In the following excerpt, I introduce the method to William and Nicki.
They apply it to one difference. As when I deal with their communication, several repetitions are required before the couple can resolve
longstanding conflicts without the counselor's assistance.

First, they were taught that conflict resolution involves two steps:
problem identification (and agreement by the spouses about the statement of the problem) and problem negotiation. In the following excerpt,
we initially try to identify the problem, then use Fisher and Ury's method
to solve it. I explain Fisher and Ury's rationale, and the partners are
helped to identify their interests, brainstorm possible solutions, evaluate
which are the most promising, and agree to try one promising solution.

Session Dialogue*

T: Let's talk about the trust issue.

H: Well, it's come up, I guess most recently, but it's come up a number of times in the marriage by . . . I often take clients out to have
dinner or lunch, for that matter. Nicki is quite aware of who I go
out with wining and dining people. It's a family business. That's
how we see it. But the issue in terms of trust is questioning who I
go out with, or places that I go. And I think that's inappropriate.
We've been married a long time and it's like, how dare she question me? I think that's the core.

W: How dare I? he says. He does have clients. Usually, it's "Nicki,
the clients are coming home tonight. Have something prepared."
This time he goes to Chez Pierre with Michelle-my-Belle. . . .

H: [Interrupts] I called you that day to say we were working late on a
proposal and when we finished, we would go out to a nice restaurant.

W: *We've* never even been there. That's the most expensive restaurant in town.

---

* In this transcript, **T** introduces the therapist's comments, **H** indicates the
husband's (William's) comments, and **W** indicates the wife's (Nicki's) comments.

H: But what I'm trying to figure out is how dare you question me.

W: You never took any other client there. At nine at night? Who eats dinner at nine at night? Every night you want dinner at six.

H: It just so happened that we worked throughout the evening. But I called you and told you this.

W: That day. He called me that day, at work.

H: You know you and I have never had a problem with me being out with someone or being involved with someone else if it were business-related.

W: Yeah, and you even had cologne on!

H: Nicki, I wear cologne every day.

W: You *don't* wear cologne every day.

H: You even bought me Calvin Klein.

W: You don't wear it every day. You don't wear it every day!

H: Yes I do. I do!

T: Let me interrupt. Nicki, what would you like to see happen?

W: I don't think he should go out on dinners like that any more.

T: What would you like to see happen, William?

H: To not be accused about conducting my business. Particularly when it's up front, and a family situation, like it's always been.

W: Family!

T: Okay, [to Nicki] so you think he shouldn't go out to dinner and [to William] you're saying that you can go out and she shouldn't accuse you.

H: Right.

T: So, the way you have the disagreement set up, the only way that you can resolve this is if one person gives up. The only way William can be satisfied is if you give up your demand that he never go out to dinner with another client. The only way that . . .

W: [Interrupts] Not as long as he's married to me.

T: [Continues] So the only way that William can be happy is if he does go out with a client, and furthermore, that you don't ever accuse him again about, about what? About unfaithfulness? Is that a concern?

W: Is it?

H: It's not for me, Nicki. I'm conducting business and the money I make, I bring home for us.

W: How are you conducting business in a candlelight French restaurant?

T: Let me interrupt. We're not really making any progress to resolve this. It's framed as an impasse. It's framed as a win-or-lose situation. Somebody's got to lose if you continue to think this way. You're in a head-butting situation where nobody can win.

So . . . what I'm going to do is to have you behave in a way that is very different from the way you usually behave. This is not like something you would do forever and ever. This is like, you break an arm and you put a cast on it and let it heal. And the cast is very unnatural. You don't make a healthy arm by putting a cast on it and wearing it for the next twenty years. But when you have a broken arm, you do things that are unnatural to allow that to heal. So, I'm going to ask you to try to go beyond the positions that you have staked out—the position of no dinners out, no accusations—and try to figure out what's behind those positions. How did you arrive at that position to meet the interests that you have . . . ?

Now, Nicki, think of what interests you have that have led to the position you've taken: that he shouldn't go out. What are you really wanting to accomplish? What interests are you trying to satisfy?

W: Well, I guess it makes me feel insecure when he does that because he doesn't compliment *me* or take *me* out to dinner.

T: Good. So, one of the interests you have is you would like to get from him some kind of validation that makes you feel secure instead of insecure.

W: Yes.

83

T: William, what kind of interests do you have behind your position?

[Discussion continues for about fifteen minutes.]

T: Let's see. So now we have a couple of lists. And the way I understand it—see if you all understand it this way—is that you have two major interests, William, behind the position you took. One of your interests is that you want to be sure Nicki affirms your trustworthiness. You feel you have a history of that and you would like for her to somehow acknowledge that. The other interest is that you're worried that if you stop taking business clients out altogether, that will damage the finances in your business and therefore have a negative impact on both of you. And so whatever the solution you end up working out, you want to be sure that you are able to conduct business without suffering financial losses.

Nicki, as I understand your interests behind your position, you want to feel secure. You don't want to feel threatened. So, whatever the solution is to this, you want to somehow feel that you are in a secure position. Second, you want to feel valued as a woman. You mentioned some ways William might do that, like spending money on you, complimenting you. But however he does that, you want to feel that he values you as a woman. And then the third interest is that whatever the solution is, you don't want to feel like you're being taken for granted, that he's just proposing a solution. Somehow you're receiving consideration.

Now, you each have some major interests that you want to be sure are met with a solution. So what I would like for you to do is to use your creative minds, the same creativity you would apply in your business or your profession, to try to come up with some kind of *different* solution that meets all these needs or some way of communicating that meets these needs. What do you think?

[Later, the discussion continues.]

H: My point is: I've never given you any reason to question me.

W: I know that. It's not that I distrust you. It's just that it was so different. I just felt really . . . it just made me think, why is he doing that? But maybe if we did things together more often I wouldn't feel like that. When I'm sitting at home just, you know, wondering what you're doing and how come we never . . . . Maybe if we did things more often I wouldn't have thought anything about it.

T: Let me interrupt here just a minute. I noticed how fast it passed, your telling him that you knew that he didn't—that he really wouldn't—have an affair or anything like that. You said it and then you went on. I think that's the very thing you were looking for—that assurance from her. It seems like, I've noticed both of you doing the same thing. You seem to have a lot of positive things that you think about each other, but you get involved in presenting your side of things and you say them and then you go on and they don't get noticed because of the brushfire that's going on elsewhere. Anyway, I don't want to distract you from this problem-solving task. But I just wanted to bring up that I noticed how you do affirm each other without making a big deal of it, kind of understated.

Nicki made a suggestion, and I don't want to divert away from her suggestion. Her suggestion was that you go out more. So that would make her feel better. [Looking at Nicki] That would make you feel more valued, make you feel more complimented, more secure. It would meet the interest you have to make you not feel taken for granted.

W: Right.

Discussion

In the excerpt above, Nicki and William were involved in an emotional argument. My challenge was to help them get past the emotionality and turn their discussion into a productive problem-solving session. I first attempted to break up the pattern of the argument, justifying my imposition of another way of interacting by using the metaphor of the cast on the broken arm.

I explained Fisher and Ury's method briefly—actually, probably too briefly—and got Nicki and William to identify their interests. As in the present case, this usually requires coaching for the couple to learn to identify their "interests."

Nicki finally proposed a workable solution—that William and she go out to a fancy restaurant periodically, affirming Nicki as a secure woman and leaving William with the flexibility to continue business dinners, which he believed to be crucial to the success of his business.

After the second session, from which the previous excerpts were drawn, the actual couple experienced a sense of increased warmth and competence at dealing with their problems. They felt that they had begun to learn a valuable problem-solving method that they could improve with repeated use.

A third session had them employ the method to work with a different problem. They left the session feeling optimistic about their prospects, and they even mentioned that they might want to end therapy prior to the agreed-upon ten sessions. I cautioned them that relapses often occurred. Importantly, couples can rarely learn different communication (i.e., the intent-impact distinction) and different conflict resolution (i.e., Ury and Fisher's method) in only one or two sessions devoted to each. Rather, like a computer program that iterates toward a solution, the counseling session repeats important lessons across sessions.

In the week after the third session, William and Nicki had an explosive disagreement during a two-hour automobile trip. Nicki became so angry that she hit William on the arm and shoulder.

At the beginning of the fourth session, William announced that he intended to move out "for a while." He had already rented an apartment for a month. Nicki was hurt that William had acted unilaterally. During the fourth session, she became angry and again hit William. Intensely embarrassed at her loss of control, she left the session angrily. I followed her and asked her to return to discuss the incident. She refused and stormed away. Fifteen minutes later, she returned to the office where I was continuing to talk to William.

Nicki asked if I would counsel her individually about her inability to control her anger. I told her and William that I saw myself as *their* marital counselor and that it would not be wise for me to counsel her individually. I referred her to an excellent Richmond therapist. She agreed to see him, and we suspended marital counseling until she had worked with him to control her anger.

After two months, William and Nicki recontacted me to resume marital therapy. Session 5 was used to review their efforts to communicate and solve problems using Ury and Fisher's method. After session five, William moved back into the home.

Session 6 was a productive session on conflict management. Both William and Nicki were delighted that Nicki had been able to hold her temper so well during the recent month. Both felt that they were better able to deal with their differences productively and to handle conflict whenever it arose without it mushrooming into destructive angry outbursts.

AN INTERVENTION TO DEAL WITH INTIMACY

Rationale

By the time we were ready to deal with intimacy, William and Nicki had attended six counseling sessions working on communication and conflict. Despite having less conflict and communicating better, the couple still reported feeling little warmth for each other.

In the present session (session 7), we agreed to discuss their patterns of emotional support. Overall, I wanted to accomplish two goals in that session. First, I attempted to use the physical space within the counseling room as a metaphor for their psychological experience of intimacy and distance. Second, I wanted to rekindle positive feelings of empathy and support within the session.

Session Dialogue

T: You've told me that you seem to be doing better, not having as many disagreements, not losing your temper as much. Yet, this feeling of emotional separateness that you've had over the last couple of years is still there. Although you're not having as much conflict, there is not a real romance and love that you can feel.

W: Seems like we interact less now that we don't fight.

T: That's always a problem. When you're fussing, at least you are in contact. So, something has to be done to get you some positive contact. What I'd like is for you to pretend for a minute. Use this room as some kind of space, a picture of how the emotional closeness feels in your relationship. That wall and this wall—when you're against each wall—that's like the farthest apart you could possibly ever get. You have no contact—zero. You're just never speaking, never doing anything together. And let's say that hugging in the middle is like the extreme emotional closeness that you would expect. How would you portray your relationship right now? Stand wherever it is.

[They rise from their chairs and move to a position that is about two-thirds of the room apart.]

T: Okay, how does that feel? Does that feel about right? So it looks like you're fairly far apart, but it could be a lot worse.

W: It could be worse. We're doing social things together. We're not emotionally close but we're socially there.

H: It's like we have our own lives in a way. We're dealing with the kids separately. She still works at night, and I still work during the day. But . . . we're just not talking about things that are important to us or even problems that we talked about before.

T: Show me where you would like to be.

[They move hesitantly together and embrace.]

W: Like this.

T: Now, you both have very busy lives. With three kids, it's hard to be like that all the time. What do you think is the best shot you could probably get, given that you have all these things going on in your life? How close could you get?

[They release each other but continue to hold hands and stand close to each other.]

H: I think at least at arm's distance or something—to be able to con-nect.

T: And how would that feel? Would that feel still too far apart?

W: It would be manageable.

T: But not ideal?

W: No, not ideal. But I could live at least knowing that sometimes when we get closer, usually we're like this.

H: At the same time, it's nice for her to be at a distance because we can do what we need to do in terms of our own lives then, at some time come back and be closer. That seems more natural. It feels natural to me.

T: Okay. So, ideally you would like to be hugged up tight, but practically you think that having some distance is still about the best that could possibly happen.

W: I think *some* distance; he thinks *more* distance.

T: So you think there is a difference in the amount of closeness that you would like. You would like more than William?

W: I prefer to be closer.

T: Is that your perception also?

H: Yes, for the most part.

T: Okay, let's move our chairs to the distance that you feel you are apart right now.

[They move their chairs, then sit down.]

T: What would have to happen to get you closer together?

W: Talk more. Be there for each other more.

T: Okay, talk more, be there for each other more. [Looks at William]

H: I think talking about specific issues that came up or things, events that have happened in our lives, whether they are with other family members or experiences we've had with the kids. . . . [Names other potential topics of conversation]

T: So, if you were going to talk more, William has named many things it would help to talk about. What else besides those do you think it would help to talk about?

W: Our hopes, our dreams, our goals for the future. We used to talk about it all the time, every day, what we were going to accomplish and even though we're older now we still have hopes and dreams for ourselves and for our children. Now, we don't even talk about that. I'd say the weather is the most intimate thing we talk about.

T: Would you feel comfortable talking about your hopes and dreams right now?

W: Yes.

T: Would you? [looking at William, who nods] Let me move myself out of the picture. You talk about things that you want to have happen.

[They talk about their daily lives for about three minutes.]

T: Right now, how close do you feel?

[They move their chairs closer.]

T: It helps to know you're talking about things you would like to accomplish. It looked to me that your children pull you apart but at the same time they give you a source of common value that pulls you together. It's like a rubber band. At times it keeps you apart but also helps you snap back together. Especially as you focus on how you want to give your lives to them. I didn't want to interrupt you. What other kind of dreams are you having?

H: I have dreams of sending them to the best schools, so we must work hard so we can afford that. That's a dream. I know you share that. Our parents struggled. We've talked when we got married, that we didn't want to have to work two, three, four, or five jobs. That's why I went to graduate school, so we can afford the things we like. I want our kids to be able to do the things we didn't do. I guess that's a dream of ours.

W: But sometimes we get too caught up in it, and we forget that there's more to life than just giving our children material things. I guess *I* have a dream of us all going on a vacation together. I saw that goofy movie with the whole family, and they go on their vacations together. All those things happened to them, but they still pulled together as a family. I don't see us doing that really. When was the last time we took a vacation?

H: We should. We've talked about traveling around the world. You've been places abroad. I've been places abroad. The kids have learned about geography. Tim is going on thirteen now. He's talking about where Egypt is.

T: I hate to interrupt you. I noticed how the whole emotional climate is different when you do things like this than it was. The anger just isn't there. Your faces are relaxed. You're looking positive and looking up. I think you both seem to have a sense that it's important for you, that it's good for you, to do this. Of course, you can't have the same conversation all the time. One of the things that might get you closer together is to take time to do this more often. The problem with a busy schedule is when can that happen?

H: Maybe it's reasonable for us to sit down and talk about the things we want to do and knowing that we're both busy and we've got things going.

W: I just think also that the nights we're both off at the same time that we, well . . . it seems that we're together, but we're not together.

H: I'd agree with that. So you think we're kind of off doing our own things. . . . I just think it's nice that we talk about this because it's been a while since we talked like this.

W: It's been a long time.

T: It sounds like you're feeling closer again. How are you feeling now? Move your chairs. [They move very close.]

W: I don't know if I feel like touching yet, though.

T: But you feel close?

W: Yeah.

H: Well, I do. [His hand starts playing with Nicki's arm.]

T: I remember when you first came and we were talking in that assessment session and you were talking about the romance you wanted to get back. This gives me an idea of William's flirty little romance. I thought that was very touching.

Discussion

In addition to using the session to create more empathy and to make the couple aware of their intimacy-enhancing and distance-producing behaviors, I approached other portions of their intimacy in subsequent sessions. In the following session (session 8), we dealt with their sexual relationship. They talked freely about how they made love and about their enjoyment of lovemaking during the first eight or so years of marriage.

Nicki began to complain about feeling physically "irritated" by William's fingers during sexual stimulation. She attributed the irritation to feeling hurried and pressured because she and William were under considerable time pressures. The complaints and the time pressures had made Nicki and William mutually cut down on the frequency of their lovemaking until at the present time, they made love only about once every two or three weeks. Often that experience was not enjoyable because they became too aroused too quickly, and frequently, Nicki still felt irritated by William's sexual caresses.

I described the cycle they had maintained—withdrawing from lovemaking until they felt very arousable, then having unpleasurable sex because they were too arousable, so they withdrew from further frequent sexual contact.

They agreed to attempt to break the cycle by having sexual relations more often—at least two times a week during the next two weeks prior to session 9. They planned four specific times when they could make love between sessions. They agreed to make love four times even if they felt irritated or if they did not have a good experience with their sex.

They expressed concern that their stress levels would still make their lovemaking feel hurried. Expression of that fear led to a discussion of their harried, overextended lifestyles. They agreed that their time commitments needed streamlining, but time ran out in session 8 before they could revamp their schedules to include more co-active and intimate time.

AN INTERVENTION TO DEAL WITH CONFESSION AND FORGIVENESS

In the last few minutes of session 8, we had reflected briefly on the hurts that each partner had experienced over the last few years. Both partners agreed that they harbored some residual anger and bitterness. I suggested that we needed to deal with forgiveness in the ninth session. Both agreed.

I then asserted that confession precedes forgiveness and assigned them to reflect, prior to session 9, on times they had hurt their partner recently. In the following session, occurring two weeks later, they confessed those times to each other, which would perhaps allow them to receive the partner's forgiveness.

The ninth session began with a review of the homework—to make love four times. They reported successfully accomplishing the assignment. The first and second times were not entirely pleasurable, but the third time was "a dream." The fourth time was not as spectacular but was "good." William and Nicki reported enjoying each other sexually more than they had for years. They said they intended to continue making love about twice weekly.

We talked briefly about streamlining their schedules. Both said they needed to reduce their stress, but both were at a loss as to how their lifestyle could be simplified.

Finally, I asked whether they had prepared during the week to confess times when they had hurt their partner. Both had spent considerable effort preparing. William had prepared a list, and Nicki said she had thought and prayed often about her part.

Session Dialogue

T: As you know, there's power in forgiveness. So what we want to do in this part of the hour is talk with each other about some times that you've hurt the other person. Let me move out of the way and have you talk with each other. People do this differently. Some people find it helpful to hold hands, to bind themselves together with that touch. What I'd like for you to do is to try *not* to offer instant forgiveness. If you've built up these pains over two or three years, it's usually hard to instantly forgive the other person because they say their sorry. So, I really want you to think about what the other person is saying and decide to forgive or not, depending on your thinking.

W: I'll start. . . . I'm sorry that I lose my temper all the time—sometimes worse than a child, I guess—throwing a temper tantrum. I won't do it anymore. And I'm sorry that I hit you—a few times. All the times. I'm sorry for hitting you.

H: I have my list here, and I have two things. I decided I would like your forgiveness for provoking you. At the dinner party when we had guests over, I said some not-so-nice things to you that I shouldn't have.

W: That's okay. It doesn't matter. I knew it was business.

H: I'm glad you're so forgiving.

W: What else?

H: Well, that's one. Another one that I have is asking your forgiveness for the dinner. Even though it was business, I was wrong, I probably should have called you. I even have one more. Being negligent with the kids. I know there was one instance where I sort of just took off and thought they'd be okay, and you came home early and were just in an outrage. I felt terrible as a parent and as a husband, that I wasn't owning up to my responsibilities. So I ask your forgiveness. That's what I've been able to come up with so far. I'm sure there are other things. So, Counselor, those are what I came up with.

T: It's my sense, after hearing both of you, that you have thought about some of the times you've hurt the other person. I'm sure over a period of two or three years, this probably just touched the surface. But what I was impressed about was your willingness to actually say, "I'm sorry. I was wrong under these circumstances." It just seemed to me that you both had real care and concern for each other. I guess that was encouraging to me to see that. What did you think about this?

W: I didn't really think he was going to say anything. He never admits that he was wrong or that he did something to me. I was really surprised that you [to William] did that. I wasn't going to say anything else, but I know I've done a lot of things to push you away or ignore you, make little snide remarks. That's something I'll change in the future.

H: You know, I was thinking that—I didn't think I'd be this emotional [wipes tears away]—sometimes I sort of push at you. I know that's my style. You tell me that all the time. You say you don't like it, but I continue to do it. A lot of times I've thought that's not right, but I did it anyway because I was sort of tired, I guess. But I was thinking, this was difficult to come up with these three, and I know there are other things, but these are the three that stuck. I know these things need to be corrected, and I'm willing to take a stab at it so we can enjoy each other and get on with our lives and so I can tear this up and I won't need a list.

T: I think you have shown a lot of courage in admitting things that are not easy to admit to each other. I'm sure that you'll hurt each other again. It's part of being people. I hope that your memory of this—of confessing these things to each other—will make it easier next time not to hold onto that hurt until it gets to be a bitter feeling, that it'll make it easier to right away admit when you know you've done something to hurt the other person.

Discussion

As is often the case, forgiveness has the power to heal hurts.[8] In this session, neither Nicki nor William expected to become as involved as he or she did. Yet sincere repentance can set the stage for healing the brokenhearted. This was an excellent way to end our formal contacts. Only the final evaluation session remained.

DISPOSITION OF THE CASE

The final evaluation session took place after a three-week break. I presented William and Nicki with a report of my perceptions of their relationship since beginning marital therapy six and one-half months previously. Overall, they attended three assessment sessions, nine therapy sessions, and the final assessment session. Nicki had attended seven sessions of individual psychotherapy for controlling her anger, and the couple had remained separated for two months while Nicki was in therapy.

In the two and one-half months since William had returned to the home, their relationship had not been without conflict, but they reported more liveliness, intimacy, and sex than in the previous three years. Both also reported more control of anger.

William attributed his anger and loss of temper to high levels of stress at work and home. He had formulated a plan for keeping stress at a more manageable level. Nicki attributed much of her anger control to premenstrual syndrome. When she perceived rejection from William near the beginning of her menstrual period, she reacted with anger. Both William and Nicki were especially sensitive to not getting under stress near the beginning of Nicki's period.

I acknowledged how hard William and Nicki had worked to conform their life to biblical patterns of behavior. I suggested that they create a special anniversary event that clearly signaled to each that they were beginning anew with their marriage. I called this the "Joshua intervention," recalling how Joshua built a memorial to the Lord after crossing into the

Promised Land (Josh. 4:20–24). They elected to go skiing for a week at Wintergreen and to set aside that week each year as a reminder of God's faithfulness in bringing them through their marital crisis.

Follow-up at Two Years

Approximately two years later, I saw William and Nicki at a production I attended at their church. They described their marriage as having "gotten back on track." They remain happily married. No doubt their marriage has tensions, but they seem better able to cope with pressures after marital therapy than before.

CHRISTIAN OR NOT? WHAT'S THE DIFFERENCE?

William and Nicki were committed Christians. I have used the same method with couples who were not Christians. There are some differences when the method is applied with Christians and with non-Christians.

With Christian couples, I usually am asked about my religious beliefs and values at the beginning of therapy, whereas with non-Christian couples I am rarely asked. The frank expression of my Christian values in therapy with Christian couples usually promotes a good working alliance. I assure people that I am an active Christian while not giving a lot of unasked-for information about specific beliefs. When couples inquire directly about specific beliefs, I answer forthrightly. I usually interpret their inquiries as a need for assurance that they are entering a "safe" therapeutic environment, which I believe to be an entirely appropriate concern. Occasionally, partners have other motives for asking, such as trying to make me the arbiter in a power struggle over theology or trying to avoid entering therapy by setting me up as unqualified to be their counselor because I flunked their theology test. However, I have found these darker motives to be rare. When they occur, and if I detect them, I try to deal with the motives early in counseling.

Second, with Christians I use Christian concepts directly. I may also use techniques developed in pastoral psychology. For example, I may discuss their understanding of wifely submission and husbandly headship. Or I may ask them to speculate on the history of their commitment to Jesus and liken it to the ups and downs in their commitment to each other. If a high value on Scripture is in line with the partners' values, I may assign partners to study and meditate on Scriptures that might be relevant to their marital difficulties. I may discuss Scriptures with them, but I generally respond to rather than initiate such discussions. I may also assign couples to read writings by other Christians. With Christians, I may or may not discuss religious issues, depending on my clinical judgment concerning whether the issue is (a) a power struggle that the partners are using to try to triangulate me, (b) an avenue that is likely to sidetrack therapy, or (c) a sincere misunderstanding or disagreement that has therapeutic implications.

Third, with Christians, I may (or may not) pray with clients depending on the clients' expectations about what will happen in their counseling with me, whom they know to be a Christian. Naturally, I pray *for* my Christian and non-Christian clients, and I usually tell them that I pray for them. Non-Christians usually simply interpret my statement as an expression of concern for them, while Christian clients know that there are spiritual effects of prayer beyond the mere psychological.

With non-Christians, I counsel essentially the same as with Christians, except that I do not use as many explicitly Christian interventions. I am clear about my Christian beliefs and values, but try to assure the clients that I will not impose my values on them. Since non-Christian clients are not as likely to bring up religious topics, I cover such topics less, though even nonreligious clients bring up religious issues at times. When I express my religious beliefs or values, I carefully preface them with statements such as, "Of course, I'm coming at this issue from a Christian position, and I believe . . . ."

One goal I have with all clients is to aid their spiritual development, or at least not damage it. I believe that couples come to a *marital therapist* primarily for help with their marriage. Thus, they want competent help. Secondarily, couples choose a *Christian* therapist because they trust him or her to give counsel that is motivated by Christian love, guided by Christian principles, and help them shape their marriage into the covenantal relationship God expects of marriage.

At times, the Christian marriage counselor cannot simply help restore peace within the marriage if nonbiblical patterns of behavior exist—such as violence, infidelity, incest, drunkenness, and the like. Like Jesus, the Christian marital therapist then comes not to bring peace but a sword (Matt. 10:34–39). At those times, the therapist may be more concerned with the salvation of the individuals than the restoration of the sinful marriage. Under most conditions, though, marriage therapy can proceed in parallel with and can even assist individual spiritual development.

EDITOR'S COMMENTS

Paul Tournier, the famous Swiss counselor, once remarked to me that he didn't like counseling with more than one person at a time. One person, he said, demands the counselor's full attention. To counsel with two people at the same time and to be aware of the interaction between them is very difficult.

But marriage counseling, by its very nature, involves at least two people who most often are seen together. Dr. Worthington handles the complexities of two-person counseling well and introduces several novel approaches into his work.

First, unlike some other Christian counselors, Dr. Worthington addresses spiritual issues only "when clients are amenable, when clients bring up spiritual concerns, or when spiritual issues clearly need to be addressed for effective therapy." I am inclined to think, however, that spiritual issues *always* need to be addressed (at least briefly) for therapy to be effective. Can counseling really be called Christian if spiritual issues are able to be ignored completely, even though the counselor seeks to use techniques that are "consistent with Scripture but need not be derived explicitly from Scripture"?

Notice that the author seeks to clarify his position near the end of the chapter. He makes a valid point that discussion of religious issues sometimes become "(a) a power struggle that the partners are using to try to triangulate (the counselor) . . . , (b) an avenue that is likely to sidetrack therapy, or (c) a sincere misunderstanding or disagreement that has therapeutic implications." Each of these three could be therapeutic issues in themselves, however—issues that could be creating tension in the marriage and should be considered.

Second, this chapter makes several references to the role of perception in counseling. A husband, wife, and therapist may each perceive the problem differently. Part of effective therapy involves helping individuals understand each other's perceptions and guiding counselees as they change their perceptions. This issue of perception would seem to be an important variable that often appears to be ignored by counselors. Marriage counseling is likely to be ineffective if the husband and wife retain strongly different perceptions of their relationship and marriage problems.

Third, Dr. Worthington gives unusual attention to assessment. His reasons for doing so are convincing, and his written critique of the case after the third session is likely to be appreciated by most couples. This is a time-consuming activity that shows the counselor's special dedication to couples and his courage in committing his initial conclusions to paper. Notice, too, that the author sets a time limit (ten sessions) near the beginning of his work with the couple. A time limit may give hope and help motivate couples to work more diligently on the relationship, but there must be flexibility. Some problems can be dealt with rather quickly; others take much longer.

Fourth, many (but not all) marriage counselors will agree that individual therapy with one of the partners is not wise if both spouses are being seen together for marriage counseling. If a marriage counselor does do individual therapy with one spouse, care must be taken to insure that the other spouse does not in any way feel left out.

Fifth, did you notice how often the counselor interrupts the couple? Some counselors would not do this, but Dr. Worthington clearly wants to stop useless haggling between the spouses. He appears to perceive himself as a teacher who, at times, teaches his counselees how to function better. It could be argued that all counseling is a type of teaching. But teachers, of course, differ in the way they approach their "students." Some may resist being interrupted, even when the interruptions are polite, as they are in this case.

Sixth, this case illustrates the value of moving about and making use of the physical space between the participants. This is a technique that allows people to express themselves nonverbally and, as the case shows, it can be used effectively, especially when you are working with more than one counselee.

Finally, I was impressed with the "Joshua intervention" that was mentioned near the end of the case. This helps to cement the new learning and to remind the counselees of their progress. Christians would relate especially well to the biblical example. This gives Christian input that Dr. Worthington might not interject otherwise.

CHAPTER FIVE

COUNSELING ANOTHER COUNSELOR

David E. Carlson

Editor's note: *In this chapter, David Carlson presents some unique perspectives on Christian counseling. The client is another professional counselor who was involved in an affair with a co-worker who, incidentally, was also a counselor. Unlike most other cases in this book, where the authors have presented a previously terminated case, Mr. Carlson got the client's permission* before *therapy began and has included the client's somewhat surprising post-therapeutic reaction to the counseling process.*

David Carlson, president of Arlington Counseling Associates in Arlington Heights, Illinois, has a B.A. and an M.A. in sociology from Northern Illinois University, a B.D. from Trinity Evangelical Divinity School, and an M.S.W. from the University of Chicago. He is a diplomate in clinical social work and has trained at the Family Institute of Chicago, the Family Learning Center of South Bend, Indiana, and the Experiential Family Therapy Program affiliated with the Department of Preventive Medicine and Community Mental Health at the University of Illinois in Chicago. He taught for several years at Trinity College in Illinois and more recently was on the faculty of Trinity Evangelical Divinity School.

David Carlson's previous publications include a book in the Resources for Christian Counseling series: Counseling and Self-Esteem.

TIM IS A COUNSELOR WHO CAME to see me because he was in conflict about his marriage. He was involved with a female counselor who was his co-worker. Like many affairs, Tim's infidelity began innocently. Tim and his co-worker would have a cup of coffee to review their work. A mutual attraction developed, and they began to spend time together nonprofessionally. Eventually they became involved sexually and Tim moved out of his home, leaving his wife and children. Interestingly, Tim's father had abandoned his family; this made me wonder if Tim was reenacting his own abandonment.

Tim came to see me for individual counseling because he and his wife had seen me for premarital counseling. Following his marriage, Tim had also come to see me for some unfinished business related to his abandonment by his father and overcontrol by his mother. He also wanted help with a history of procrastination and being late for appointments. We came to understand these behaviors as a way of expressing anger and fighting a sense of being controlled. These family-of-origin issues included engulfment and abandonment, failure to separate and develop his own unique self, i.e., individuate, manipulation by caretakers to get their needs met at Tim's expense, self-destructive ways of dealing with anger, inability to identify and ask for his own needs to get met, and irresponsibility in managing finances, time, and relationships. These issues were worked on in counseling with some improvement, but they were not resolved at the time he terminated his counseling. As you read through the process you will see that these became the content of his current counseling. I view the affair as a symptom of these unresolved family-of-origin issues.

Now, five years later, Tim called for a consultation. From the message he left with my secretary, I thought he was asking for a professional consultation on one of his cases. But when he came to my office he asked me, "Do you think you can work with me?" Tim's concern was, "You worked with Lori and me. Can you be objective in working with me and not feel disloyal to my wife?" The first session was used by Tim to decide if he could work with me. Because I was a Christian, he wondered if I would be able to counsel him without judging him for his affair and help him make sense out of his decision to leave his wife.

I told Tim that I was pro-marriage and that as a Christian I would not support him in an affair. I affirmed that I was willing to work with him to understand the affair and make some choices about his marriage. Could he work with me knowing my values and beliefs?

When I asked Tim for permission to publish his case, he responded rapidly. "Okay, you know I want to feel special," he said. "I'm a pleaser, you know. How could I turn you down?"

"Yes, that worries me. I wonder how writing up the interviews will affect therapy. Will you be able to be spontaneous and not monitor your responses?" I questioned.

"I think so. I've got some pretty serious things to talk about with you. It's not like I'd have an audience."

"True. I'm also concerned about your being scared when I get close to you emotionally. Will you feel intruded upon or violated when I report those intimate thoughts, feelings, and interpretations?"

"I do get scared when you get close emotionally, but I trust you. I know you won't betray me. I settled that in our first interview."

SUMMARY OF MY COUNSELING APPROACH

I am basically an insight-oriented therapist who begins with the client's "here and now" and works back to the client's "where and when." My starting point is, Where is the client? What is this person experiencing now? Why is the person seeking help now? What is happening in this person's life, relationships, work, family, and inner world that is causing pain?

I approach each person with a set of five questions[1] that gives me perspective on what I need in order to be helpful. These "outcome" questions help the client tell the therapist what the focus of treatment needs to be. They are questions that provide both counselor and patient with a reference point during therapy. The content is reviewed and the answers revised and developed throughout treatment. I use the outcome questions as a framework to guide the interview process and to evaluate counseling progress.

A basic assumption in my counseling is that people seek counseling because something is missing in their lives. That "something" is frequently an unchanged behavior, an inexperienced feeling, an unfulfilled need, an unachieved dream, an unpleasant memory, an unsatisfied relationship, or a frustrating circumstance. Usually people seeking counseling have exhausted their ways of coping. They may have even lost sight of what it is they want.

Asking, "What do you want that you do not now have?" is a productive starting point. I seldom begin with the common question, "What is the problem?" because that emphasizes the negative and is of little help in moving the person toward a positive resolution. I have found that focusing on the goal or desired outcome generates a feeling of hope that life can be different. Also, it is sometimes easier to know what you want than to know what is wrong.

"How will you know when you get what you want?" is the second question I explore in the first session. Not knowing what a person wants is common for a client seeking help. Therefore, I spend time helping the person define what he or she wants before helping identify what he or she will see, hear, feel, or do when the desired state is reached. Notice that the answer to the question "How will you know when you get 'it'?" is answered by sensory (hear, see, feel, taste, smell) experience.[2]

"How will your life be different?" is my third question.

My intent is to learn what the client's expectations are. Are the desired changes achievable, and will they bring the desired positive effects?

Frequently, clients are unaware of what gets in the way of experiencing their desired state. Asking the fourth outcome question, "What stops you from getting 'it'?", helps explore the blockages and informs both counselor and client what needs to be faced and overcome. When asking the blockage question or any of the outcome questions, I try to be as specific as possible. The word *it* is seldom used when asking questions about the desired state. As the counselor identifies his or her understanding of the client's desired state, the client is able to affirm or correct the counselor's understanding of the goal.

"What do you need in order to get what you want?" is the fifth outcome question. In my early years as a therapist, I would forget to explore what resources the person needed in order to achieve the goal. This is a fundamental mistake that results in frustration for both the counselor and client because the goal is identified but the resources are not identified or developed. The problem cannot be solved or the goal realized without resources. "What do you need in order to achieve your goal?" is a question that facilitates the exploration of resources that need to be developed and identifies those which the person has and may not be using.

These five questions provide a direction for the counseling. They create a working framework and give both counselor and client hooks on which to hang and organize the interview.

My job as counselor is to help the person think about his or her behavior, feelings, needs, dreams, memories, relationships, and circumstances in ways that bring understanding, relief, and effective ways to live. Frequently, the person has lived life unconsciously and has no sense of the connectedness between one's behavior, affect (feelings) and thoughts. B.A.T. is an acronym for behavior, affect, and thoughts. I use it to remind myself of these three areas to explore in counseling.

You will probably not be surprised to learn that the client often feels and believes that life does not make sense. This is because he or she is not a whole person, i.e., behavior, affect, and thought are not connected. When one's B.A.T. is connected and lived out congruently, we describe that person as being integrated or whole.

Discovering the developmental experiences, deprivations, or historical life events is key to understanding how and when the client lost connectedness. I use Erik Eriksen's eight life stages as one way of understanding my client's story developmentally.[3] As most counselors are aware, Eriksen conceptualizes human developmental tasks into eight polarities. They are (1) Infancy: trust versus mistrust, (2) Early Childhood: autonomy versus shame and doubt, (3) Play Ages: initiative versus guilt, (4) School Ages: industry versus inferiority, (5) Adolescence: identity versus identity confusion, (6) Young Adulthood: intimacy versus isolation, (7) Adulthood: generativity versus self-absorption, and (8) Senescence: integrity versus disgust/despair. These developmental tasks are conceptualized in other ways. For example, I listed in the introduction to the case several issues that need to be addressed in my client's therapy. These are developmental needs or tasks. Any developmental task that has not been completed at the appropriate age is unfinished. These unfinished developmental tasks or needs continue to influence a person's perceptions, relationships, and coping abilities throughout life.

I also use permission statements (e.g. You have a right to be curious, You can think and feel at the same time, You can be responsible for your own life) to help me assess a person's developmental needs.[4] The client is given a list of permission statements and asked to pick which one he or she would most like to have heard from his or her parents.

I find Winnicott's four selves useful in thinking about my client's developmental experience.[5] The (1) Lost Self is the client's personality that was repressed in order to survive in his or her family. Repression is an unconscious process (defense) of pushing feelings, needs, perceptions, and memories out of consciousness to avoid pain. The (2) Disowned Self is also an unconscious process of ignoring one's feelings, needs, perceptions, and behaviors that are unacceptable to the most significant people in the client's life. The (3) False Self is the public personality that results from the developmental experiences of losing and disowning one's (4) Real Self (feelings, needs, sensations, memories, perceptions, and behaviors). The False Self is the personality that was used to adapt to the pain of growing up in the family of origin. This public personality was very useful in the past to survive.

Because insight is sometimes not enough to produce change, I also use an experiential approach. Clients may be able to hear or see what needs to change but need to connect the perception to feelings. When these feelings are blocked or repressed, an experiential approach is helpful.

Experiential counseling is helping the client get in touch with feelings and then express those feelings with deep breathing, loud sounds, and vigorous motion.

My counseling approach is rooted in the belief that I am Christ's representative in this client's life. I am not good parent or spouse. I am not rescuer, I am not knight or prince on a white horse, I am not magician or miracle worker. I am another human being who offers to be with my clients in their pain, to empathize with them without reinforcing their distorted perception or encouraging a sense of infantile entitlement. My role is to encourage them to accept responsibility for their growth without blaming parents, God, circumstances, etc., to challenge them without creating shame or humiliation, to confront them with their own values without obligating them to my agenda.

As Christ's ambassador in my client's life, I am responsible to create a healthy atmosphere that is safe, nurturing, and understanding. The helping relationship needs to be a place where the client can find and expose his or her Real Self and learn to be Real Self in relating to me as therapist. As therapy progresses, the client is then encouraged to be that Real Self in his or her relationships outside of counseling. This is a therapeutic goal. My aim is to be Christ to my clients in the way Jesus was to the woman at the well. She left her water pot and invited the men in her city to "Come, see a man who told me everything I ever did" without making her want to run and hide (John 4:29).

I desire to be the kind of person who helps hurting people respond the way prostitutes, tax collectors, and sinners experienced Jesus. They welcomed Jesus to their gatherings without fear of judgment, attack, or ridicule. Jesus did not have to first say to sinners, "Fear not" for them to feel safe. They could hear Jesus say, "It is not the healthy who need a doctor, but the sick" (Matt. 9:12).

THE INTERVIEW PROCESS

Tim came to the second interview with a question he wanted to answer: "Should I stay in my marriage or leave?" As a Christian, my belief is that people should stay in their marriages. But as a counselor, I have been trained not to tell someone what to do. This is a dilemma I face every day. This case will show how I attempt to honor both roles and beliefs.

I could have answered Tim's question biblically and theologically in a few minutes. Yet that would not help Tim deal with his question and answer it for himself. If I told him what to do, he might have compliantly agreed without facing the personal and marital issues that made him want to leave in the first place. Or he might have rebelled against my response, giving himself no opportunity to find happiness in his marriage or to learn how to apply his Christian faith to his personal struggles.

To help me with this dilemma, I reminded myself that whatever response I made would not guarantee that Tim chose his wife over his colleague. Tim claims, "It is not a choice of choosing one over the other. It is choosing my wife or not." With this conflict settled in my mind (I still struggle in my heart with wanting a simple, immediate way to affect the changes I want clients to make and the ones I think Christ and Scripture declare) I chose to ask him, "What is the issue here? You seem confused as to what you want to do."

Notice that I did not ask him, "What should you do?" Nor did I remind him that he claimed to be a Christian and I did not understand that there was even another possible choice than his marriage. This is an illustration of "beginning where the client is" rather than beginning where the counselor is. I wanted to know what was going on inside Tim that led him to ask the question, "Should I stay or leave my marriage?" While these kinds of life situations have biblical and theological answers, the questions usually do not arise out of biblical or theological doubts.

Tim's struggle, like so many people's struggles with sin, is rooted in emotional and relational disappointments and frustrations. Some readers may fear that perceiving sin this way would minimize the seriousness of sin or the destructive consequences of sin. Surprisingly for most clients it provides a way of looking at sin that makes the problem understandable and workable without denying their feelings or conflict.

Tim's response to my question, "What is at issue here?" surprised me. "I feel like a fake! No, I *am* a fake. Being straight is hard for me."

"Being straight is hard for you? I don't understand."

"I can't tell anyone what I think and feel. I can't tell Lori that I have never been happily married to her." He talks about being an actor more than a person. Tim begins to cry. This is very rare for him. He usually presents himself as very emotionally controlled. When I ask, "What are you feeling?" I don't get an answer right away. He looks away from me, seemingly unable to look me in the eyes as he has been doing. Hesitatingly, softly he responds, "Sadness, shame."

"Sad and ashamed for being an actor more than a real person?"

"Yes."

"What would it be like for you to be a real person?" I am asking the "evidence" question since he is telling me his goal, to be real. I want to know if Tim knows what it means to be real. Here I am looking for sensory descriptions, i.e., what he will see, hear, feel, do when he is a real person.

Tim tells me he will be real when he can tell the truth, when he can express his feelings and thoughts without fear of rejection, when he will not please others at his expense and when he will be able to choose what he wants rather than give in to others' desires. I am impressed that he is aware of what "being real" is. He has given me behaviors and feelings that will change when he is real.

I ask if he is aware of what blocks his being real.

"Fear."

"Of what?"

"Of not being liked, of rejection!"

"How did you learn that being real results in not being liked?"

Here Tim reminds me of living with a mother and two aunts who were perfectionistic and demanding. These three women alternately indulged him and demanded of him. "I learned to be nice, to smile, and to be compliant as a way of getting along."

"Yes, I now remember the story. I also remember how being nice helped you get along with women authority figures in your past job."

He laughs, "Oh, you remember her?" (his previous boss).

"Yes, and I remember how the other staff members got angry at you for the favoritism you seemed to generate with her. What did gaining her favor cost you?"

"Myself, being real."

"Wow, that is quite a price to pay. Is it worth it?"

"I think that's why I am here. It is not worth it at work or in my marriage."

Here I make a guess based on what he has told me about his life and marriage. Normally I would not offer this interpretation in the second interview, but I had a previous relationship with Tim and information about him so I thought the risk of his rejecting it was low. "Tim, I have an idea. I don't know if this is true or not. But as I listen to your history of being controlled by mother, aunts, and women bosses, is it possible that your desire to leave your wife is part of your attempt to be yourself and stop letting people control you, kind of like being able to say no for the first time to a woman?"

"I never thought of it that way, but it sure sounds like a possibility."

"It is my experience as a counselor that people marry each other as a way of working out a relationship that they could not work out with their parents. Would you be willing to look at your marriage to Lori as a way of trying to master your ability to get close without being dominated and controlled by a woman?"

"Yes, I think so. I can see that in other people's marriages, but I have not thought about that as a dynamic in my marriage."

"Tim, I've been reading a book that argues, 'People marry spouses who resemble their significant caretakers in both positive and negative ways.' Have you heard of the book by Harville Hendrix, *Getting the Love You Want*?" [6]

"Yes, in fact I'm reading it now."

"Okay, so you are familiar with the idea of marrying your problem parent?"

"Well, I haven't heard it put that way but it sounds right."

"Tim, it seems to me that when you were in for counseling previously you were struggling with some of the same issues—how to be yourself, how to stop being a pleaser, how to be your own person. Does that seem right to you?"

"Yes, I guess I don't learn too fast."

"Is it helpful to put yourself down?"

"There I go again."

"Well, I'm not going to let you get away with it here. Let me take you back to the idea of working out a relationship with Lori that is not like the compliant, passive/aggressive one you had with your mom and aunts. I want you to think this week about what it would take for you to be straight with Lori. That will be our focus next session."

A week later Tim came on time for his appointment. This is significant because it was not his usual pattern in making any kind of appointments on time. We had discussed this possible problem in the first session because Tim was concerned about my reaction to his arriving late. I told him that as long as he paid me he could come late for his appointment. Coming on time tells me Tim's motivation for counseling must be high and his resistance to facing himself and his inconsistencies must be low. I commented on his "being on time" because I wanted to check out his motivation and recognize that this represented a significant change in his behavior from our previous counseling.

I observed, "Tim, I remember that you had a habit of making commitments and then claiming to 'forget' them. We talked about how that was a way of saying no indirectly. I see this as an issue of being real. What is your pattern now in saying yes when you mean no?"

"I think I am doing that less, but it still happens from time to time. I still procrastinate, but I am better at not doing that."

I could have focused on how much better he is doing, but I thought a more important point to pursue was the connection between his passive-aggressive, withdrawing-avoiding behavior and the affair. "I wonder if your conflict over whether to stay or leave your marriage is part of this pattern of pleasing and procrastinating?"

Tim agreed that his staying in the marriage was out of fear of hurting Lori and his need to please. But he also felt he was an obligation to his wife.

I didn't understand what he meant, so I asked, "How do you get the message that you are an obligation to Lori?"

"Well, she mothers me."

"How's that?"

"She controls the money. I have to turn over my checks to her and then I have to ask for money. I have to account for everything I spend."

"And that makes you feel mothered?"

"Yes, she also makes me feel like I'm a spoiled child. She wrote me a letter. Incidentally, she now knows about the affair. She said she could be out of the house by August and I should make plans. She affirmed her commitment to me, and I think I'm the one who should leave."

"You should leave because . . . ?"

"Well, I'm the one who has had the affair. It would be easier for Lori and the kids to stay in the house. I owe them that."

"Can you leave the house without feeling like a victim?" (Other responses I could have made here were, You've decided to leave the marriage? or You feel like you ought to suffer for having an affair? or You feel like you owe them something but you are not willing to give them yourself?) I chose this question so we would focus on the side of him that gives away what he wants. This keeps us focused on his goal, learning to be real.

"Victim, hmmm, I have never thought of myself as victim; but now that you say it, that is exactly how it feels to be married to Lori."

"So, your choices as you see it are, you can either be hurtful to Lori and the kids or hurtful to yourself?"

"Yes, that's the way it feels."

"I'm thinking this dilemma is pretty common for you. For example, it is not only whether you or Lori stay in the house, but it is whether you stay in the affair or not."

"True."

"Tim, it sounds to me like we are talking about boundaries here. How do I please others without hurting myself, how do I give to others without playing victim, how do I accept responsibility for my behavior without accepting blame?"

Tim agreed that his boundaries were nonexistent and that he easily gave them away.

"I know we haven't talked about the last homework assignment, but I want to give you something else to read about boundaries. It is a little pamphlet we and our clients have found helpful. Do you know the name Rokelle Lerner? She wrote *Boundaries for Co-dependents*."[7]

"I think I make a conscious decision to not be straight," Tim confessed at the beginning of the fourth session. "I'm like a chameleon; I change with whoever I'm with. It feels like I lose myself or give up on myself."

"It seems to me that not being straight is your way of trying to have boundaries. You agree to meet someone or do something, but that is only an immediate response. Are you saying that many times you consciously agree but that you seldom intend to keep your commitments?" I identify this as passive-aggressive, a term he understands diagnostically and can apply to himself.

"Yes, I can't say no and feel good about it."

"Can you say yes any easier and feel good about it?"

"Apparently not. I never thought of it that way."

"If I am hearing you correctly, what is at issue here for you is your struggle to be accepted and autonomous. It is like a catch-22; you haven't figured out a way to get both at the same time, so you lie as a way of buying time until you can figure a way out. Interestingly, you seem to be able to charm people into accepting your 'forgetfulness.' And yet that does not set you free. Do you think you're not free because you know that you have lied to get autonomy?"

"Well, I feel a lot of shame when I'm not straight. I've been reading Buber about 'I-Thou' relationships. My relationships are 'I-It.'"

"Tell me what you mean by an 'I-It' relationship."

"Dave, I can't even be straight with the woman I'm having an affair with. I either treat her like an object or myself as an 'it.' I play games with people. I pretend that I am present, but I go blank."

"So when you're with people who ask you to share yourself with them you go blank rather than feel the scare of closeness and possible demands or rejection?"

"Yes, I feel really empty inside."

"I wonder if you are really empty inside or if you have found a way to not feel the pain of not being able to ask for what you need in relationships."

Here Tim begins to cry. I sit quietly for a few moments waiting to see if he will put his feelings into words. He wipes the tears away, sits up straight, and looks at me with a slight smile. When he says nothing I ask, "Can you tell me what you were just feeling?" For whatever reasons Tim is unable, maybe unwilling, to say what he is feeling. I offer this observation: "It seems like you are not empty inside. There are some pretty strong feelings inside. Would you be willing to keep track of the strong feelings you have this week and report in the next session?" In previous counseling Tim has worked with the feeling recognition chart, so I do not spend time introducing him to the six primary feelings or how to fill out the chart. (For a copy of this chart see my book *Counseling and Self-esteem.*[8])

Tim looked depressed as he came for the fifth session. His posture was slouched, shoulders rounded and falling forward, his head somewhat bowed; eye contact was brief and his cheeks sagged as if he were carrying a heavy weight. He did not shake my hand or say hello with his usually upbeat enthusiasm.

"What's going on?" I asked. I often begin an interview by inviting the client to tell me what is happening for him or her in the moment. Or I ask clients to tell me their current emotional state by saying, "What are you feeling?" Or I may observe what I think the person is showing me by labeling the emotion, "You seem scared/angry/sad/happy/excited/tender."

Tim told me, "I don't feel listened to."

"By whom?" When I asked this question I was worried that he didn't feel listened to by me.

"By Lori and my boss. I'm feeling crushed and invaded."

"It sounds like you're feeling abused."

To this response Tim told me that his mother tried to kill him twice. As he told the story he expressed no observable emotion. I wondered what it would be like to have my mother try to kill me twice. I shuddered with fear and anger and asked Tim, "Where is your emotion? I hear you telling me that your mother tried to kill you twice, but I see no emotion."

Hearing this, Tim begins to cry softly. I wait for him to experience his feelings before asking him to put his feelings into words. "What are you feeling?" I want to know if he can identify his feelings and then express them verbally.

He tells me he is feeling sad. "Yes, let yourself feel sad." I wait for him to continue his feeling experience. He turns away from me, hides his face in his hands, and curls his legs up sobbing heavily. "Good for you. I'm so glad you can feel the sadness."

Tim continues to cry and to hide. I wonder aloud, "What are you hiding from?"

"I'm feeling so vulnerable and shamed."

"Yes, feeling emotion does feel vulnerable. What is the shame about?"

Tim is still crying. "I feel shame when I feel. It is the same feelings I had when I wet the bed until I was ten years old." Tim describes the humiliation he felt at not being able to control his bladder. Then seemingly out of the blue he volunteers, "I decided at age eleven that I would not experience anger."

"That's interesting. How did you decide that?"

Tim has now turned back to face me, but he is still crying. "My aunt Irma took away all my possessions as punishment. When I got mad she took more away. It was no use; expressing anger didn't get me anywhere."

"So you decided expressing anger was hopeless?"

"Hopeless, yes. When I was six I frequently went to bed crying and asking, 'Am I going to make it?'"

"Make it, as in live?"

"As in live. I felt I was a bad person who was going to die. I couldn't please my aunts enough." Tim then exploded into a rage, hitting himself, then the couch pillows, yelling, "It isn't my fault, it isn't my fault, it isn't my fault." If Tim would have continued to hit himself, I would have stopped him and directed him to hit the pillows. I encouraged him to keep hitting the pillows and to scream, "It isn't my fault."

When Tim stopped hitting the pillow, seemingly exhausted, I pursued his cries of protest. I had an idea of what wasn't his fault, but I asked him, "It isn't your fault for what?" because I wanted to make sure he made the connection of thought to feelings. As he expressed his understanding, I also encouraged him to say it aloud to his mother, "It isn't my fault that your husband had an affair." This message was directed to his mother for blaming him and wanting Tim to die for the father's affair and abandonment of the mother. Hitting a pillow and verbalizing the feelings is an example of experiential counseling.

Sobbing, Tim said, "It isn't my fault for being born."

"Of course not. You are so right. What makes you feel guilty about being born?"

"Remember, I told you that my mom tried to kill me twice?"

"Yes, I remember."

"Well, she tried to abort me because she didn't want me. I feel blamed for being born."

"How do you know your mother didn't want you?"

"She and my aunts have told me. When my mother was pregnant with me she discovered that my dad was having an affair. That's when she tried to kill me the first time."

"What are you feeling now?"

His crying intensifies. "It feels so good to be heard. But I want to scream."

"Go ahead, scream."

Tim shuts down emotionally. He stops crying. "What just happened Tim?"

"I can't scream. I'll make a fool of myself."

"You aren't feeling safe enough to scream?"

"I can't scream in front of you. Besides, someone will hear me."

"And then you'll feel ashamed?"

"Worse than that, I'll be humiliated, punished."

"Here, in relationship with me?"

"My head knows better but my heart says I'll be treated just like my aunts treated me. It's nothing against you, Dave, but I feel like I'm going to be hurt."

"I'm glad you can tell me your fear. Could you tell your aunts your scare?"

"You mean today?"

"Well, yes, I was thinking about expressing here in the office what you wish you would have told your aunts. Would you be willing to do that?"

COUNSELOR'S COMMENTS

I have seen Tim weekly for seven months. He initially gave up his affair following a discussion we had about the impossibility of giving his marriage a fair chance while in an affair.

After three and one-half months of therapy he moved out of his house but not into the house of the woman with whom he was having the affair. I asked him, "What does leaving your wife and kids mean?" His response was to the moral issue. "I know it is wrong." He seemed to leave an unspoken "but" out of his statement, so I asked, "but . . . ?"

"But I can't stay. I'm not right. My feelings are not okay. I wanted the relationship to end before I married."

"Are you saying that you felt coerced into the marriage, sort of 'gave in' to Lori's control of you and now that justifies your leaving?"

"Dave, isn't it ever okay to end a relationship?"

"Tim, you know how I would answer that question. If I make the decision to stay or leave, you are then in another relationship where someone other than you is in control."

Tim responded that he was in my office because he knew that I would not control him. His best friend, however, who is a Christian, confronted him about leaving his family. Tim felt anger and shame but was not *manipulated* into deciding to go back home. I interpreted this to Tim: "One part of you knows leaving your wife and kids is wrong. Yet the issue seems to be an emotional one for you. Standing up to your best friend is like saying, No, you're not going to control me."

"Exactly."

Two months after this exchange Tim moved back home. Part of his decision seemed to be his wife's ultimatum, "move in or I divorce you." He also was asking himself, *Is an individual more important than a marriage?* Tim said, "I can't live with myself without trying again."

As therapist, I felt strongly about his moving out and equally strongly about Tim moving back with his family. I acknowledged these strong feelings to Tim. In these situations I assume my feelings will be picked up by the client and I don't want them to influence the client's decisions. I want the client to make his or her own decisions, as Jesus allowed the rich young ruler to decide for himself. I also want to maintain as much objectivity as possible so I can help the client understand himself or herself and make the decision. The client has to live with his or her decisions. In this case, I was concerned about Tim's compliance on the one hand and his tendency to rebel on the other hand. If I influenced his decision, Tim was then victimized by another's desire, and this repeats his family-of-origin experience that contributed to his marital problems. Getting Tim to comply without really changing his mind would be a hollow victory. It has been my experience that it is frequently a temporary victory, too.

I did not leave the spiritual issue out of the interview process. I explored Tim's faith. He acknowledged that he is ambivalent about Christianity. It seemed to me that ambivalence characterized his emotional experience in every relationship. "Tim, you say that you feel ambivalent about Christianity. As I hear you describe your relationships they all seem to be ambivalent. It doesn't surprise me that you would also have mixed feelings toward God."

Notice that my style of interviewing was to relate Tim's marital struggle with his relationship in the affair, with his work relationships, and then to his relationship with God. It is within this framework that we continued to explore the meaning of his affair and leaving the marriage.

The question that I kept asking Tim was, "How are your current feelings and behavior similar to what you experienced in your relationship with your mother and aunts?" Tim's relationship with his abandoning father is also a focus of treatment. "How is leaving your wife and kids a reenactment of your father abandoning you, your mother, and brother?"

The diagnostic assumption here is that we unconsciously repeat the traumas of our childhood in adult life. This tendency is true regardless of the spiritual life of the client. That is, a person can be a Christian, consciously living his life dedicated to Christ, but still have to deal with the unconscious temptation to repeat the character of the parent-child relationship.[9]

WHY IS THIS COUNSELING "CHRISTIAN"?

I am Christ's ambassador to my clients. I am the Christian, a person who trusts Jesus' death and resurrection to pay the penalty for my sin. My counseling is "Christian" because I represent Christ to my clients. I may use explicitly biblical or Christian language with my clients. I may pray with my clients. I may sing or quote hymns. I may suggest Christian literature to read. I may evangelize. I may invite confession, repentance, and restitution. I may use spiritual warfare and praying. However, what makes my counseling Christian is my relationship with Christ. To paraphrase Colossians 3:17, Whatever I do in word or deed, I do to the glory of God.

My counseling is not Christian because I believe certain doctrines about the nature of God and man. Using certain techniques found in Scripture does not make my counseling Christian. Playing a specific biblical role, e.g., prophet, pastor, or priest, does not make my counseling Christian.[10]

But this activity does not make Christian counseling. Much of what claims to be Christian counseling focuses on *content*, biblical and Christian, or *behavior,* sinful or not sinful. Counseling is more than the therapist focusing on content or behavior. It is discovering the internal processes (both conscious and unconscious) by which the client is living his or her life. Counseling is helping the person understand these processes and recognize the destructive consequences that result. It is helping the client develop resources to change the problem content and behavior. My counseling is Christian because I am willing to be "Christ" to my clients, to walk with them through their dark valleys, to understand them without judgment, to speak the truth in love, to be a real person with them. I am willing to treat them as I would treat Christ (Matt. 25:35–36). This is what makes my counseling Christian.

I use biblical stories to illustrate my interpretations whether or not the client is a Christian. I ask about the client's faith because this is a possible unused resource in dealing with his or her unresolved conflicts and unrealized goals. Many times the client's faith in and view of God are distorted and inadequate, and this opens the door for me to introduce my faith and my God (assuming mine is not distorted and inadequate) and the gospel that is truly "Good News": God loves you; he will not condemn or abandon you (Rom 8:1–2, 31–39). All of this is in the context of the client's experience of me as a person who desires to understand and support him or her. Safety, empathy, and choice are three hallmarks of therapeutic relationship. When these are established, the client is able to hear what I have to say spiritually because I have been God's representative in his or her life. I may be the first safe, empathetic, and choice-affirming relationship the client has had. I also may be the first person who represents God in a way that is loving and non-punitive, different from the client's experience of father, mother, or caretaker.

What makes my counseling Christian? Christ living in me and embodied in what I say and how I relate. This is incarnational helping.

How Has This Case Turned Out?

Tim has terminated treatment while he makes a job change. I asked him to read this chapter and give me feedback. After reading it, he wrote a response saying that he regrets giving me written permission to publish his story before reading the draft. He feels imposed upon and angry that I requested that he sign the permission to publish his case "knowing that I [Tim] did not even read the paper yet."

I was feeling rushed to get the paper to the publisher and apparently conveyed this to Tim. I had asked for Tim's permission to use his story before I accepted the writing assignment. Even though we processed his feelings then, apparently my beginning with what I needed (my agenda) rather then being sensitive to where Tim was at (his agenda) was negative. If I could replay the request to sign the permission to publish, I would tell Tim what I needed and ask if there were anything he needed before he signed. This would have gotten to Tim's issue of needing to read the material before he signed and also avoided his anger at me for not being with him in his pain. Tim wrote:

I could have refused, I own that. . . . I had many questions running through my mind at that time. Does Dave think he better get me to sign this now or I'll refuse later? This is real important to Dave.

Is he wanting to avoid a situation where he will be "asking me for something" and put me in a position of "control" over him?

These questions in Tim's letter presented an interesting observation for me to consider. I am not consciously aware of feeling this, but I will consider it. I wonder if this reflects Tim's feelings about our relationship. Am I an imposer and controller in this relationship? I need to check this out. The letter continued:

Doesn't he [Dave] trust me, that I would not play games with him? These are my questions and fantasies—but I end up still feeling disrespected by you. I do feel hurt, David. Am I way off base? Am I overreacting and feeling "the Big Hurt"—i.e., reenacting my "abandonment issues" with you? @#¤!%•†#

How can I consider Tim to be off base when he tells me he feels disrespected by my rushing him to sign the permission form? I don't feel disrespectful toward Tim, but the "message sent is the message received." Therefore, as the sender of the message, I have to take responsibility for what the message is from the client's perspective. I also must consider if Tim has deeper ambivalences about giving permission to tell his story.

Tim asked me to change some of the identifying information because as I wrote it his confidentiality was not protected. I agreed to make his suggested changes. He also asked me to consider my behavior and attitude in the next-to-last session before his break from counseling. He wrote:

As a colleague—some questions for you: (1) Are you avoiding this client? (2) Are you over your head? Can/will you admit to this client that there are strong counter-transference issues going on here? (3) Your paper is a reflection of your struggle regarding staying with someone "because" you are married. Once you choose, that's it! The marriage is more important than the individual. What did this client touch off in *you*? (4) Are you afraid of a lawsuit because [you think] "I made a mistake in how I handled this case"?

You were so %@¤!%•†#@ off base with me that session. And the real crap is *you were not even aware of it when we met the next session.* You were *surprised* by "my concerns, perceptions, feelings, and fears." Were you really?—I know you are sharp and perceptive.

Were you hoping I would just not mention anything and hope it will pass? Your "mistakes" with me in the second to last session are forgivable—you had an off day, much was on your mind, etc. But for you to be "unaware" of your behaviors and not start off the next session with: "I was really off base last week," or "Can I check out with you how the last session was?" This is almost [written very small on purpose] UNFORGIVABLE. . . .

After several more paragraphs Tim wrote,

Well, now that I have calmed down a bit, my intention of all that stuff I just said may be to try and hurt you—like I feel inside. Some of it, I know, does not belong to you. You can blow off most of it. But I do challenge you to consider some of that [stuff].

Wow—several pages later! My initial intention was only to write a one-page "short and sweet" comment regarding my concern of "confidentiality." I didn't know I had all that stuff in me. . . . I want you to hear what I really think, how I really feel. I did that on those earlier pages.

Right now I believe I must face you still. I will call for an appointment once I know my new schedule.

I think I need to send this letter to you David. There is no way I could say all that stuff to your face. I need to send it, then face you—and talk about it. I won't be able to take back stuff—because its on paper.

What is my reaction to Tim's angry response? First, I am glad I asked him to write a response. I am not surprised that he is angry because he conveyed those feelings to me in the counseling session. Second, his request for a change in identifying information was helpful. In the original draft I gave too much specific information that could have possibly made him known. Third, his questions to me, from the perspective of being my colleague, tell me our relationship is unequal and he does not feel he has power or choice. He is shifting roles from being client to colleague when he asks me to consider his questions. This is significant.

I first hear this as Tim's attempt to reestablish balance in our relationship. This felt imbalance may also be a reflection of the imbalance he feels in the marriage relationship. Tim concluded his note to me with these words:

Lori appears to be "adjusting" to life without me. It is clearer to me now than ever before: "I [Lori] needed you for your money and for you to fix things around the house."

Her money is still coming in—and she can get others to fix stuff for her.

It didn't matter who I was in that marriage. It has been difficult in some respects mainly regarding the kids; but I am still glad I am out. To be me and loved because of or in spite of me is important.

It seems possible that my posture of being for marriage leaves Tim feeling that I am not for him. Remembering the statement in his note, "the marriage is more important than the individual," I wonder how I have conveyed to him that he is less important than his marriage. I do not believe that a person is less important than the marriage. I believe a person cannot have a satisfying and fulfilling marriage without being a real person, i.e., someone who knows, loves, and values himself or herself, who is able to express what he or she feels and ask for what is needed, and who has a positive identity. This is a major issue to reconsider with Tim.

He is absolutely right when he says that this paper is a reflection of my struggle, but not a struggle with my marriage or choosing to stay married. I am struggling with my ability to stay objective, to be priest and not prophet, to help Tim consider that he has not yet made the connection between his own abandonment and rejection and how he is treating his wife and kids. My struggle is how I can stay with his process, explore his values and needs, expose his resistances, challenge his defenses of projection, displacement, and denial without having to fight myself as therapist. Cognitively, Tim sees the issue but is unable or unwilling to let the parallel inform his decision to stay in the marriage. His note to me helps me understand that he sees his wife as the problem. He is merely getting out of a relationship with a woman who cannot make him feel free to be himself, loved and not used.

When Tim returns to therapy I will begin with his note to me and his feelings of being disrespected and controlled. I will encourage Tim to look at how he participates in victimizing himself with me, his wife, friends, and employers. He sees himself as powerless in saying no to others and in being free to be himself.

At work, Tim is standing up to his boss. The fact that she is a woman may reflect what he wishes he could do to his wife and mother. He is proud of himself and excited that he is not "caving in." I am hopeful that this positive experience will be used by Tim to "stand up" to other women in his life, including his wife, without leaving her (abandonment) or being False Self (passive-aggressive). Unfortunately, Tim was dismissed from his job (rejected for being himself), which reopens the childhood wound and the marital pain.

To be real is a great risk for any of us. There is always the possibility that our Real Self will not be accepted. Tim is apparently feeling this rejection in his relationship with me. It seems that Tim is willing to risk telling me what he has had a hard time telling the significant people in his world. I am excited about his willingness to risk further rejection with me by agreeing to return to therapy. It is within the therapeutic relationship that healing can take place.

When we have worked on our relationship and Tim is feeling safe and free to be himself, I will then encourage him to learn how to believe in his own value. I'll also encourage him to accept the legitimacy of his own needs and feelings, ask for what he needs, express what he feels without shame, and set limits on people who get too close to him. I hope he will learn to separate the past abandonment and rejection from the present marital relationship, and experience his relationship with God as freeing rather than demanding. But the biggest challenge for Tim is to accept responsibility for his own victimization. He claims he did not choose Lori as wife, that she forced him into the marriage. Tim is unable or unwilling to see how he participates in relationships that make him feel controlled. Without claiming the choices (conscious and unconscious) he made and is making, Tim is programmed to repeat his passive-aggressive life. An affair or a new wife will not change his internal processing (denial, rationalization, projection) that leaves him feeling victim.

I feel sad as I review this case. I am thinking of how Tim and I are like Jesus and the rich young ruler (Mark 10:17–27). He comes to Jesus with a genuine question and a sincere desire to have it answered. But he wants the answer on his terms. Jesus' answer makes the rich young ruler feel sad; the cost is too great. If I am able to communicate any message to Tim I want it to be, "What you are hanging on to (False Self) is not the treasure for which you are looking (Real Self). Jesus did not come to take away your fulfillment, he came to give you life abundantly. Both of us know that you have not found that. And you wonder if it is possible. I assure you that with God it *is* possible."

If I could ask Jesus one question about the rich young ruler it would be, "How did you learn to let people go their own way without feeling sad or attempting to control them?" I am still learning to let go.

EDITOR'S COMMENTS

When he first agreed to make a contribution to this book, David Carlson suggested that he use dialogue material to illustrate his clinical interventions instead of giving a lengthy verbatim report and commenting later. This "reader-friendly" approach gives a running commentary on what happened throughout the course of therapy.

At the beginning, the counselor mentioned his pro-marriage viewpoint and asked if the client were willing to work with someone whose values might be different. Mentioning this near the start of the counseling process is important (and good ethics) in a case that is so clearly value-related. You will notice, however, that the counselor at no time forced his values on the client, even when there were opportunities to do so.

Mr. Carlson calls himself an insight-oriented therapist; but he shifts to his "experiential approach" when counseling needs a change of direction. Here again we see the need for counselor flexibility in the choice of methods. Notice, too, that the author makes several suggestions that other counselors could find helpful. These include:

- the five basic questions that can help effective counseling get started;
- discovering early in therapy what personal, interpersonal, and other resources the client has at his or her disposal to help achieve therapeutic goals;
- giving counselees permission to be curious, angry, frustrated, or feeling other emotions;
- being careful to understand the client's perspectives and to begin "where the client is rather than beginning where the counselor is";
- helping counselees recognize that when they ask questions about what is right or wrong biblically, often these are more than theological questions needing a biblical answer; often such questions come out of "emotional and relational disappointments and frustration";
- occasionally giving interpretations, but leaving this until a solid rapport has been built, then giving the interpretations in a way that says "this is what I am wondering . . ." instead of as a firm viewpoint;

• telling the counselee openly, "I'm not going to let you get away" with unrealistic thoughts or irresponsible behavior; and,

• working on the diagnostic assumption that we unconsciously repeat the traumas of our childhood in adult life—whether or not we are Christians.

Near the end of his commentary, Mr. Carlson gives his perspective on what makes his counseling Christian. If you read this section carefully you will get a concise statement of the nature of Christian counseling. It comes from a seasoned counselor who has thought about this issue, discussed it with his professional colleagues, and continues to put it into practice. Notice his view that the Christian counselor represents Christ to his or her clients. "I am not good parent or spouse," we read. "I am not rescuer. I am not knight or prince on a white horse. I am not magician or miracle worker. I am another human being who offers to be with my clients in their pain. . . ." This is a good perspective for all people helpers.

Having read this case, you probably have admired David Carlson's honesty and courage in presenting a case that was not completely successful and that ended, at least for now, with an angry response from the counselee. Here is a chapter written by a Christian counselor whose therapeutic skills are first rate and whose knowledge of the counseling art is superior. When the selected case did not turn out as expected, the counselor presented it anyway. "That's what happens sometimes," David said to me shortly before we sent the book to the publisher. Even though he could have chosen from a host of counseling successes, the author of this chapter stuck with this less successful case, despite the outcome. For this he must be applauded.

Whatever you may think of the counseling methods presented in this chapter, surely you will agree that David Carlson has taught us a valuable lesson about Christian counselors. Sometimes we see people change as a result of our work; sometimes we do not. That can leave us feeling sad and reluctant to let go; but Christian counselors continue to serve and give assistance, with God's help, even when some of our counselees don't seem to get better.

CHAPTER SIX

THE USE OF HYPNOTHERAPY IN COUNSELING A CHRISTIAN

Robert R. King, Jr.

Editor's Note: *In the whole field of Christian counseling perhaps there is no more controversial issue than the subject of hypnosis. Many committed believers shy away from its use, skeptical about its effectiveness and uncertain about its appropriateness for Christians. A few believe that hypnosis is satanic and the antithesis of Christian counseling. Others, like the author of this chapter, are dedicated Christians who feel no such hesitation in using hypnotherapy.*

Robert R. King is a Californian whose B.A. degree is from University of California, Los Angeles. His M.S. is from the George Washington University, and his Ph.D. in human behavior is from the United States International University. He is a licensed marriage, family, and child counselor (MFCC) in the state of California, a certified hypnotherapist, adjunct professor of pastoral care at Bethel Theological Seminary West, and co-owner (with his wife Mary, who is also a licensed counselor) of Healthy Relationships.

In addition to his counseling practice and teaching, Dr. King serves as executive secretary of CAPS, the Christian Association for Psychological Studies, Inc., an organization of Christian counselors. He can be contacted at P.O. Box 628, Blue Jay, California, 92317, and is interested in receiving copies of written guidelines for trance inductions, hypnoanalysis procedures, hypnotherapy worksheets, or extasis (hypnosis) summary sheets.

THE CLIENT WAS A CHRISTIAN WOMAN in her mid-thirties. As a Christian, she believed in Jesus Christ as Savior and was growing in her relationship with Jesus as Lord of her life. Her persuasion was evangelical, somewhat charismatic, but not at all dogmatic about the gift of speaking in tongues. She had been married for sixteen years and was the mother of a son and daughter, both approaching adolescence. She was intelligent, articulate, dedicated, believed in a Christian set of values—including the sanctity of marriage and the importance of the family—and was active in church and community activities. She had leadership abilities.

She came to my counseling office on the recommendation of the family's medical doctor, who was also a Christian. I had previously (and since) cooperated with the doctor in making referrals to him of clients whom I believed needed medical assistance and/or a complete physical checkup, and receiving referrals from him of patients whom he believed needed psychotherapy and/or a psychological evaluation. The client in this case had to be brought in by her husband because she was "very sick" (her own words) and could barely walk unassisted. Her husband had an arm around her waist to help support her as she walked haltingly into the waiting room. As I greeted her she appeared exhausted and depressed. She had an unenthusiastic smile, offered a limp hand in greeting, and spoke in a soft, hesitating voice. The weather was cool and thus her layered clothing prevented an accurate assessment; but even so, she appeared to be quite slim (I suspected anorexic) and to weigh no more than 100 pounds, perhaps less. She was about five-feet four-inches tall, although that was difficult to estimate because of her exhausted condition, slouched posture, and her leaning on her husband; he was obviously quite concerned, although somewhat irritated. Because of his irritation, I suspected his wife's illness was a recurring situation.

Indeed it was. After inviting them both into my office where, I told them, "you can be comfortable and we will have privacy," the following major conditions or situations were brought up during a ninety-minute consultation. (The first session was a *pro bono* consultation, which our counseling service offers when appropriate. The client, who will be identified by the pseudonym "Martha," was ashamed of seeking help, and obviously needed some degree of rapport with me and assurance of confidentiality before she would consider coming in for counseling. It is worth noting that such needs are not at all unusual, in my opinion. This is especially true for Christian clients who are devout and who have had some input—perhaps from a church, pastor, book, or Christian friends— that ". . . all you need is more faith and to confess your sins. You don't need psychological 'mumbo-jumbo' to experience the abundant Christian life.")

a. Martha thought she was "fat and ugly." Actually, she was very underweight and had quite attractive facial features and hair.

b. She had abdominal pain, slight chest pain, and a "band of pain" around her head.

c. She had experienced several miscarriages in previous years, but had two children from pregnancies during which she had had hormone shots.

d. She felt "like a failure" to her family, church, and community.

e. She had been and was addicted (my term) to a cola drink because of the caffeine in it.

f. Some women from her church had imposed themselves upon her and conducted a ceremony and fervent prayer to exorcise the "demons" that they (not the client) believed were causing the problems and illness.

g. Eating had been an issue in her family of origin.

h. She had periodically used diet pills that were diuretic and thus had lowered the potassium level in her body.

i. Normal menstruation had ceased at times, not due to pregnancy.

j. She said, "I want to get my health back . . . [a positive statement!] and to become well so that I can be a mother and wife again." (This shows a sense of duty as motivation.) "I don't want this cycle to keep on repeating. I want to be free of it forever!"

I admit using that last statement as a means of encouraging Martha to come in again soon for counseling. "We could explore what has been going on in your life," I said. "With wisdom from the Holy Spirit, we can discuss the truth, and the truth will set you free." That suggestion, which was an application of a biblical reference, connected, and Martha agreed to come in for counseling.

SUMMARY OF COUNSELOR'S APPROACH TO COUNSELING

I do not embrace any particular approach of counseling (or psycho-therapy) *in toto;* nor do I reject any mode of therapy out of hand, including those developed by "secular humanists." (Those words are in quotes because they are, in my opinion, not only inappropriate labeling, but are also redundant.) Rather, I use "multimodal therapy," a term I prefer to "eclectic," since the latter sometimes can be "hash" or, as Lawrence J. Crabb, Jr., says, "tossed salad." Perhaps my application of "multimodal therapy" could more accurately be called "Kingian." That identification is meant to be honest, rather than self-aggrandizing, and is in line with what I have recommended to all interns whom I have super-vised and all pastors whom 1 have taught in pastoral care and counseling courses. That is, take your last name and add "ian" to it to identify your approach to counseling and serving people who are hurting and need help. Not only would that be honest; it would also recognize each ser-vant (child) of God as unique.

I am a licensed marriage, family, and child counselor (MFCC) in the state of California, which also means being qualified to provide "psychotherapy" as defined in state law, regulations, and attorney-general decisions. In addi-tion, I am certified by California to use hypnotherapy as a counseling modality. I was fortunate enough to attend three different, accredited graduate schools—fortunate because the multimodal approach was devel-oped during the graduate-school experiences, and I could avoid settling on one major theory and application of psychology. Thus, I have had thorough training in such counseling modes as (in alphabetical order) cognitive, com-munications theory, family systems, gestalt, hypnoanalysis, hypnotherapy, logotherapy, pastoral care and counseling, psychodynamic, psychological testing, rational-emotive therapy, Rogerian or nondirective, and the treat-ment of sexual dysfunction. Less thorough training has been experienced in axiotherapy, behavior modification, biblical counseling, bioenergetics, cov-enant, decision-making, humanistic, neuro-linguistic programming, psychoanalytic, reality, strategic (i.e., short-term), and transactional analysis.

Every counseling procedure I use is "screened through the grid," so to speak, of my Christian faith, beliefs, and values. It should be noted that my denominational background is primarily baptistic, which of course means there are some biases in my Christian "grid." To be specific, it means such biases as: "once saved, always saved"; the Christian counselor is saved, not perfect; the Christian counselee needs to be nurtured and encouraged in a fellowship of believers; spiritual maturity is a journey; speaking in tongues is not a measure of spiritual maturity; disorders and difficulties being experienced by the counselee are not necessarily a result of that person's sin; not everyone is healed; "trials and tribulations" are normal experiences of life; prayer and fasting can be beneficial in healing; wisdom is available from the Holy Spirit; and just because I don't understand a person's behavior or situation doesn't necessarily mean that unconfessed sins and/or demons are involved.

My interpretation of counseling experiences, the "failures" along with the "successes," is that a trusting and accepting relationship between counselee and counselor, based primarily on empathy (not sympathy), is usually more important than the counseling methods used. However, that should never be an excuse for inadequate training.

In summary, my approach to counseling is multimodal, "Kingian," professional, based on biblical principles, to be a burden-bearer (Gal. 6:2), and to be in constant prayer and seeking godly wisdom from the Holy Spirit.

Verbatim Dialogue of Counseling

Introductory Session

(The day after the initial consultation)

T: Hello, Martha. I'm pleased that you decided to come in for counseling. I believe that if we work together we can discover what's been going on and why, and then the truth will help to set you free.

C: I'm not so sure of that. [pause] I feel ashamed about coming here—I shouldn't need help. I have to get things done; [pause] I have to, for my husband and children.

T: So you feel guilty about having problems and not doing the things you think you should be doing for your family? [pause] Let's go in my office [we were in the waiting room] where you can be comfortable and we will have some privacy.

C: Where do you sit?

T: Nothing has my name on it except the nameplate on the desk. You try out any seat you want and pick the one where you'll be able to relax and collect your thoughts. [Martha looks around, considering several choices. She finally picks a recliner chair.]

C: Do you sit here?

T: Sometimes, if a person prefers the couch. However, today and whenever you want when we meet, that recliner is yours.

C: [sitting, pause] Oh, I like this! [pause] Are you sure it's okay?

T: Of course. You seem concerned about what I might want, as if other people's needs must be met before yours, and then yours comes in a lousy last.

C: [pause] Of course. Isn't that the way it's supposed to be?

T: Not if it means you're trying to save me, or your family, or the world from experiencing life as it really is. You might think about the idea that Jesus said to love your neighbor as yourself, not *better* than yourself or to act as if you're nothing.

There was no verbal response, but the client sat back in the recliner, relaxed, and appeared to be thinking deeply. After about a minute of silence, I briefly discussed my approach to counseling, the topic of confidentiality, and other preliminaries designed to both inform Martha and to put her at ease. The emergency session the day before had seemed to be an inappropriate time for such an introduction and discussion.

T: You look, sound, and act depressed.

C: [Nods agreement]

T: I was blessed to have two courses from Viktor Frankl, one with only twelve students, where he instructed on a simple procedure of questions and answers about everyday events and feelings to

diagnose depression and get a handle on what's likely to be causing it. Would you be willing to answer about a dozen or so
questions and hopefully help us get a handle on what's causing
your depression?

C: Whatever you say.

I questioned Martha for about half an hour, using what I call the
"Frankl factor-analysis of depression," a procedure unpublished to date,
at least in English translations. Some of Martha's answers or statements
included: "I'm afraid of getting fat," "I'm afraid of dying," "I have to get
things done," and "I know when things are real or unreal." I immediately informed Martha of the results of the analysis.

T: It's probably no news to you that you are depressed. You scored
thirteen points out of a possible fifteen, which means you are
more than moderately depressed, possibly deeply depressed. Fifteen points would be the pits. You scored five points for
endogenous depression, a fancy way of saying your body chemistry is out of whack and is a major factor in your being depressed.
[I noticed that Martha gave a sign of relief. She had been holding
her breath during the first part of the statement.] You scored only
two points of reactive depression, that is, in reaction to your life
situation. However, you scored six points due to negative thinking about yourself and your handling of what's going on. [I
purposefully avoided the word "neurosis" learned in Frankl's
course, based on the belief that Martha would not be helped by a
label of "neurosis" or "neurotic."] In other words, you probably
give yourself a hard time—you're probably very critical of yourself—and that's a major part of your feeling depressed.

C: You mean I'm not crazy? The women who insisted in praying over
me said I was demon-possessed. I hated that. Then they said I
lacked faith when I didn't get well.

T: Of course you're not crazy, any more than I am! [We both
laughed.] You're depressed, which feels terrible, but it's not a sin
and you don't have demons! Since you are a Christian, you are
filled with the Holy Spirit, and ". . . the one who is in you is greater
than the one who is in the world" (1 John 4:4).

C: [Silence. Relieved expression on face. Breathing is normal.]

T: Your doctor [the one who referred Martha] has already pre-scribed medication. [Martha frowns.] I bet you don't want to take it—think you shouldn't need it.

C: [Laughs and nods agreement.]

T: I know your doctor; you know your doctor. He's a godly man who truly cares about you. [I knew that to be the case.] The medica-tion will probably only be temporary, to help your body chemistry get corrected while at the same time lifting your depression to the level where we can find out what that depression is telling you. Okay? And those diet pills have been sucking the potassium out of your body and I bet your doctor doesn't know you're tak-ing them. How about not eating so much if you want to lose weight instead of taking those pills?

C: You're not going to make me eat?

T: No, that's your decision.

C: [Pauses with puzzled expression.] Anything else?

T: Well, have you ever thought of taking a vacation from church? With "friends" like that prayer group, who needs enemies? You can still pray or read the Bible if you want to.

C: [Smiling] When do you want me to come back?

T: In about three days. Let's make an appointment. I'll contact your doctor, if that's okay, and tell him what we discovered about your depression. Also, we'll continue to cooperate with his guidance on medication.

C: Okay.

Seven conjoint sessions were held during the next month, since: (1) I believed that the family system, especially the marital relationship, was a major factor in Martha's depressed condition; (2) Martha's husband had to provide transportation, at least until she was feeling well enough to drive and her doctor had determined the medication did not interfere with her driving skills; (3) I wanted to work with both Martha and her husband, to avoid either one becoming the "Identified Patient"; and (4)

Martha's husband needed to learn about and gain a greater understanding of depression, thus reducing his irritability and impatience about the situation.

First Counseling Session with Martha

(After greetings and preliminary remarks)

C: I'm feeling better lately—have been sleeping better and I guess the medicine is helping.

T: That's good to hear. You're on the road to feeling okay. However, remember that like any journey, there may be detours, dips, and potholes. Progress is rarely steady, so you won't need to be discouraged if you have some times when you feel depressed.

C: I thought I'd be practically okay by now. [I actively listened to Martha's feelings of impatience, her wanting to be busy again, and her belief that "quitting means failing."]

T: What do you do to get a "pick-me-up"?

C: How did you know? I used to drink three six-packs a day of Diet Coke when I was busy . . . actually I was anorexic. But now I've cut way down . . . I'm trying to cut down but I'm afraid to get off!

T: [Silence. I did not question what "I've cut way down" meant, not wanting to get into a parental role of checking up on what Martha drank or ate.]

C: I've been busy all my life—had to, but never got any praise from Mom, only criticism. Dad wasn't around much—busy working—a brilliant engineer. I had a bad fight with him when I was sixteen. I would have been happy being a nun. [Martha then reveals the ups and downs of her marriage. They need not be repeated in this narrative.]

T: How are things going now, and how have the conjoint sessions affected your marriage?

C: Things are better lately. He's more understanding. But I haven't totally forgiven him [for the past].

T: It sounds as if forgiving others and yourself has been difficult in the past. Also, you have remarked several times that some things don't make sense to you, even about yourself.

C: [Nods agreement with pensive expression.]

T: When our behavior doesn't make sense, sometimes it's because we are automatically reacting to things that have happened, maybe many years ago, things that we may well have even forgotten consciously. If that's the case, the use of hypnosis in therapy can often make sense of how the past affects us in the here and now. Also, hypnosis usually brings about understanding much quicker than traditional talk-therapy.

C: [Looks interested; does not show any fear or concern in her affect.]

T: I have been trained extensively in the use of hypnosis, have been certified by the state as safe to turn loose on the public, and have even taught hypnosis workshops at UCSD extension courses. The type of trance I would teach you would be one in which you would be in control—I would have no control over you, nor would I want any. Would you consider experiencing hypnosis during our next session?

C: Would it be okay for a Christian. . . ?

T: Yes, I believe so; otherwise I wouldn't use it in counseling.

C: Whatever you say.

T: Whatever you're willing to experience in counseling, not whatever I say. There is a handout in the filing cabinet in the waiting room that summarizes what hypnosis is and is not, and when to use it and when not to. I'll give you a copy to take home and study. Then if you have any questions, fire away at the beginning of our next session and I'll answer all your questions so you'll feel confident and safe about experiencing hypnosis.

(A copy of the handout is included at the end of this chapter.)

Third Counseling Session with Martha

Martha was not ready to experience hypnosis during the second session. Instead, she wanted to talk about her childhood and family of origin.

However, she was unable to remember anything before being a teen-ager, and could remember only a few events as a teen-ager before becoming seventeen years old. That was very frustrating to her, because she wanted to remember growing up. Undoubtedly it had been painful, because the few memories she could talk about were primarily about not being appreciated and being criticized for what was not done by her, or for making mistakes.

T: Hello, Martha. I'm glad to see you. Please have a seat wherever you'll be comfortable. [She chooses the recliner.]

C: Thanks. [Pause] I'm on a protein diet; I want to lose more weight. I've already lost four pounds. Everybody's upset with me, and I'm feeling rebellious.

T: It's like there's a power struggle over what you eat or don't eat and about your weight.

C: Yeah.

T: [I share a story about a friend who used to push her food around the plate and sneak some to the dog, which fooled her family.] She won that fight! She fooled them!

C: [Laughing] I know.

T: Are you ready to experience hypnosis and get some knowledge about your past that could help you win the power struggle you're in now?

C: Yes.

T: You're already relaxed in that recliner, so you're on the way already. . . .

C: I really like this chair . . . wish I had it.

T: You do, every time you come in for counseling. Maybe I'll give it to you in my will someday!

C: [Laughing] But I hope that will be a long time from now.

T: Same here. Do you have any questions about hypnosis that were not covered by the handout?

C: No, no questions. But I'll be in control?

T: Absolutely. I'll teach you a simple way, just by lifting your arm, where you can control the depth of the trance you'll be enjoying and how you can come out of it anytime you may want to. Okay?

C: Okay.

T: Let's continue now. One of the things I'll be teaching you is how to relax deeply—self-hypnosis, if you want to call it that. First, let's find out what your special "cue" for relaxing is. Do you have any questions about what I mean?

C: No, sort of like a "trigger"; that's what a "cue" is?

T: Yes. For example, think of something you really enjoy doing. Imagine yourself doing it. You don't have to tell me what it is. [Martha smiles, has a pleasant expression, and is very relaxed.] See? That's a cue—you thought of something fun and then you smiled automatically. Now, as for a relaxing cue. Is there a place you have been, or have seen in a picture, or is there an event or color that you would automatically associate with being relaxed?

C: [Pause, relaxed] Yes, yellow—pastel yellow. That is so relaxing.

T: Fine, we will develop that and reinforce it as your cue to relax anytime you want to. Are you comfortable?

C: Yes.

T: Be aware that you are free to move, to talk, to change positions, whatever is needed to remain comfortable while remaining in a trance, perhaps getting even more deeply into a trance. Also, if you want to talk with your hands, that will be fine with me. Most of the stuff you see on TV or in a movie about how a person gets stiff, or like a zombie when experiencing hypnosis is a bunch of baloney!

C: [Laughing] That's good to know.

T: Also, you heard me say "experiencing hypnosis" instead of "being hypnotized." I won't hypnotize you, you'll experience it yourself with me as just a guide. I won't have any control over you, nor do I want any. You'll be in control. Do you agree?

C: Yes, that's fine.

I then helped Martha to experience a deep trance, using a modification of procedures developed by the late David Elman, a master at hypnosis.[1] The modified Elman method is reasonably fast (usually takes five to fifteen minutes the first time, depending upon both the subject and the therapist). It has built-in observation points, so the progress of the induction and depth of trance can be monitored easily by the therapist; and it is a gentle, nondirective method. Only two verbatim parts of the induction as it occurred are given below.

T: I just noticed that your eyes opened slowly when you were supposed to be pretending they could not be opened. That's fine, because you proved you are in control. Now, as you let them close again, pretend—tell yourself—that no matter how hard you try to open your eyes, they just won't do it! That might even be amusing to you as you experience the power of telling yourself "can't" or "won't."

C: [Eyelids flutter, but do not open. A determined expression appears, then a smile.]

T: That's wonderful. Now let your eyes remain closed; stop trying so hard to open them, and let the relaxed feeling in the muscles that control your eyelids seep downward through your entire body, as if gravity were irresistibly pulling that nice, relaxed feeling down to the tips of your toes.

C: [Very relaxed affect, breathing deeply, slowly, and regularly. A slight flush is on the cheeks.]

T: Now I'm going to count backwards, from ten to one. Each time I say a number, you can become more deeply relaxed. You won't even have to think about relaxing—it will happen naturally. And once in awhile, between numbers I'll read a verse of Scripture, if you would like.

C: [Nods head in agreement.]

T: Ten. You're enjoying breathing deeply, becoming more and more relaxed, into a deep, beneficial trance. Yet you're in control. All you have to do if you want to come out of the trance is rotate your right forearm upward from the arm of the chair. Straight up will be completely out of the trance. Resting on the arm of the chair will allow a deep trance, and any one of a thousand positions of your arm between up or down will give you precise control to any depth of trance you feel safe in experiencing.

I then counted from ten to one, interspersing Scripture in the countdown. Martha entered a deep trance. The following verses from the NIV Bible were the ones I read to Martha:

Peace I leave with you; my peace I give you. I do not give to you as the world gives. Do not let your hearts be troubled and do not be afraid. (John 4:27)

The Lord replied, "My Presence will go with you, and I will give you rest." (Exod. 33:14)

I will lie down and sleep in peace, for you alone, O Lord, make me dwell in safety. (Ps. 4:8)

And the peace of God, which transcends all understanding, will guard your hearts and your minds in Christ Jesus. (Phil. 4:7)

Jesus looked at them and said, "With man this is impossible, but with God all things are possible." (Matt. 19:26)

And I will ask the Father, and he will give you another Counselor to be with you forever—the Spirit of truth. The world cannot accept him, because it neither sees him nor knows him. But you know him, for he lives with you and will be in you. (John 14:16, 17)

T: How do you feel? You can answer and remain in the trance.

C: [Softly] Wonderful. Really relaxed.

T: You're a great "subject," as we say in the study of hypnosis. You make it easy for me to be your guide. [Martha smiles.] Now, if you would, please imagine that you are nine years old. [Martha had remembered in an earlier session that at nine years of age she had sworn she would *never* be fat.] You are at a county fair or a circus.

C: Yes. [smiling in pleasant reverie]

137

T: You are in the "fun zone," walking around, when you see a brightly colored building with a sign on it that says "The House of Mirrors." The barker out front perhaps reminds you of someone. There is music and loud laughter coming out of the building. The barker says, "Come on in, Martha, it will only cost a quarter and you'll have a million laughs."

[Pause] So you pay a quarter and go in the entrance, even though you feel persuaded against your will because you don't really know what's inside and you hear some shrieks, not just laughter.

[Pause. Martha has a troubled expression on her face.] As you enter a short hallway from the entrance, you hear the music getting louder and you see a mirror on the wall. You look at your reflection and you like the way you look, because the mirror is flat and gives an accurate reflection.

[Pause] Then you turn a corner, following the hallway, and you see another full-length mirror. Only this one is curved in deeply in the middle, like a cave, and you look short and fat. You look ugly, but you stare at the mirror, fascinated yet repelled. [Martha now moves in the recliner with an agitated expression on her face.]

Finally, you go farther, the hallway now twisting and turning like a maze. Then you see another mirror, only this one curves out and you look tall and slim, even skinny. What a relief after looking so fat and ugly! But is it really you? You're beginning to get confused. You rush on, and you're surrounded by mirrors at every turn. Some are wavy. Some are concave, some are convex, either vertically or horizontally or both. You no longer even know what you look like, because all the reflections have confused you. As you finally find the exit and rush out, people standing outside laugh at you as you bolt out of The House of Mirrors!

C: [Breathing rapidly and shallowly.] Oh, that's horrible.

T: [Putting hand on Martha's arm to reassure her.] Yes, it is horrible to not know what you really look like. And since you enjoy reading, you probably remember what William James wrote years ago. He said other people are like mirrors to us, and how they act or react forms a reflection, so to speak, forming a concept in our mind of who we are.

C: That's interesting—hmmm.

T: Yes, and if you think about it, many such reflections are as if they came from the mirrors in a house of mirrors in the so-called fun zone, because many of their biases and demands are just as distorted as the glass on those mirrors.

[Pause] And even an expensive, well-made mirror is just a reflection that doesn't show your appearance accurately. It's just a mirror-image. Think about it, and you'll discover the only accurate image of the way you're created.

Now, believe it or not, our time together is over for today. I'm going to count from one to five, the reverse order of the trance-deepening procedure, and then I want you to count six through ten so you'll be fully alert for a safe drive home or wherever your next destination may be.

One. You're commencing to stir around a bit if you feel like it.

Two. You're enjoying breathing deeply and comfortably and naturally.

Three. Your mind is clearing; it is integrating all you have remembered and imagined with what you already know about yourself, because you're the world's best expert on Martha.

Four. Your body is feeling relaxed yet refreshed, and you are learning more about your body as an integrated part of you.

Five. As you open your eyes, you're noticing how you feel. How do you feel, Martha?

C: Relaxed but ready. That was strange but wonderful. But was I hypnotized? It didn't feel like it.

T: Look at the clock on the wall.

C: Oh, my goodness! Where did the time go? A whole hour gone already? I guess I must have been.

T: And Martha. . . .

C: Oh, yes—six, seven, eight, nine, ten!

T: Remember the self-hypnosis. If you ever feel anxious or up tight, you can sit down or lie down, breath slowly yet comfortably and naturally, and softly say "pastel yellow" as you close your eyes. You'll then be relaxed, in a trance if you need be. Then spend a couple of minutes—that's all it takes—and think about positive, affirming events or plans. Also, you might want to remember some favorite Scripture verses.

C: Okay.

Sixth Counseling Session with Martha

Not all sessions involved hypnotherapy; just about a third to one-half did. There had also been a total of nineteen conjoint sessions by now. However, Martha reported that relaxing on her own via self-hypnosis, using her cue, was wonderful. Also, the medication was helpful and the depression had moderated so markedly that it was no longer a focus of counseling. Further, Martha's cue was being used during hypnotherapy sessions to help her achieve a deep trance in about two minutes, sometimes less.

The sixth session focused on coping with stress of life, conflicts in relationships, and keeping track of who really "owns" the problems and conflicts that arose or, in some cases, had been present off and on for years. Only the following dialogue at the conclusion of the session was of particular interest to the counselor and is therefore presented. Martha is experiencing a deep trance.

T: "Then you will know the truth, and the truth will set you free" (John 8:32).

When I used the usual procedure for Martha to come out of the trance, she did not open her eyes. I erred in assuming the reason was that Martha was in such a deep, relaxing trance she did not want to come out of it. I should have inquired about the reason for Martha not opening her eyes. Instead, based on the aforementioned erroneous assumption, I further erred in once again using the normal procedure with Martha, and she opened her eyes at the count of "five."

C: I was scared to come out of the trance.

T: I didn't realize that. I goofed and I apologize for being insensitive to your feelings. Do you wish to enter a trance again right now and find out why you were scared?

C: No, I think I was scared—even fighting hyperventilating—of the truth.

T: Okay, we'll find out more in the future, but only when you're ready to deal with it.

C: [Nods agreement.]

Seventh Counseling Session with Martha

C: [About a third of the way, i.e., twenty minutes, into the session] I don't think I'm fat and ugly now. [Martha had actually put on about fifteen or more pounds since the first session ten months ago.]

T: How do you feel about that?

C: Pretty good, actually; but I would panic at anything more than 112 pounds. I weighed 92 pounds the first time I came in to your counseling service!

T: I noted that, but didn't see any reason to make an issue of it.

C: Thanks.

T: You're welcome. Now, how about some more trance work? [Martha agreed and was into a deep trance in less than two minutes.]

T: Are you interested in stories?

C: Oh, yes, I've always liked stories.

T: Good. Once upon a time—that's a good way to start a story, isn't it? Once upon a time there was a tall pine tree in a forest. A squirrel wanted to eat a pine cone, so he chewed the stem and the cone dropped to the forest floor, splitting open. One of the seeds that was scattered landed under the overhang of a huge, granite boulder, where the squirrel didn't find it.

C: [Relaxed, breathing deeply.] Oh.

T: The seed was warm, because it was summer. However, as it lay there day after day, night after night, the days became shorter, the nights became longer, the air became cool, and leaves from nearby oak and dogwood trees fell on the seed and covered it. The leaves made it dark and the seed became frightened.

C: [Sympathetic expression.]

T: Then one day it snowed, the first of several times during a long, cold winter. The seed and the leaves on top of it were soon covered, and it became so cold the seed thought it was dying.

C: Poor baby [concerned expression on face].

T: And in fact the seed did die, in a way, before life could come and it could become a pine tree.

I completed the story, which took about ten to fifteen minutes more. There is inadequate room here to give the story verbatim, and probably it would not be completely accurate because I made it up as I told it. The main points made in the story are worth mentioning, however, because they were meant for Martha to identify with and to have hope. The main points were (1) the seed was warmed by the sunshine in spring, put down a deep tap root, and a sprig burst upward to meet the warmth of the sun; (2) the large rock, which had at first protected it, was now in the way; (3) some animals nibbled on its bark and almost killed it; (4) other trees, large and small, made fun of the little tree and ridiculed its appearance as it had to grow at an outward angle before it could be free from the overhanging rock and reach for the sun; (5) storms occurred, but the strength of the tree enabled it to survive, while an old, brittle tree and an oak that was so hard it would not bend very much were knocked down by a storm; and (6) the tree finally soared to tremendous height and beauty, and provided food and a haven for birds and squirrels.

During the story I occasionally used deliberately confusing language, so it was not clear whether I meant "the sun" or "the Son." Martha had tears trickling down her face as she heard the story.

Ninth Counseling Session with Martha

Martha was still on medication (Tofranil and Mellaril), but at a reduced dosage. Coordination with her medical doctor was ongoing.

C: I'm feeling better.

T: You look it, too.

A few minutes later Martha was in a deep trance. At the conclusion of the deepening count from ten to one, the following Scripture was quoted:

"For God did not give us a spirit of timidity, but a spirit of power, of love and of self-discipline" (2 Tim. 1:7).

C: I don't know what love is, how I should feel.

T: Perhaps it's more than a feeling. [I then read 1 Cor. 13:1–13.]

C: [Pause] Hmm. Some of those are doing things.

T: Yes, I agree. Speaking of love, remember "For God did not give us a spirit of timidity, but . . ."?

C: Yes . . .

T: Perhaps you would be willing to imagine something that has three legs. It could be a stool, a table, an easel, whatever.

C: Yes, I've got it. [Martha didn't say what "it" was, but that didn't matter.]

T: Now imagine one leg represents love, another power, and the third, self-discipline. [Pause] Imagine the leg of love is very long and the legs of power and self-discipline are short stubs. What happens?

C: It falls, out of balance.

T: Correct. That kind of love is probably just feeling love, very powerful, but eventually mere sentimentality because it is unbalanced. Now imagine the leg of power is really big, and love and self-discipline are stubs. [Pause] That kind of power becomes tyranny, control over others, perhaps eventually paranoia.

Now imagine the leg of self-discipline is big, and power and love are stubs.

C: Whoops!

T: "Whoops" is right; the whole thing falls over! That much self-discipline or control can become perfectionism, or obsessive-compulsive, or being afraid to make a mistake. [Pause] All three in balance—power, love, and self-discipline—can be God's gift. What do we do with it?

C: [Expression of pondering is on Martha face.] It's . . . it's . . . it's all about power, isn't it? Who's the boss? Who's in control?

Additional Sessions

Hypnotherapy and hypnoanalysis[2] were applied during the tenth, fourteenth, and sixteenth counseling sessions. There is inadequate room and there is no need to describe them verbatim. The following features were noteworthy, however: (1) I told Martha the old story of the ugly duckling; (2) I told a story about a little lost plant in a greenhouse that almost died, then was nurtured into health;[3] (3) a story was told about a beautiful, talking doll that couldn't talk for a while because someone in the family wound her up too tight; and (4) a story was told about a caterpillar that "died" and then became a butterfly, able to spread its wings because of warmth and strength from the sun (Son).

Seventeenth Counseling Session with Martha

C: I guess I love myself, because I'm making changes.

T: [Responded affirmatively, then guided Martha into what appeared to be a very deep trance.] Imagine that you're in a building that is statuesque and safe, sturdy but not so hard as to be brittle, on a strong but "floating" foundation, so to speak, that can even enable the building to ride out a severe earthquake. [Pause] The building has as many stories or floors as your age. You are in a large room on the top floor. There are windows on all sides, but with draperies in case you want them shut for any reason, and the view is spectacular. [Pause] Are you able to imagine that?

C: Oh, yes, and I like it.

T: Good. The large room you are in is furnished and decorated by you, exactly the way you want it. You even ignored advice from others who thought they knew more about you than you do. Some people on the outside try to decorate the inside, but even professional interior decorators often don't ask you what you want, or what your personality is.

C: How true.

T: In this room there is a "communications control central," so to speak, with a mainframe computer connected to computers on every floor of the building, telephones, climate controls, lighting controls, sound controls, observation cameras—you name it.

You're able to control and monitor whatever you want to. [I knew that Martha operated computers expertly.] Is that okay?

C: I like that.

T: As you're there on the top floor, seated comfortably in communications central, you become aware—even if you're not quite sure how—that each floor in the building has a story—maybe several—to tell. And you're also aware that one floor in particular has a story—perhaps in the archives that can unlock the truth to set you free. Can you imagine that?

C: Yes [but with some apprehension in tone of voice].

T: So you get up and walk over to the elevator. Of course there's an elevator in such a tall, well-designed and constructed building. You push the "call" button, since you're on the top floor, and hear the elevator approaching. It arrives, stops, and the doors open. The elevator is just the right size and the decor and lighting are to your liking. There is a mirror on one wall that gives an accurate but not perfect reflection. [Pause] Are you ready to take the elevator to the floor where there is something very important to remember, to learn from?

C: Yes.

T: Good. You're willing to take the risks of learning. You step into the elevator. Then, without having to think consciously, you reach over and push the button for the floor where you know there is some very important information. The doors close smoothly, and the elevator starts smoothly downward—smoothly—downward, passing floor after floor. The elevator slows, stops, and the doors open. You exit the elevator. What floor are you on?

C: I don't know. It's so dark, like a basement. But it's warm. There's a baby there—something's gone wrong, me and her—we're not born. [A few tears trickle down Martha's face.]

T: [Thinking to self, not talking.] *Oh, dear Lord, this can't be it! She's in the basement? The basement? The womb! It can't be, this is not logical. And there's someone else there?* [Praying silently, while Martha cries gently and makes periodic remarks, such as "Pretty girl" and "Don't die!"] *Dear Lord, this is awesome. May* *the Holy Spirit comfort Martha in this painful trip into the past. The womb? How can it be? Father, I confess that some of the biggest mistakes I have ever made in counseling have been to pray for wisdom and then to doubt what was revealed, only to have it confirmed weeks or months later. I apologize. Thank you for forgiving me. Please continue to reveal the truth, and comfort Martha. Amen.*

C: Don't die. You're so pretty. I should be the one to die! [Tears]

T: [Concerned about a full-blown abreaction developing, I placed my hand gently on Martha's left forearm. She was breathing irregularly, shallowly, sometimes holding her breath. Her pulse was rapid.] You only need to remember enough to set you free from the tyranny of the unknown. Remember, this is a memory, and you can be free from abreacting, from reexperiencing it. Now, in a few moments I am going to count slowly to sixty. It could be sixty seconds, or sixty minutes, or like sixty hours, whatever you need, because time can be compressed or expanded by your mind, at least as you experience time. During the time I count to sixty, you will be able to integrate, to make sense out of, whatever you remember and how it has affected your life. You probably will be able to resolve it, at least get a handle on it, during the time I count to sixty.

C: [Calm expression, but still a few tears] Yes.

T: One [pause], two . . . [about a minute and a half elapses, during which Martha's breathing becomes more regular and her pulse, visible on her neck, slows] . . . sixty. There, have you integrated it? Does it make sense?

C: [Nods head affirmatively.]

T: Good. Please be aware that of course I don't know for sure what you just learned and integrated. It can remain private, if you wish. I don't need to know everything to be your guide. Tell me only if you want to, and if so, only as much as you want to.

C: She was my twin sister. We were touching each other, holding hands, I think. She let go, she died before we were born! [Angry expression on face and in tone of voice]

T: And you've tried to be perfect to make up for her, because you think she should have lived and you should have died instead of her.

C: Yes! And nobody was satisfied with me. All I ever got was criticism! [Tears]

T: That's really heavy. Perhaps that's enough for today . . . I'm wrung out just from hearing about what happened, and you must need some "time out" to process and assimilate these memories at a more gentle pace.

C: [Nods]

T: You push the "up" button to call the elevator, but it's been waiting for you and its doors open right away. You get in, the doors close, and the elevator automatically moves upward toward the top floor. As you pass by floors, you realize that some of them might also have events in the archives for you to remember, including some very pleasant ones. The building has a rich history, a unique history. The elevator approaches the top floor, slows, stops, and the doors open. You step out of the elevator into the top floor.

The view is beautiful; somehow it seems clearer than ever before. You notice there are other buildings around—some taller than yours, some about the same height, some shorter. You notice that some have been well maintained, while others have not. You also realize that you can refurnish, redecorate, even remodel your building because it is strong, built well, and has classic features. You enjoy the view, you appreciate the self-control available to you through communications central. Also, it even has a satellite dish on top so messages can be sent back and forth with the world, the heavens, even. Do you like the building?

C: Yes.

T: Are you comfortable in it?

C: Yes.

T: Good. Now I'm going to count from one to five . . . [Procedure as described before is used for coming out of a trance.]

T: How do you feel?

C: Whew!

T: I'll say! If it's okay with you, I'll close with a short prayer.

C: That's fine.

T: Dear heavenly Father, thank you for the privilege of working together with you and Martha. We pray for wisdom and strength as, indeed, the truth is setting Martha free. In Christ's name, amen.

C: Thanks.

T: Thank *you*. You're a brave woman. You're a survivor. You're going to make it.

Twenty-third Counseling Session with Martha

By this time Martha was well on the road to recovery. Her weight was normal (about 115 lbs.), depression was no longer a problem, she was assertive but not aggressive, and her relationship with the Lord demonstrated stronger faith and her being perceived as a loved child of God. She also was eating appropriately, even though some of her family members irritated her by questioning her too much about her eating habits.

C: I'm angry about being "parented" about what I eat.

T: I would be, too. [Pause] However, have you ever considered letting it be their problem instead of getting into a power struggle? It takes two or more persons to have a conflict—a power struggle. Perhaps we could discover the origin by visiting the past, and then putting it into an adult perspective.

C: Sounds interesting. Let's do it. [Martha is in a deep trance within a minute or so. The counselor's guidance was needed only minimally.]

T: We're going to build a bridge to the past. The bridge is an "affect bridge," so to speak. You know how even when you're not experiencing hypnosis that a feeling, or a song, or even a gesture can bring to your conscious awareness an event and the same feelings from years ago?

C: [Nods head in agreement.]

T: We're going to build the affect bridge based on your feelings when someone *tries* (they really can't do it, can they?) to control your eating, usually trying to make you eat more. Now you're going back in time to an occasion when someone was hassling you about eating or how your body appeared.

C: [Angry affect] I don't want to do it! You can't make me. I'm never going to be fat!

T: You're very angry because someone is trying to control you about such a basic thing as eating and how your body looks.

C: Yes! [Emphatic tone of voice, angry affect]

T: Now hold on to the feeling. It's becoming a bridge. Pages on the calendar flutter backwards—months—years—as if a breeze were blowing leaves in the fall. You remember a previous time when you felt exactly the same way—angry, frustrated, about someone controlling you. [Pause] If you wish to, tell me about it.

C: [Haltingly] We have to move again. I'm in high school. I'm starting in my fourteenth school! I feel so angry, insecure—controlled. Why doesn't anybody ask me whether or not we move? State to state . . . it's terrible!

T: [Marveling about how different events can be related because of the emotional response] So being angry about moving, being controlled, vowing never to be fat—the one thing you can do in this power struggle and to get even is to not eat.

C: Yes. It's a power struggle . . . and I'm going to win.

T: Indeed. And perhaps there are ways you can "win" without "losing." [The word "losing" is intended to have a double meaning. Pause] Power . . . love . . . *self*-discipline or control. . . . You're doing great. Now, the bridge to the past spans many years, if you're ready, as you remember an earlier time when you experienced the same feelings [Pause]. Where are you now?

C: In kindergarten. The very first day! The teacher was mean, always criticizing and telling me what to do or what I couldn't do!

T: Just like . . .

C: . . . Mother! I didn't want to be born! She should have made it [her twin sister who died in the womb and was stillborn as Martha was born]. I'm so angry and upset!

T: [Touching Martha gently on her left forearm] Yes, you're angry. You haven't had much control over your life. Always trying to be perfect, to make up for your lost sister. Being criticized for mistakes or for what you didn't do. Being uprooted and moved and going to fourteen schools without ever being asked. This is a memory, though. It is not happening again. Now, as an adult, you have self-control, balanced by love and power. Can you believe that?

C: [A big sigh, then breathing regularly. Facial expression becomes calm.] Yes, I think I can. I'll try.

T: No, don't "try." That powerful word implies failure. What if you were to say, "Dr. Bob, things are getting better and I feel like we're friends. Could you and Mary come over to our house for dinner?" and I answered, "I'll try." Do you think Mary and I would come over to your house for dinner?

C: No.

T: You're right. "Try" has built-in failure implied. The little red train didn't say "I'll try," it said, in rhythm with the driving piston and the clickety-clack on the rails, "I think I can, I think I can, I think I can. . . ."

C: [Laughing] I think I can.

T: Good. You *can* do it. You can learn from the past, where your feelings of frustration, anger, false guilt, being controlled, rebelling . . . where they all came from and how they were reinforced until they and your reactions became practically automatic. Now, as an adult, you can keep track of who really "owns" the problem and you can exert self-control or discipline, balanced with power and love. You are an adult, not a little girl who is being controlled.

C: [Nods head]

T: Now, I want you to take some time right now to visualize what you are going to do and say in the future when someone attempts to control you. You've been a good student of "active-listening" and "I statements," so you might want to use these tools. I will be quiet now while you visualize, even hear in your head, what you as an adult can say or do. [Silent for about two minutes or so]

C: Okay. [signals same with hand gesture]

T: Wonderful. You know, of course, that you can only control yourself, that you can't control what other people may say or do. In fact, you even have limited control left concerning your kids.

C: Isn't that the truth!

T: Fortunately, yes. I said "fortunately" because you remember what unreasonable control and criticism did to you as a kid. And you've told me some wonderful things about your kids, too, not just the hassles.

C: Oh yes, they're beautiful!

T: [The arousal procedure detailed before is repeated.] How do you feel?

C: Six, seven, eight, nine, ten. Wonderful! Confident! Freed! [Said with emphasis.]

T: Good. I told you early on that I'd be working myself out of a job, that you would never become dependent upon me as "the answer man." We've gone from counseling sessions two or three times a week, to weekly, to every other week, and soon you'll be on your own, with the Lord's strength and wisdom.

C: It's been a miracle. I'm even liking—loving—fellowship again. You know, that was good of you to give me permission to take a vacation from church. I even felt judged and criticized there, especially by the "holier-than-thou" types.

T: Yes, I know the feeling. That's unfortunate, that sometimes where we need to be encouraged and even mourned with, we get judged, even shunned. But I must confess that I forgot that I suggested a vacation from church, even though you're not the first client to receive that permission.

C: Oh, Dr. Bob, you forgot?

T: Yes, as we have discussed, I am not perfect and . . .

C: . . . that is okay! [laughing]

T: Right on! And there is one more situation that I think you need to deal with before we conclude and go on an "if-needed" basis. I think you will be released completely when you are able to forgive your twin sister for giving up and dying. That's some "wisdom" from the Lord, in response to prayer, that I've been denying for several sessions.

C: So have I!

T: Let's consider it for our next session, if you're ready.

C: I'll think about it.

Twenty-fourth Counseling Session with Martha

There is no need [nor is there room in this chapter] to give a complete verbatim of this session. Martha achieved a deep trance and then the therapist used the metaphor of the building, as described above for the seventeenth session, to have Martha deal with the issue of forgiving her sister. Again, Martha went to the "basement" of the building. Again, I was awed by what happened. It should be noted that I introduced an additional setting, a metaphor. I had Martha imagine there was a movie entitled *The Life and Times of Martha* that she could not only see, hear, and understand, but that she could also control by slowing down the "projector," or seeing still frames, or even speeding it up. The purposes were twofold: (1) to make the memories less traumatic by having Martha be an observer instead of just a participant, and, (2) to give her even more control. Some dialogue from the latter part of the session follows.

T: So it appears that you were actually the stronger of the two of you; you survived.

C: Yes, that makes sense, but it's been hard to believe. She was so wonderful.

T: I believe you. However, being so wonderful, would she want you to be perfect to make up for her death or would she want you to live your own life? [Admittedly a risky question]

C: [Pause] To live my own life.

T: I think so, too. Now, can you understand why she died? Consider everything that went on as you were growing in the same place.

C: [Long pause] Yes. [Barely audible]

T: Now I'm going to give you all the time you need to forgive your sister for giving up, and those persons who over-controlled you for many years. I'm not even going to count to sixty. I'm prepared to wait as long as you need for forgiveness and understanding to take place. Okay?

C: [Nods affirmatively.]

T: [Silent, completely silent; praying, but not audibly.]

C: [Five minutes later, tears flowing] Everything's okay now. We're going to see each other again in heaven, I'm sure.

T: That would be a wonderful reunion! [There is no use commenting on what heaven may or may not be like. The "elevator" transports Martha back to the top floor, then the typical arousal procedures are used.]

C: Six, seven, eight, nine, ten.

T: How do you feel? [Even as the question is asked, Martha has the beautiful, composed expression one sees in Madonna portraits. Awed, I already knew the answer.]

C: Wonderful. At peace. Understood. Forgiving and forgiven. It's a miracle!

T: Indeed. [We then prayed. If my memory is correct, since it was not in the case notes, it was the first time we prayed audibly together. The prayer was one of praise and thanksgiving.]

COMMENTS BY THE COUNSELOR

In addition to the remarks interspersed throughout the dialogue, the following comments about what was done are offered.

1. I imagined myself in Martha's place, as difficult as it was. Thus, empathy and trust were developed.

2. Martha was not labeled the "identified patient." While she certainly had severe problems that needed to be dealt with, considering her the "IP" would have been detrimental to her, to say nothing of being inaccurate. The irritation in her husband's affect during the initial consultation, even though he was very concerned about Martha, was a clue that the "family system" was involved. I also suspected that the systems in the families of origin (both Martha's and her husband's) were actors in the drama that was about to unfold.

3. The "identified illness," if I can use that term, of anorexia nervosa was never diagnosed or dealt with directly by me. I strongly believed it would be counterproductive for me to enter what was perceived as a "power struggle" by telling Martha she had to eat properly to get well.

4. The identified illness of depression was dealt with directly and openly. I purposefully told Martha what the diagnosis was and how it was obtained. The prognosis was presented with reasonable hope. The cooperative assistance of Martha's family doctor, and his initial referral as a loving authority figure who was a Christian and could be trusted, were very helpful and providential.

5. Conjoint counseling was used frequently, in line with my bias that family systems and marital relationships profoundly affect every aspect of our lives, i.e., spiritual, physical, and psychological (sociological, if you prefer). There were twenty conjoint sessions and one private session with Martha's husband during the course of psychotherapy. They were interspersed with forty-one private sessions with Martha.

6. Hypnosis was introduced when I thought it would be an appropriate method of discovering the "hidden truths" more quickly and much more accurately than psychoanalytic procedures, nondirective Rogerian

therapy, or any cognitive approach. I consider hypnosis to be the treatment of choice when feelings, experiences, and behaviors do not make so-called "logical" sense.

    a. It was explained, introduced, and then used in a noncoercive way. Hypnotherapy and hypnoanalysis are powerful "tools"; I would never use them without the client's agreement and permission.

    b. The trance-induction method used was permissive, and I taught Martha the arm-raising technique so she could be in control of the hypnotic trance.

    c. Self-hypnosis was taught so Martha could gain self-control over depression and negative thinking (which had produced anxiety, at times exacerbating depression) between counseling sessions. She reported often how helpful self-hypnosis was.

    7. I told stories to Martha during the majority of sessions when hypnosis was being experienced. Several were made up (usually before the session, but sometimes during the session), some were old stories from children's books (e.g., about the ugly duckling and the little red train), and some were borrowed, albeit modified to fit Martha's needs, from Wallas.[4]
Several years ago it dawned on me while reading the New Testament that Jesus did not give advice or preach sermons the way most seminaries teach pastors to do. I couldn't even find an alliteration in any of Jesus' sayings. Instead, he told stories his listeners could identify with and thus apply to their lives without making lists of thoughts and behaviors. Since then it has never ceased to amaze me how much people get out of stories when in a trance, often far more than I had hoped for, often making connections with the past that I had never dreamed possible.

    8. Metaphors and ambiguous (or double-meaning) words were used often during the hypnosis sessions. The building metaphor was powerful with Martha, as it has been with many other clients. The client identifies with the building "that has as many floors as your age." The "communications control central" represents the person's brain, with conscious and automatic controls (self-control) built in. Each floor represents an age. The "archives" represents memories. The choice to remodel or redecorate

represents the ability to change. The possibilities in the metaphor of the building (and other buildings, which represent other persons) are almost limitless. Also, the metaphor of a movie theatre is powerful in viewing personal history and changing the way it affects the client. The client can become the audience, the participant, the projectionist, and even the producer of a future movie. Of course, such a metaphor can be used positively only with persons who believe it is okay to go to the movies. Some Christians don't.

9. I prayed for wisdom frequently. Even so, as noted in the narrative, I at first doubted the truth revealed because it seemed too strange to be possible. Doubting was a mistake. Even when I have ventured in the past to verbalize some "truth" and it has been either off-target or presented too soon for the client to accept, she (or he) has disagreed and corrected me with no hard feelings. With empathy and absence of judging, the counselor can be wrong and not cause a problem.

10. I frequently checked on Martha's "journey" to ensure that she could assimilate therapeutically what was being learned and that I wasn't pushing her too fast. By contract, my nature and cultural training is to solve problems and be impatient with lack of progress.

11. Post-hypnotic suggestions were used to suggest to Martha that learning would take place between sessions, that godly wisdom would be given to her, that she could exert self-control, and that she was not to become dependent on me as an "answer man."

12. As Martha recovered from depression, was no longer obsessed with food and her body weight, and was functioning better, the frequency of counseling sessions was deliberately reduced. Also, I affirmed to Martha that "I am working myself out of a job," thus paving the way for our "separation" when my counsel was no longer needed. The final session included appropriate review, summary, closure, and a fond farewell.

Reasons the Counseling Was Christian

Simply stated, the counseling was Christian because a Christian "burden-bearer" established a relationship with a troubled person in a way that facilitated resolution of the disorders being experienced by the burdened person. Sometimes I think it does Christian counselors, and the people whom we counsel, a disservice to try to define Christian counseling in detailed theological and psychological language. Further, I do not believe there ever will be *the only* godly way of Christian counseling, because both Christianity and psychology are fragmented into so many schools of thought based on different theological, denominational, or psychological theories and methods of counseling. Thus, I propose the simple definition offered above. Some brief comments are offered by way of explanation.

I am a Christian. To me, that means that I believe Jesus Christ is my Savior who paid the penalty for my sins, past, present, and future. Also, it means that the journey of life includes attempting to have Jesus be Lord of my life in obedience to him. That means that the counseling I do is "screened through the grid" of my Christian beliefs and is based on both biblical guidance and professional training.

Perhaps equally important in counseling, my being a Christian means that I do my best to perceive each person through the eyes of Jesus, so to speak, although admittedly far from perfectly. In theological yet practical terms, it means that each person who comes to me for counseling is: (1) created in God's image, no matter what his or her appearance or behavior may be, and thus has inherent, basic self-worth and dignity; (2) needs to love and to be loved; (3) needs to understand and to be understood; (4) has a concept of morality; (5) has some creative ability; (6) has some "gifts"; and (7) can experience health in wholeness as normal, as the way it was in the beginning, when liberated from the wages of sin by Jesus Christ.

My counseling with Martha was also Christian in that she was (and is) loved as a sister in Christ. That basically defined the burden-bearing relationship. Thus, I did not attempt to define her sins because the "log" in my eyes would have caused blindness to my own sins. Biblical principles were foundational, and only Scripture verses that were affirming and comforting were read or quoted. More than enough Scripture verses that were condemning had been verbally hurled at Martha in the past, both far and near, for me to judge her with selected Scripture.

The counseling was also Christian because prayer was ongoing, as referred to in the dialogue of this account.

Last, but not least, the counseling was Christian because one of the results (but it was not the first or even second goal of counseling, I will admit) was that after Martha was set free by the truth, her relationship with God was strengthened and she thus could serve him more effectively in everyday living.

A Personal Postscript

As a counselor and neophyte author, I want to acknowledge the courage of the editor in accepting this chapter that gives an account of using hypnosis in Christian counseling. We are both aware, sometimes from being criticized by some brothers and sisters in Christ, that there is judgmental concern about the "heresy" of psychology. Many Christians are suspicious of psychology and hypnosis, some because of the pronouncements and books of such brothers and sisters in Christ as Jay Adams,[5] David Hunt,[6] and Martin and Deidre Bobgan.[7] Even more severe is the condemnation from some about hypnosis as a treatment modality, since hypnosis is considered to be in the same league with fortune-telling, divination, sorcery, and other such blasphemous activities.[8] I can't afford the time and effort to rebut the arguments of these critics, but my response, if it were to be developed, would be based on the biblical evidence that Satan is the accuser of brothers (Rev. 12:10). Thus it is sad when brothers (and sisters) accuse other brothers (and sisters) of not being Christian in their methods of burden-bearing. A more reasoned response has been written by English.[9]

Again, simply stated, the counseling was Christian because "a Christian 'burden-bearer' established a relationship with a troubled person in a way that facilitated resolution of the disorders being experienced by the burdened person."

HOW THE CASE TURNED OUT

The case turned out well in that during the almost two-year span of counseling: (1) the depression Martha experienced lifted and did not return, even when additional difficulties occurred in her life; (2) the anorexic condition and Martha's obsession with food and with her appearance gradually disappeared; (3) Martha was no longer devastated by or rebelled against unjustified criticism and/or judgment; (4) she became more aware of her inherent self-worth as a child of God, created in the divine image; (5) she dealt with the past, forgave all concerned, and is achieving (it's a lifetime journey, in my opinion) a balance of love, power, and self-discipline; (6) Martha's relationship with the Lord was strengthened; and (7) she is functioning well. Life is not without its "trials and tribulations," of course, which she now understands and is able to accept, even meeting them head-on.

Counseling also turned out well in that I learned once again that I am not a healer, the Lord is. I also learned that Christian counseling is a privilege, a challenge, a ministry, a burden, a joy, and an opportunity to serve.

Also, since I am on sabbatical from providing personal psychotherapy and marriage and family counseling, Martha and her husband recently resumed conjoint counseling with a Christian colleague of mine to work on some issues that bubbled to the surface again. When Martha experienced healing that, of course, affected the "family system," and that is now being addressed. I am confident the "system" will be healed and all family members will benefit, including those in the next generation.

EDITOR'S COMMENTS

With all of its diversity, it is not surprising that Christian counseling includes some techniques and approaches that are controversial. Dr. King presents some of these issues in this chapter.

Quite frankly, I struggled about whether or not to include this case. I have never used hypnosis in my own counseling, and over the years I have tended to be skeptical about its effectiveness and legitimacy as a technique for use by Christians. Nevertheless, I respect the fact that a number of my professional colleagues—men and women who are committed, growing Christians—*do* use hypnotherapy, without hesitation. Surely there is value for all of discuss this issue openly and to decide, for ourselves and before God, whether this or any other method is suitable for use by believers.

Clearly, Dr. King is no novice as a hypnotherapist. He has taken the time and energy to learn the technique professionally. This is a good model for any of us. Christian counselors should not utilize this or any other technique they do not understand well or know how to use effectively.

In addition to the use of hypnosis and visualization—another controversial method—Dr. King's chapter illustrates additional aspects of Christian counseling.

First, the author acknowledges that most of us use therapeutic approaches that are at least partially molded to our personalities. You might want to follow his suggestion, put "ian" after your last name, and let this be your approach. Be careful, however, that you do not let this become an excuse for incompetence or lack of familiarization with therapeutic methods. Dr. King clearly recognizes his own uniqueness, but demonstrates the importance of mastering good counseling skills.

Second, this case illustrates the use of storytelling. Jesus taught in parables, of course, but this has not been done often in traditional counseling. Sometimes a story can convey a message that more straightforward comments cannot convey. By telling a story, we often can deal with difficult issues in a safer way that is less threatening to the counselee. This, in turn, reduces defensiveness. Of course, stories can be misinterpreted and sometimes the counselee misses the point. When a counselor is careful to avoid these dangers, however, the use of parables can be powerful.

Third, the therapist in this case recognizes that family members are often a part of the counselee's problem. For this reason the counselee was seen with her husband on several occasions. Only some systems theorists would use hypnosis, but all would accept the fact that the family unit needs to be treated, not just the individual who "carries" the problem.

Fourth, Dr. King makes mention of his efforts to avoid a power struggle with the client. Others had tried forcing her to eat, but this therapist, in contrast, dealt with more basic issues, and the eating problem took care of itself. This does not always happen, but sometimes when an underlying core problem is the focus of counseling, the more obvious presenting problems disappear.

You may disagree with Robert King that hypnosis is a powerful tool. You may feel uncomfortable with the use of prayer or Scripture during the hypnotic trance. But we cannot appreciate the complexities of Christian counseling, even as practiced by evangelicals, if we reject methods before looking at them carefully. I hope this chapter will challenge your thinking—as it has mine.

HYPNOSIS AS A THERAPEUTIC TOOL

1. **What is hypnosis?**
    A. It is a natural, common experience.
    B. It is an induced state, an altered state of awareness that is different from both sleep and normal, waking consciousness.
    C. It is characterized by increased awareness, focus of attention, and concentration.
    D. It is a state in which there is increased suggestibility. That is, the "critical factor" is bypassed by the appropriate and desired degree.

2. **What is hypnosis NOT, or what does it NOT do?**
    A. It is not a form of sleep.
    B. It does not cause loss of consciousness.
    C. It does not enable someone else to take control of an individual's mind.
    D. It does not cause an individual to give away secrets.
    E. It does not cause an individual to become more gullible.
    F. It does not cause an individual to remain in a trance, or to be unable to come out of the state.
    G. It is not something the therapist does to someone. The therapist is the guide, so to speak, while an individual experiences hypnosis.
    H. It is not magic.

3. **What are some of the characteristics of a person who is experiencing hypnosis?**
    A. There is increased concentration, increased focus of mind.
    B. There is increased susceptibility to acceptable suggestions.
    C. There is relaxed muscle tone, but sometimes with jerky, hesitant movements.
    D. The pulse is rhythmic and slowing to a reduced pace.

E. Respiration is slower and eventually shallower, although breathing deeply is not precluded.

F. Eyelids may flutter, eyes may tear, or whites of eyes get pink.

G. Body warmth may increase generally or in a localized area.

H. A person may feel like laughing.

I. The digestive system may gurgle.

4. What are some of the therapeutic uses of hypnosis?

A. It can enable an individual to learn to relax quickly and effectively.

B. It can help an individual use the power of his or her mind for emotional health rather than emotional distress.

C. It can help an individual use the power of his or her mind for physical health and comfort rather than illness and pain.

D. It can be of assistance in medical and dental treatment and surgery.

E. It can assist in making desired behavior changes.

F. It can help an individual achieve spiritual growth.

5. When should hypnosis not be used?

A. It should not be used for amusement or entertainment.

B. It should not be used if it might cause damaging emotional trauma to an individual.

C. It should not be used without first being completely explained to the individual who will experience it.

D. It should not be used to remove a symptom or pain that has value, or is needed as a defense.

E. It should not be used to give inappropriate suggestions of any kind.

6. Who can be hypnotized?

A. Most people can experience hypnosis to a variety of depths.

B. Generally speaking, highly motivated, intelligent individuals make the best subjects.

C. A person who can concentrate, and focus attention, is usually a good subject.

D. Children who are able to focus attention and use imagination usually are good subjects.

7. **Additional remarks**

A. There is nothing to fear from hypnosis, particularly when used ethically and professionally.

B. Critics of hypnosis often remark, "No one knows why it works." However, no one yet knows exactly how or why aspirin works, but we continue to use it because we know it does work.

C. Hypnotherapy is not a universal panacea. It is no more curative than the other psychotherapies. Its chief value as a therapeutic tool is that it can be a relatively rapid method when compared with more orthodox psychotherapies. Also, it can be used to reach certain disorders that are ordinarily resistant to conventional psychotherapy, such as disorders controlled by the subconscious.

D. Remember, hypnotherapy is not a "magical gesture." It is simply one more tool, albeit an effective one, a therapist can use to help troubled persons.

CHAPTER SEVEN

COUNSELING A FUNDAMENTALIST FAMILY WITH A SON WHO HAS AIDS

James L. Powell

Editor's note: *Counseling can be filled with surprises. Sometimes we begin with one problem and soon find ourselves dealing with entirely different issues.*

This was the case with Sally, a woman who was referred because of her obsessive thoughts, compulsive behaviors, and deep feelings of inadequacy. Once again, the counselor began with a cognitive behavioral perspective, but as more and more counselees got involved, the approach began to look increasingly like family systems theory. The change in emphasis began when her son's AIDS was discovered. The entire family, not only Sally, benefited from the counseling and experienced psychological and spiritual healing.

The counselor, Dr. James L. Powell, is president of Psychological Studies Institute in Atlanta. PSI is "a nonprofit educational institution founded to promote training, research, counseling, and service in the field of mental health from an interdenominational evangelical perspective." An ordained minister and licensed clinical psychologist, Dr. Powell has his A.B. and M.Div. degrees from Duke University and a Ph.D. from Georgia State University. His specialty is in clinical-community psychology.

———————————

GRACE, BY DEFINITION, ALWAYS CARRIES an element of surprise because it is not expected or earned, but is God's unmerited love toward us. Grace was the answer to the presenting problem by Sally as she was referred by her pastor. Sally suffered from obsessive-compulsive traits, so burdened by her search for the perfect that she often did not achieve the possible. She was in a long line of people who discovered that grace was the answer to their problems of perfectionism: the apostle Paul, Martin Luther, and John Wesley. Out of their own psychological struggles, God used these saints of the faith to proclaim that each of us is loved *despite* ourselves, not *because* of ourselves. The initial task in therapy was to see that Sally experienced this same healing, but the task soon became more complicated.

Sally was an attractive, trim, fifty-five-year-old woman who had masked her anxiety by the use of obsessive thoughts and compulsive behaviors. She had become unable to perform many tasks of daily living—cooking, or even cleaning off the dining table so it could be used for meals. Life had become an almost unbearable burden. She and her husband were not wavering in their faith, though. They were members of a church known for strong biblical teachings, and they were active in leading Bible studies. Sally, however, was becoming more obsessive about memorizing enough Scripture.

Sally never felt adequate. This was part of the basis for her perfectionism, and was made more problematic by her father, a professional man, who divorced her mother when Sally was five. She never had much contact with him after that. Her mother had never been willing to show many emotions; but with the divorce, the situation deteriorated, and her mother was in a psychiatric hospital for some time. Sally lived with her grandmother during this period.

Her mother, when not in the hospital, sought peace of mind through fad religions and cults, none of which gave much comfort to Sally. Searching for a solution to her own problems, she felt drawn to a life of helping, and became a nurse. She did not pursue this vocation long because she met and married Harry, a strong Christian man. She reflected that had she not become a Christian, she did not know how she could survive.

Harry was a long-suffering man with his wife and family, but hard-driving in his work. He was in middle-level management with a large national corporation, and he had proved his worth to the company many times by his hard-minded business sense. He had earned his Cadillac by extra work, including the work he brought home.

Much of Sally's stress and anxiety was being expressed physically. She was referred to me after her medical doctor had recommended biofeedback and therapy as a possible way of getting control of her somatic, or physical, complaints. In assessing Sally for therapy, a psychological test, the Minnesota Multiphasic Personality Inventory, was administered. The test results showed she had difficulty with anger, was sensitive to rejection, and was frustrated by not getting her needs for attention and approval met. This anger may be turned inward so that the individual ceases to engage in activities that generate pleasure. Her stress was very likely to be expressed by physical symptoms. Even minor stress might cause difficulty in memory and concentration and result in impaired judgment. Under stress, her relationships with others would likely be irritable.

People whose MMPI profiles are like Sally's most often have experienced rejection or desertion by fathers. The sensitivity to rejection and lack of approval in the present is the result of the rejection in childhood. People with this profile frequently have work histories in which they fail to achieve full potential. Similar problems often exist in marriage, where they are often passive and dependent. The profile is common in people who worry a great deal, have highly individualized thinking, and exhibit low energy. Here was our client, then. How could healing occur?

THERAPEUTIC APPROACH

I work from a cognitive behavioral perspective drawing strongly on the scientific psychological material of psychology, seeing science as discovering God's order in creation. Behaviors and emotions, however, are not seen as resulting directly from stimulus events, but are the result of the intervening variable of belief system. Individuals act or feel a certain way because of their interpretation of events, not because of the situations they encounter. If individuals tell themselves the truth, they are free to have more choices. If they are still rehearsing the self-statements and perceptions of not being adequate, of needing to prove themselves, then their behavior will be distorted and their feelings will be maladaptive for achieving abundant lives.

The task of therapy, from such a perspective, is first to help individuals clarify the distortions, untrue self-perceptions, and views of the past, and then to learn to tell themselves the truth. To develop more adaptive responses, they may need to "unlearn" old habit responses, develop new social skills such as assertiveness, and learn to deal realistically with themselves within the bounds of the created order. They may need to learn to function within the limits of nutrition, rest, and exercise. The use of technology such as biofeedback can enable individuals to see on a meter what stress is doing physiologically to their bodies and to learn again how to relax, assisted by actual physiological measures for the feedback.

If the client can begin to see with the mind of Christ, then he or she can discover new freedom in Christ and can live more effectively. Distorted perceptions and maladaptive habits come from experiences in the past.

Therapy sessions help to make sense of what a person perceives and how that supports his or her current ways of feeling and behaving. Therapy helps the person decide if perceptions are the truths he or she wants to believe. If not, then the individual prayerfully seeks out new truths and the possibilities that God has for him or her.

The process of therapy is a mutual journey between the client and the therapist, with the client being the expert in his or her own history and belief system and the therapist being the guide who can help clarify the client's own assumptions and the self-statements that influence his or her life. The journey becomes a pilgrimage toward health and wholeness, and eventually to holiness.

This approach takes seriously the biochemical and biological levels of behavior, intervenes at the psychological level, uses referrals to both physicians and ministers, as needed, and keeps the client informed about the process. I assume that what the clients tell themselves about the process of therapy is important in the healing process. The approach also looks at social systems and how they reinforce current behaviors.

In the case that follows, the early stages of therapy focused on learning to cope with the anxiety and lower the defensive behaviors. Behavioral programs were designed to overcome some of the obstacles to effective living. Biofeedback was used to assist with the relaxation and pain reduction. The marriage began to improve, and some of the therapy worked on developing better skills for enjoyment of each other, communicating more effectively, and resolving conflicts. Just when hope was increasing, and God's grace seemed so real, a new issue emerged that seemed to challenge the couple's deepest Christian beliefs.

Sally's husband Harry introduced the subject of their son, John, the third of their four children. He had been something of a black sheep who had not finished college and who currently was working in construction. Harry began to elaborate about the son's alcoholism and, with much difficulty, talked about the son's homosexuality. For parents who had come from a conservative religious tradition, this behavior was a sin that bordered on being unpardonable.

On the night before this session, John had told his parents he was going into the AIDS unit of the hospital. The shock was immense. Neither of the parents had slept the previous night. Harry had held Sally in his arms most of the night as she sobbed. In the therapy room they struggled to bring some rationality into this event. Only in his mid-twenties, John now appeared to be under a death sentence.

To make matters worse, in his mid-teens, John had renounced their church, and recently he had joined a church that the parents labeled as a cult. They worried about John, about his soul, and about their responsibilities as parents. John was seeing a therapist who was also homosexual, and they were upset and confused by that. Could a homosexual do anything to help their son? The family was in crisis. Insight therapy was not needed at this point. Life was at the bottom, and they needed crisis intervention to help them restore the family to its previous coping level. Their support system was not working, so a major goal was the restoration of a support system when everything, including God, had seemed to have left them. The following dialogue comes from this crisis session.

THERAPIST: You have been through many traumas with John, but you had not expected this one.

HARRY: I was the one who delivered John. Sally didn't have time to get to the hospital; so I brought him into the world. But I never expected anything like this. The only thing I know to do is to kidnap him as soon as he gets out of the hospital, and then he will be away from those people.

SALLY: We don't want him to associate with those people any more. Maybe if we had been more adamant earlier, then. . . . [She sobs.]

THERAPIST: You tried to help before, but now you question whether you could have done more.

HARRY: We should have done more . . . but I don't know what we could have done.

THERAPIST: So you are saying that you did all you knew how, both praying for him and talking to him.

HARRY: Yes, but it wasn't enough. And now he has AIDS.

SALLY: And he did it to himself. He caused AIDS by what he was doing. But why did he do it?

THERAPIST: You feel angry because his illness is a result of his involvement in a homosexual lifestyle, something you have warned him about for years.

SALLY: But he wouldn't listen. We would invite him to church, but he would not go with us. We raised him to go to church.

THERAPIST: You did what you could as a parent, but that did not seem to be enough.

HARRY: But we are going to correct that now, even if I have to kidnap him from the hospital. He will not set foot in his home again. He doesn't need his so-called lover and his so-called friends. He needs his family.

THERAPIST: Have you talked to his lover?

HARRY: No. I haven't talked to Joel for some time now; it was a couple of months ago, I guess, when I delivered the piano that John wanted. Joel helped us carry it off the truck.

THERAPIST: What is their relationship like?

HARRY: They are very close. John thinks Joel is one of the greatest things that has ever happened to him. That is why we have to keep them apart. It is his homosexual friends that got him into this, and they must be avoided. God certainly wouldn't want John to be compromising his life now.

THERAPIST: What does John want?

SALLY: John wants Joel to take care of him and bury him in that so-called church that both belong to.

THERAPIST: Does Joel love John?

SALLY: A sick and sinful love.

THERAPIST: What happens when you try to witness to John?

HARRY: He turns us off. He talks about the hypocrites, and he says there are more true Christians in AA than in our church.

THERAPIST: Do you remember what Jesus did with the woman caught in adultery? She was a sexual sinner. What would you have done with her?

HARRY: But she was heterosexual.

THERAPIST: Yet she was a sinner. How would Jesus witness to John? And to Joel?

HARRY: But John needs people who really love him.

THERAPIST: Does Joel love John?

HARRY: Yes, but it is a sinful love.

THERAPIST: Does John need to be surrounded by people who love him? People who love him enough to love the sinners who support him and care for him?

HARRY: I had never thought of it that way. I wonder if we could make a difference on both John and Joel.

THERAPIST: But don't try to con either. The love that Jesus had was actual love for the person, not the sin.

HARRY: I do love John, and actually, if he weren't homosexual, Joel is a really nice person. He is an artist, and his business is growing. He does really good work. Yes, I think I can be a witness, but it won't be easy. I can do Evangelism Explosion easily, but this is my son with AIDS.

SALLY: John may not let us get close. He has been pretty angry at us at times.

THERAPIST: What do you believe you need to do?

SALLY: I guess all we can do is try . . . and pray. I am willing to try.

THERAPIST: Let's summarize. You now feel that kidnapping is not the answer, that his relationship with Joel is important to him, especially now facing AIDS. And you are willing to allow the love of Christ through his Holy Spirit to work in your lives to allow John to be part of your lives again, even if he is still supported by friends you don't like.

HARRY: I don't believe as Christians there is anything else we can do.

THERAPIST: Before we finish our session, let us lift this issue before the Lord as we pray.

After the prayer, both Sally and Harry were visibly calmer. They had a plan now; they knew they had support from our counseling services through our twenty-four hour crisis line, and they left with expectation. The shocking news that a loved one is dying leaves a helpless feeling. But they were able to determine a way of being in ministry to their son. In their son's hour of desperate need, they would help him to continue to be supported by those who loved him. The courage needed to do this came from their strong relationship with the Lord.

A therapy session not long after this intervention plan included both Harry and Sally and two of their sons. The sons, Will and Joe, had severed most of their ties to John, but also to the family, particularly to Sally. The following segment demonstrated their anger.

JOE: Mom, you have so many problems of your own that I feel you have no time for me. I have just given up on our relationship.

SALLY: But you have never told me this before.

JOE: We have never been able to talk.

SALLY: I tried to talk.

JOE: I heard you talk about how sick Grandma was, how sick you were, and I wasn't going to get sick to get your attention. It was easier to say nothing.

THERAPIST: You wanted your mother's attention and love, but gave up trying because it seemed easier than being able to talk in this family.

WILL: You bet. You don't talk about John, you don't talk about things that make a difference. It hurts less if I don't come home often, and I don't.

SALLY: But I wanted to talk.

WILL: But I didn't know that, and I don't know that now. Dad, you were always working, and Mom, you were more involved in the church than you were in my life.

JOE: John may hurt and be angry, but I am, too. Would you call a meeting at a therapist's office for me?

HARRY: Your mother and I really do love all of you. If we have not been perfect, at least we tried. I was trying by not saying more. I didn't want people upset. I can stuff my issues and go on, but maybe that hasn't worked well for the family.

JOE: I have felt deserted. God gets his share. What's left over for me? I still don't know about church and God.

THERAPIST: This family has tried to be so nice that everyone has been hurt by not dealing with many issues. John's illness is forcing you to look at the family, and now you have some opportunities for change. One good change is that you feel safe enough here to talk about your anger.

JOE: And Mom is listening. It's crazy, but I feel the closest to Mom that I have in a long time.

THERAPIST: True intimacy and closeness means you are free to be yourself and share feelings. Both of you are caring enough to listen.

SALLY: I never thought about it that way. By trying to be closer to the kids, I was actually distancing myself.

HARRY: Maybe God is the same way. He tolerates my getting angry at him. I just hope that we can work through this anger that John has. He will only let me get so close, and he is quiet much of the time.

As more openness developed in the family, more closeness followed. The family was beginning to pull together because of the crisis of John's illness, but they were learning to relate in a different way. The old patterns of conflict avoidance were being replaced with an attempt to understand. In a later session some work was done on anger around the concepts in Ephesians 4.

HARRY: I never thought about my avoidance of anger as sinful until we talked about the biblical command to be angry, but sin not. I was so worried about avoiding sin that I did not deal with my anger. I took it out on myself.

SALLY: It is still hard for me to believe that God will not reject me for getting angry. It is not just letting the sun set on my anger that I have avoided; it is letting it rise or shine on my anger, as well.

THERAPIST: In the letter to the church at Laodicea, the behavior that gets God to spit the people of the church out of his mouth is not enthusiasm or anger, being hot or cold, but apathy, being lukewarm.

HARRY: I am concerned that while we were enthusiastic about the church and the work of the Lord, and while we tried to model biblical principles in our lives, by avoiding talking about our anger we communicated an attitude that our children took as rejection or apathy.

SALLY: But I had always thought that if I talked about conflicts with the family I would be rejected by them, and surely God would reject me for not being a more loving person. This is a strange notion you have—no, I guess that the Bible has—that love and closeness can be expressed through our anger. I wish we had known this earlier to use with John, but we need to do what we can. He needs to understand this, too. We will talk to his medical doctor and get permission for you if you will go and talk to him in the hospital so he will be prepared for a family session.

This technique is called cognitive reframing, taking a concept that someone uses in a maladaptive way and helping him or her to view it differently, more realistically and truthfully, so that more adaptive behavior will result. The liberation of the biblical word on anger was amazing for this family. It gave them the assurance that the new tools they were developing for strengthening the family and confronting the critical issue of John's illness were part of God's plan.

The visit to John's room was revealing. He was stable psychologically, responding physically to the treatment for the pneumonia, but was not trustful about the family. The motivation was high, but he was not going to choose between his friends and his family. He believed his family would prohibit his support system from having contact with him if he became involved with the family again. Prior to the recent changes in the family, that perception would have been correct.

JOHN: You will never get my parents to change their minds about me. They will never accept me. I regret that. I can't leave my friends now; they are all that I have. And some of them depend on me to help them get to AA meetings. Except I don't know when I will be driving my truck again.

THERAPIST: You sound motivated to get closer to your family, but you sound doubtful that anything short of a miracle of God will cause that.

JOHN: Not their God. He hates me. I haven't even been in their house, thirty miles away, in four years. Mom has never been in mine. Dad has been there once. Their God hates me and my friends.

THERAPIST: Are you willing to risk a meeting with your family and me to talk? I can reassure you that I believe they are more open to talking than you realize. They are working on their own issues, and they want a relationship with you.

JOHN: I wish that could happen. I am not really close to any of them. Only my sister is easy to talk to, and she lives out of state.

THERAPIST: I am glad you can voice your doubts to me.

JOHN: But you listen.

THERAPIST: Let's see what we can do to encourage your family to listen. I believe you have much to talk about.

JOHN: I want our meeting to be on neutral ground. Not at their house. I don't want to be kept from Joel and my friends.

THERAPIST: Depending on how well you do, the meeting can be here at the hospital or at my office. How does that sound?

JOHN: I don't know if they will come. Only Dad has been to the hospital yet, and he doesn't say much. Do you think Mom will come?

THERAPIST: Each of you says that you are willing to try. That alone sounds like progress, for each of you are talking about the problems of talking.

John was not willing to talk about the disease or his death at this point, but he was facing more than he had in the past. He was doing this without alcohol or drugs. This did, indeed, represent progress. His medical progress was slow; so the next session with the family was scheduled for the hospital. Sally, Harry, John, and I met in a small office on the main floor.

THERAPIST: What expectations do each of you have for this meeting?

HARRY: I want us to be a family again, one in the Lord, working together during this difficult time.

JOHN: I have my own church, but I want us to be a family.

SALLY: But we *are* a family.

HARRY: And you are welcome to come home anytime.

JOHN: I have my home. I don't want to be controlled and to disappoint you again.

SALLY: We want you to be with people who really love you.

JOHN: Joel loves me, and he accepts me for who I am. All I do is disappoint you.

SALLY: But we do love you.

JOHN: Then why don't you accept me as I am?

SALLY: Because it is wrong.

JOHN: See. It is hopeless.

[Silence]

THERAPIST: One of the problems is whether loving John means accepting his lifestyle.

HARRY: John, I love you, but I will never accept being gay as anything other than sin. But I love you.

JOHN: How do I know you are not trying to trick me?

THERAPIST: Think back to the Bible. Who was the man after God's own heart?

JOHN: It was David, and I am not perfect like he was.

THERAPIST: Yes, it was David, and yet he was far from perfect. He lusted for another man's wife, arranged for the murder of that man, and until Nathan pointed the finger at him, David did not even realize what he had done.

JOHN: Dad, do you believe that?

HARRY: I am trying to.

JOHN: I don't think you or Mom can do it.

THERAPIST: Are you willing to risk finding out?

JOHN: I don't know. I don't know if it is possible. I have tried so hard so long.

THERAPIST: What reassurances do you need from them?

HARRY: We can pray about it.

JOHN: That is your thing. If you want to, go ahead.

After more discussion, a prayer time was held, but John did not participate. He was quite reluctant to risk trusting, even with religious convictions behind commitments. The whole situation was revisited about four weeks later when John was out of the hospital. He was invited for a meal at his parents' home, but was refused the right by his mother to bring Joel. A family session was held with Harry and Sally, as well as John and Joel.

SALLY: We love you, and we know Joel is important to you, but I hope you can see why it would never work to have him come and visit at home with you. You are trying to force us to say that sin is acceptable.

JOHN: How?

SALLY: Our home is a Christian home, and we cannot approve of Joel that way.

JOHN: What way?

SALLY: We love you. You know what way.

JOEL: John, why don't you go and visit alone? I understand.

THERAPIST: You originally had trouble understanding the importance of this relationship to John, but once you did, you ceased trying to break up their mutual support during this time.

JOEL: John, you need your family, too. I'll understand.

JOHN: But I won't. You are included, or I won't go.

SALLY: Joel, do you really mean that?

JOEL: Yes, I want John to be happy. You don't have to approve of me.

SALLY: We do know how important you are to John. We just want to do what is right for John.

THERAPIST: You both share the same concern for John, but the differences are around defending moral stances. Each of you sees the situation differently. Each of you loves John. John talked earlier this session about how little time he felt he had before dying. Everything is important now to him.

SALLY: I only want what is best for John. I just wish he had never gotten AIDS.

THERAPIST: How then do you make decisions? What values serve the greater good of helping John?

HARRY: In a way, we need to decide what our Lord would do. He told people to go and sin no more, but he also ate with the sinners. In a way I think we owe it to Joel.

JOEL: You don't owe me anything.

HARRY: I didn't mean to offend. I know that we see things differently, but we want good things to happen for John. We feel caught between the lifestyle that we see as wrong and our concern for our son. We want him to know our love, and I believe that is your concern also.

SALLY: I am the one the family sees as unbending, but I do love John. I know the two of you are important to each other, but I have to do what is right in the eyes of God. Homosexuality is not right.

THERAPIST: I hear you wanting to support John and Joel at this time, but not wanting to do something sinful.

SALLY: That's right. I feel trapped.

THERAPIST: Have you ever had an excessively overweight person eat a meal at your home?

SALLY: Yes.

THERAPIST: Do you believe that gluttony is a sin?

SALLY: Yes, but this is more serious than overeating.

THERAPIST: Remember Romans 8:38–39 where there is a long list of things that cannot separate us from the love of God in Christ Jesus our Lord? I believe this situation is in that list.

SALLY: You don't think God would be angry at me for having Joel come as well?

THERAPIST: Sounds like you expect God to be hard, to be upset with you.

SALLY: God is a God of justice who expects us to obey his commandments.

THERAPIST: But God is also a God of love. Do you think you sometimes take your feelings about your biological father and put them onto your heavenly Father?

SALLY: I really have a hard time with God as Father. I never felt love from my father, and I wonder often if God loves me. I try to be worthy of his love.

THERAPIST: You keep wearing yourself out trying to prove that you are okay.

SALLY: I do all that I know how to do, but it never seems enough.

THERAPIST: Your father rejected you, and you worry that God can never accept you as your are.

SALLY: When I stop and think about it, I know that God loves me, but I forget about that so much of the time, especially in my daily life. I wonder if God is going to punish me for John.

JOHN: God is not punishing you for me. I did what I did, and some of it I would not change. We have had our differences, but some of the problem has been my stubbornness, not you. I didn't know about your father. Sounds like he hurt you. You have never talked about him. Would you like to tell me about him?

By confronting the issues, the barriers were beginning to fall. John began to understand parts of his mother he never knew. He began to discover that she, too, had feelings of hurt, and the identification increased between the two of them. Part of her distance from the family was not having dealt with the issues of her own father. Now John was learning to see her as a vulnerable, hurting person, and he could relate. Joel did join them for the family visit, and all felt that God approved.

After another month of sessions with Sally and Harry, a decision was made to have a family session with all the children. This was sparked in part by a call from Sue, a daughter who lived out of state. She was sensing a new openness in Sally, and she wanted to see if more progress could be made for the family.

SUE: The only problem that we have in this family is not John. We each have wanted more that we have not had. We have been busy being Christians, but we have not been able to talk with each other. We help others, but we don't always help ourselves.

THERAPIST: What do you want now from your mother?

SUE: I want to know that she will listen. I never felt I could be perfect enough to her. She would be great when I was sick or hurting, but I never felt she was there when things were better. I couldn't be in need all the time. I often felt alone.

SALLY: But I was there for you.

SUE: Perhaps as much as you could be. But I didn't always feel it then, and I don't always feel it now. You always seemed so worried that I did not want to bother you.

SALLY: I'm sorry. I was just trying to do things right for you.

SUE: You often seemed so worried about being right, that I felt I was wrong and not important.

SALLY: I never meant to hurt you.

SUE: And I was the one who thought that I was hurting you.

179

THERAPIST: The basic problem is one of communication, not good intentions. Neither of you talked through the issues.

SUE: I don't think I learned to talk about problems until my second year of college. Then it felt so good. That is one of the things that attracted me to my husband. I could talk with him. Mom, I want to be able to talk with you.

SALLY: I did the best I could.

SUE: I can forgive the past. Let's make it better now. Just listen to me; don't judge me. I wanted you to hear that I was hurt by my boyfriend, not that I was better than he was and should be able to stand suffering. I wanted to hear that you loved me, not that I could have made a B in algebra. I wanted you to know what I was like and still love me. John, at least you listened to me when I talked.

JOHN: And I often felt that you were the only one in the family who listened to me.

THERAPIST: Sally, who listened to you?

SALLY: [Sobs] I tried so hard.

SUE: [Reaches out to Mom and hugs her] I love you.

SALLY: Thank you. I love you. I love you, John. I am so scared for you. And for all of us.

Finally risking listening, and trusting that God would not judge honest exploration led to a growing closeness within the family that proved to bring much healing to the family unit. As the family grew closer, Sally and Harry began to wonder about their church family and not letting those with whom they had spiritual closeness know something of the struggle they were facing. As John got weaker, they took over more of the care, especially during times when Joel was traveling on business. The family's new-found excitement inspired them to risk being vulnerable, but they were concerned what the church would think about them because of John.

THERAPIST: When did you tell the pastor?

HARRY: We told him early, but he can be trusted and is a great spiritual leader. He continues to mean so much to us.

THERAPIST: Did you talk to him about being more public with the church?

HARRY: Yes, and he encouraged us to go ahead to tell them at a night service.

THERAPIST: What holds you back?

HARRY: That is a good question. I believe we should share the burdens of each other, but it is still hard.

THERAPIST: Are you afraid of being labeled sinful because John has AIDS?

HARRY: It just doesn't happen in nice families.

THERAPIST: What evidence do you have for that?

SALLY: None of our friends are facing this.

THERAPIST: Or least are not talking about it. What did you do wrong?

SALLY: We could have been better parents.

THERAPIST: Did you intentionally do anything to hurt your kids? Did you pray for them? Did you raise them in the church?

HARRY: We did all of that, but from our family sessions, we realize that we could have been closer.

THERAPIST: That is exciting for you to learn, but you did the best you could when you were raising your kids. God can forgive us for the things we ought to have done, just as he forgives us for the things we ought not to have done.

HARRY: I am a deacon in the church. I should have done better.

THERAPIST: God asks us to be faithful, not perfect. Now you know how David felt about Absalom, yet he continued as the leader of the people.

HARRY: I had not thought of John like Absalom. This does not make my service in the church invalid.

THERAPIST: Some people may say that it does, but where do you listen for the truth?

HARRY: Sometimes it is hard to remember the biblical word when people are peddling guilt.

THERAPIST: You're right. If you go public, you need to stand on God's word first, for many people get irrational about AIDS. Yet your pastor and both of you describe your church as supportive. What do you think you will do?

SALLY: I want us to try to talk about it Sunday night. We need to get rid of the feeling of guilt that we are carrying, and we need to allow our friends to pray with us.

THERAPIST: Getting close to people means taking risks, but you sound like you are ready to take that risk.

HARRY: I think we both are. We are growing closer together with each other as well as with the kids. John's illness has created an awareness in us that we needed more than just working in the church. We needed to allow God to minister to us in a deeper way, feeling the acceptance that we have never felt before.

SALLY: In a strange way, John's illness is bringing us closer together as a family, and closer to God. I am getting to know each of my children in a way I had not before.

CONCLUDING COMMENTS

Those remarks summarized a personal experience of Romans 8:28: "And we know that in all things God works for the good of those who love him, who have been called according to his purpose." The hidden feelings of rejection and the works of righteousness of Sally had assisted in creating a family that did the right things, except to each other. John had chosen to leave the family, struggled for several years with substance abuse, and finally contracted AIDS. He defeated himself, but toward the end of his life began to accept more of his traditional Christian teachings. He experienced Christian community within his family and from his parents' church, for their talking with the congregation brought much support. A mutual forgiveness and new life process was seen in the family.

The family needed Christian guidelines and examples in therapy, because of their excessive guilt and Sally's need to be perfect. Their faith, often devoid of God's grace for their own situation, was a major source of strength. The use of prayer, a new openness to the leading of God, and the fellowship of their church community were all part of the Christian aspects of their therapy. Secular counseling's parallel to grace is often a self-centeredness or not caring. Instead of the hollow insistence of looking after number one, the Christian counselor can help clients give up unnecessary burdens by focusing on the fact that God loves them despite, not because. Sally and Harry would never settle for a self-centered approach, for they are too grounded in biblical concepts. While they had acknowledged grace as a concept and practiced it toward others, they had not really applied it in their own lives.

Therapy became for them a laboratory where grace could be explored. From the crisis counseling session after they had first learned of John's illness, they began to discover that God had more compassion and healing than they had experienced. They did not have to carry total responsibility for John, nor did they have to separate him from his own friends and support during the difficult final year of his life. They also discovered that John's friends who had been so bitter toward religion began to change, and they became more open to Christians. This type of approach from a therapy perspective is known as unconditional positive regard, and it models in a human way what God does for us in a divine way through his grace.

Crisis intervention is also an effective tool for helping people reestablish their equilibrium, to regain their sense of being able to make decisions and move ahead. From a cognitive-behavioral perspective, the client becomes more effective in labeling the dynamics of the events so that he or she can make informed choices.

Cognitive restructuring is effective in helping to take the barriers established by man and see them through the eyes of Christ. At many points, the therapy was able to take the frustrations and make them into learning opportunities. The authority for new perceptions is the Bible. Rather than denying truth, clients are assisted to find a deeper truth. The focus on the person as being more important than the sin was a scandal of the ministry of Jesus to the pious, but pointed to the radical transforming love he proclaimed. Regardless of the sins of John or Joel, they were not to be denied the witness of a caring Christian community.

Attention to the function of behaviors within the larger system was part of a comprehensive approach. By working with the dynamics of the family system, many changes were accomplished. Work on communications helped the system become rewarding itself and began to introduce more changes on its own. The church system also provided a powerful component, modeling the love Christ had for the lepers of his day, to John who had a modern equivalent of leprosy. The family was tied back into their ongoing therapeutic community that would continue long after therapy had ended.

The final healing came from the Holy Spirit continuing to work in their lives. Out of the death of John there was healing in the family, a resurrection of mutual concern and involvement. In the death of Christ, we find our salvation, and sometimes in the death of a loved one there is new life in relationships. John's life was not in vain for the impact he had on others, particularly in the recovery community, and on his family in forcing them to examine their identity and learning to experience God's grace. Why is this Christian therapy? The redeeming love of Christ transformed the worst experience of a lifetime into a renewal of God's purpose for a family. That is the good news of the resurrection.

EDITOR'S COMMENTS

Early in his chapter, Dr. Powell mentions that from his perspective the process of therapy is a mutual journey. It is shared by the client and therapist, with the client being the expert in his or her own history and belief system, and the therapist being the guide who helps give direction to the journey. This type of thinking is likely to be welcomed, especially by clients who feel insecure about counseling and would resist meeting with a counselor who appears aloof or authoritarian.

Almost in passing, the counselor mentions the importance of nutrition, rest, and exercise. It is difficult for counselees to concentrate fully on their counseling if they are not taking care of their bodies. Notice, too, that the counselor was aware of the client's support system. Even though she and her husband were active in their church, they had no support system when they needed it most. Often, the support of family members and friends can help the counseling indirectly. When there are supporters to help between sessions, the journey to health and wholeness can be smoother.

At the beginning, the counselor used traditional client-centered (nondirective) responses. This stimulated talking at the beginning, but

Dr. Powell did not remain with this all the way through. Notice that he prayed with the client and her husband near the end of the session and at one time he summarized the contents of the session. He encouraged Joe to talk about his anger in the first family session, and he illustrated the concept of cognitive reframing—taking a concept that someone uses in a maladaptive way and helping him or her to view it differently and more realistically.

I was impressed with Dr. Powell's ability to let the family members express their feelings about the son's homosexuality, but without the counselor getting into the debate. Had he taken sides, the rapport-building in this family probably would have failed.

At one time Sally mentioned that she has problems with the concept of God as Father. Often this is true of people whose growing-up experiences at home have been strained. If one's earthly father was abusive, absent, hypercritical, condemning, or not to be trusted, it is easy to conclude that God must be the same, despite theological teaching to the contrary.

You will have noticed that Dr. Powell began and ended his chapter with mention of the concept of grace. He wrote, "regardless of the sins of John or Joel, they were not to be denied the witness of a caring Christian community." This kind of grace was seen most clearly in the life of Jesus. He showed grace to the sinner without condoning the sin. The effective Christian counselor is a believer who allows the grace and love of Christ to flow through the therapist and into the lives of hurting counselees.

CHAPTER EIGHT

AN INPATIENT ASSESSMENT
WITH A SEVERELY DEPRESSED
HOSPITALIZED PATIENT

Robert S. McGee

Editor's note: *At times, outpatient counseling fails to help and a counselee must enter a more intensive in-hospital treatment program. This chapter considers the case of a woman who was severely depressed and entered the hospital after an eight-month period of outpatient counseling.*

It is difficult to summarize a complex case in a few pages. Every writer in this book is aware of that difficulty. Mary, the subject of this chapter, experienced a number of interviews and therapy sessions. Instead of trying to summarize all of these, the author of this case history has chosen to present one interview, an in-hospital assessment evaluation. We learn other details of the case at the beginning and end of the chapter.

Robert S. McGee came into the counseling profession by an unusual route. Born in Oklahoma, he was an Army assault-helicopter pilot in Vietnam before earning a B.S. degree in journalism from Oklahoma

186

State University. His M.S. degree, also from Oklahoma State, is in clinical psychology. He completed the Mental Health Specialist Program, is a licensed professional counselor, and is founder and president of Rapha Hospital Treatment Centers. With headquarters in Houston, Rapha is a health-care organization that provides a Christ-centered approach to treatment in over twenty centers nationwide. Robert McGee's best known book is The Search for Significance.

MARY, THE SUBJECT OF THIS CHAPTER, is a twenty-nine-year-old white female who grew up in an unstable and dysfunctional family. She was unwanted by her father (who tried to get the mother to have an abortion), and grew up in a home filled with rejection, emotional cruelty, and fears of abandonment. The father had a drinking problem and left the family when Mary was about nine years old.

The mother was emotionally unstable, once diagnosed as schizophrenic, and a victim of sexual molestation, including rape. Mary had also been abused sexually (by her grandfather) and she had tried, without success, to fix her mother's many emotional, relational, and financial problems. Often, the mother was gone and Mary was left in the care of baby-sitters or various family members. She had a very low self-esteem that was complicated, no doubt, by her obesity. When she entered the hospital, Mary weighed 327 pounds. She blamed this, in part, on constant eating in an effort to "fill the empty feeling inside."

Eight months prior to hospitalization, the patient sought outpatient counseling for symptoms of anxiety, loss of sleep, a tendency to neglect daily activities, and flat affect that was interrupted at times by rage.

The outpatient counseling failed to help. The therapist focused exclusively on her behavior without examining the underlying causes. Transference and periodic role-reversal complicated the therapeutic process. Sometimes the patient became enraged with the therapist, but most of the time she acted like his caretaker, concerned about whether or not he was happy with her. After eight months of this, Mary had become severely depressed: feeling hopeless, lethargic, chronically fatigued, suicidal, and unable to function effectively.

She was admitted to the hospital for the evaluation and treatment of depression and her overeating disorder. The admitting psychiatrist noted that her attitude was cooperative and pleasant, her psychomotor activity was normal, her thought processes were intact and coherent, but her affect was constricted and sad. The admitting diagnosis: Axis I: (1) Major depression, single episode, (2) Bulimia. Axis II: None. Axis III: Essential hypertension, morbid obesity. Axis IV: Severe. Axis V: Current GAF 35, highest past year 65.

RAPHA TREATMENT

Rapha's approach to treatment attempts to utilize the discovered truths of many different theories of psychotherapy and to integrate these with the revealed truth of God's Word. The therapist assumes that three ingredients are critical in the healing process: our forgiveness in Christ, the character of God, and our identity as children of God.

The basic approach in conducting the following assessment interview was a cognitive-behavioral model. This was chosen because of the compulsive eating disorder and the patient's tendency to use intellectualizing as a primary defense mechanism. She often gave spiritual explanations for her underlying psychiatric issues and tended to perceive God the Father in a way that was similar to her earthly father—demanding, rarely approving, distant, and tyrannical. This concern about spiritual issues prompted the counselor to use prayer, scriptural quotations, and interpretations of events using "spiritual language." The cognitive-behavioral features of the interview focused on breaking through the patient's denial to facilitate identification of underlying issues, negative self-talk, and the accompanying emotions.

Early in the interview it became evident that this person had no awareness of the influence of her family systems on her dysfunction or how the family had influenced her perception of God the Father. Notice that specific references were made about the church as a source of love and acceptance. Mary had not found this in her relationships with others.

Family rules relating to performance and perfectionistic standards as represented by the word "should" were expressed often by the patient. In addition, Mary obviously was trying to break free from her responsibilities of taking care of the family. One evidence of this was Mary's immediate and inappropriate anger toward her mother. Early in the interview it was noted that Mary equates performance with being accepted. This issue of acceptance is a key concept in Rapha's cognitive-behavioral approach to therapy.

The primary motivating emotion that underlies the above cognitive structure is fear. In this case the fear is buried deeply under layers of dissociation, projection, and intellectualism. Toward the end of the interview the insight comes to light that Mary is afraid of becoming mentally ill like her mother. While this fear was rooted in the family and projected onto God, the focus on God throughout the interview provided a safe metaphor to allow Mary to explore her feelings in more depth.

Underlying themes of shame, lack of intimacy, and self-condemnation were uncovered and brought to light in the context of family dysfunction. This self-condemnation typically was described as a failure to please God through performance. By exploring these "failures" in this context the emphasis was gradually shifted to patterns of family dysfunction. This was accomplished through using language and biblical constructs to provide a safe environment where she could reveal destructive patterns. Later she was able to disentangle her views of God from views of her dysfunctional family.

The lack of appropriate sexual identity was identified early in the interview and targeted for later treatment intervention. Mary had never seen appropriate or well-functioning role models because of her distorted childhood development.

Rapha's approach to treatment is based on the therapist's ability to help people deal with a system of relational truth based on the integration described above and demonstrated in this interview. This is only a first step in establishing a basis for trust and opening the door to further healing. Speaking in the language and beliefs of the patient allows reframing of scriptural words, beliefs, and interpretations to occur without violating the patient's inherent religious affiliation. When this occurs in the context of discovered psychological truths, the power of God can be seen in a special way that provides love, forgiveness, comfort, and meaning.

The following assessment interview had several purposes: to identify major treatment issues, to evaluate family issues, to give hope for recovery, to motivate the patient for treatment, to give some initial insight to help the patient overcome her denial, and to demonstrate the power of God's love, forgiveness, and comfort in a meaningful way.

THE ASSESSMENT INTERVIEW

T: Let's ask the Lord to give us his wisdom as we talk.

Father, we thank you for the fact that you are a sovereign God. We thank you for what you have done and what you are doing. Father, we don't know exactly what you want to do and really that's up to you. And so, Father, I ask that you will superintend this time. We're going to trust you to bring up whatever you want to, knowing that you will be in the business of resolving those issues. We don't have to be fearful of talking about things that we're not ready to deal with, and we don't have to worry about coming up with anything. We can rely on you to superintend our time together. We ask this in Jesus' name. Amen.

When treatment is successful, we experience freedom—not perfection, but an ability to enjoy life and cope adequately with life's problems. Are you struggling with any issues like that?

C: It seems like I've got a lot of intellectual knowledge, but when it gets down to the heart—it stops. And I think the other area we've hit a lot is when he, my therapist, said, "You've done all your goals really good until you get down to the one about compulsive overeating and binging." That's where I stop.

T: You mentioned "compulsive overeating and binging." People who have problems with food usually have had difficult family backgrounds. They have experienced a lot of hurt and a lot of anger. Often, though, they learn to control the hurt and anger by suppressing these feelings. Sometimes, they become very analytical about life's experiences without feeling the emotions. How much do you intellectualize instead of feel?

C: Before I came here, I would've said a lot. Since I've been here I've been identifying that I'm not feeling a lot of emotion—that I'm shutting it down. Probably the emotion I feel the most about present things is that I get angry at lots of things. About past things—the anger's just gone.

T: The anger that's gone—did you ever experience it?

C: Yeah, I did. I remember being pretty rageful most of my life— slamming doors and screaming. And in the last three or four years, that wasn't appropriate in the church I was involved in, so I really worked at being happy and okay. I'm finding now that I don't do a lot of yelling and screaming anymore.

T: So to be spiritual, you couldn't experience your anger?

C: Right, or that I shouldn't be that way. I remember in similar sessions, I thought, *Oh, well, you shouldn't think that way or you shouldn't act that way. You shouldn't be talking to people. . . .*

T: So what you *should* be is very important?

C: Yes. And I'm always feeling like I'm not meeting up to what it should be, that I'm always below that.

T: Why is being what you *should* be so important?

C: To be accepted, to make sure I fit in with the crowd. And there's a couple of levels. One, I need to be in the middle of what's going on—a leader. Best example is at church—I'm not satisfied to just sit back and be the status quo or be on the fringe. I feel like I need to be right in the middle of what's going on in decisions and things like that. And then part of me really feels like if I do what I'm supposed to do, then I'm okay to God, too.

T: So part of you wants to be identified in the group as *special*. So there's something inside of you that wants to be special. And you entered a realm of living which was religious or spiritual; and to qualify as being special, one of the things you couldn't be is angry.

C: I think so. I think it's because of what happens when I get angry, that feeling of losing control when I get angry.

T: Are you scared of yourself?

C: I think I might be. It's really hard for me to identify what it is I'm afraid of, because I know that I feel it. I can see all the symptoms.

T: You did something before in your life when you were angry that you don't want to repeat?

C: The sense of the feeling that I want to break things or pull things down or slam doors and yell . . .

T: With your parents?

C: With Mom. I could never do that with Dad, although I did that some when I was older. My parents are divorced. I remember . . . I don't remember specific instances . . . but I remember slamming doors at Mom and being very angry.

T: Why were you angry?

C: I don't remember.

T: That's important though, isn't it?

C: Seems like it is. When people tell me there's a lot of resentment and anger toward Mom, I'm not in touch with any of it. She was real sick. She was demon-possessed. I went through that with her.

T: What do you mean, demon-possessed?

C: Mentally ill. She was diagnosed as schizophrenic.

T: How did that affect you?

C: It was real hard for me. It was real scary for me.

T: Scary because . . .?

C: Because things were so out of control. I never knew what she was going to do. It kind of mulls together—the mental illness and the demon possession.

T: Were you responsible for her?

C: Yes and no. I felt very responsible for keeping the family together. I remember hiding her medications from her—not her psychotic medications but her other medications, so she wouldn't overdose and . . .

T: How old were you then?

C: When I was hiding medications, I was fourteen or fifteen. When her nervous breakdown started happening, I was eleven or twelve.

T: So from eight to eleven . . . do you remember much of that?

C: I don't remember much of the year when . . . I'm not clear on when Mom and Dad got divorced. I don't remember much of the year right after the divorce. Mom said I used to come home screaming that I wished Dad had died in Vietnam instead of getting the divorce, but I don't remember any of that. I remember the school a little bit. I remember feeling rejected because we were among the few kids whose parents were divorced, and everybody would say, "Oh, where's your dad?"

T: So your dad abandoned you? And that made you angry?

C: I think so.

T: Because parents aren't supposed to abandon their children. They're supposed to take care of their children—not abandon them. He abandoned you physically. Your mother abandoned you emotionally. So you had some reason to be angry. You were getting the short end of the stick. But you don't experience that much in your emotions?

C: No, until very recently I could tell you a story without any emotion at all.

T: Was there anybody else around? Or was it just you and your mother?

C: It was me, my mother, and my brother until the nervous breakdown. Then Michael stayed with a family in Indiana. He was there long-term, but would come to see us maybe once or twice. I was always happy to take care of him.

T: Who gave *you* support?

C: The only other person that was around was this woman, Barb, and her two kids who were our age. We spent time together as a family. I know I was really attracted to Barb, but Mom and I would talk about how bad she was doing with her kids. I don't remember there being anyone else.

T: Was Barb doing that badly?

C: Yes, real bad. She was sick a lot, too. I remember her lying in bed, telling the kids to go do this and go do that. . . . She was always upset about having to be responsible for everything, so she seemed . . . she was happier and more socially acceptable than my mom.

T: But you didn't have anybody to comfort *you*?

C: Not that I know of. Not even Mom. I can remember looking for that, always wanting approval of authority figures and feeling like I wasn't getting it very often.

T: Have you *ever* felt comforted?

C: I would say not in terms of what I think it should be. I know that probably all the nurturing that's happened has been through my fellowship that I'm in now. That's been the last ten years, but . . .

T: But you've had to perform?

C: Right. So it's felt like I haven't quite made it, or that I'm being comforted for awhile, but then I'm finally. . . . And they've gotten disgusted and said., "You should get your act together," though that might not have been their exact words. I just felt like they may have been there for awhile, but then it was just too much and they'd cop out.

T: Comfort isn't based on performing for a pat on the head. Comforting, typically, is for when you really need it—which is usually when you feel you've failed, or when you've been hurt. So you don't know what it is to feel comforted, do you?

C: I'm not sure. If it's happened, it's happened in the last ten years of my life. But even in my church experience, I feel real distant. I feel like I wasn't meeting up to their standards.

T: I wonder if you don't experience the emotion because you don't know how. It's almost like you've defended yourself against your pain by not feeling it.

C: I've struggled with some of that here. What I feel is pain. What do I do with all this pain, and feeling like there's no comfort? Food's a great anesthetic. TV's a great anesthetic. I feel like my sins are anesthetics, to a point.

T: In other words, being here in the hospital takes away these things that give you comfort, but you haven't found an alternative. That may be the reason why it's so hard to give up on food and television as an anesthetic.

C: Yeah, it's so hard to give this up. And I don't feel comforted from God at all.

T: God seems very distant to you, doesn't he, Mary? You don't feel *intellectually* abandoned by God, but *emotionally* you don't know what it feels like to be comforted by him.

C: I don't. And I feel myself longing for that a lot. I've heard people talking about how they feel as though God's arms are around them, and I keep wishing, *Oh, Lord, if only I could feel that somehow . . . somehow I could touch that reality.* And yet it doesn't feel like there's any reality, it's like I grasp at nothing.

T: Do you feel angry at God?

C: At God? It comes and goes. Earlier, I was really angry at God because I felt like I'd had a really bad deal.

T: Well, you had a tough life.

C: Yeah, and you come here and see these other people and you think, *Boy, I've got it easy!*

T: But that doesn't help you.

C: No.

T: No. What do you mean it comes and goes? Sometimes you'll let yourself recognize it?

C: Eight months ago, I was really angry at God. I was furious. And I don't really think I talked to my counselor about that, but I was really trying to grasp the fact that I didn't need to perform. I tried to work at just relaxing and not performing anymore. It's kind of subsided, although I was really feeling angry again Saturday. The biggest struggle for me has been going to Scripture and seeing this wonderful verse of comfort and then reading a little bit further and seeing condemnation. If someone were *telling* me that, it would be different—but this is Scripture I'm reading, so then it gets real frustrating for me. You can't win. I hear this book saying that you don't have to perform, that you're fully accepted and totally loved, but then I look at the Scripture and it says, "If you keep on sinning . . ." and that's the category I feel like I fall into. Somehow I've missed it. Somehow I've . . . and then I get angry because I feel, *What else? Gee, what else can I do?*

T: You seem to experience a lot of shame and condemnation. In other words, you could have ten things that were positive and one thing that was negative, and you would attach yourself to the negative. It's like you have a sensor inside you that accepts shame and condemnation, yet doesn't know how to receive anything positive and accepting.

C: And I feel a real lack of being able to receive even if somebody loves me—I freeze up.

T: All you know is how to receive condemnation.

C: Sometimes I feel like I am bathed with people from my congregation who support me, bathed with positive affirmation, and yet at the same point I can't . . . somehow it doesn't go any further.

T: Which is also your fault?

C: That it doesn't go any further?

T: Yes.

C: Sure.

T: I mean, here you are and you have the best that God can offer—people who are to love you unconditionally, who are interested in your life and want you to be strong and happy—and that hasn't had its effect and that's your fault.

C: And I'm ungrateful—I've got more things than I've ever had in my life and I'm still not happy. I've got it better than I've ever had it . . .

T: But you still hurt?

C: Yes, I still hurt, and I'm desperately seeking something to fill this empty void that is *so* empty.

T: Well, part of your emptiness—your feeling of being empty, of being dead—is that you really only experience life from the shoulders up. Right? You're into your thought life. You're just thinking and there's not much of a real experience of yourself. And part of that is because you don't know . . . in some ways it's gracious of God that you have not experienced a lot of pain because you don't know how to receive comfort. Right? That would be pretty devastating to be immersed in pain without being able to receive comfort. So as a child you were abandoned, left in your pain with no comfort.

C: My whole life, from age one on.

T: How far back do you recall?

C: I recall at the age of three what Mom and I went through—a whole list of things. I had the illusion that from the time I was born until the time I was three and Michael came along, Mom was there taking care of me. And come to find out that after three weeks, Mom left me with Dad. He wasn't giving me a bottle or changing my diapers. He was switching me from baby-sitter to baby-sitter and she was gone. There was one baby-sitter who would tie me to the crib at times and pick at my dress. I was with this baby-sitter for months. Mom couldn't figure out why I kept coming home with a hole in my dress. She showed up one day out of the blue and saw me tied down to the crib so I couldn't get out. It was that kind of thing again and again and again—always switching baby-sitters because Mom would always find something wrong and she wasn't home.

T: Do you know of any sexual abuse that occurred early in your childhood?

C: The only thing . . . Mom said that there was an incident, when I was really young, where she found Grandpa in the bedroom and he had his hand up my dress.

T: How young?

C: I thought she said one or two.

T: So even from birth, almost . . .

C: Dad had wanted an abortion and was trying to get her to take a hot mustard bath because it was an old wive's tale that said it would abort the baby. Mom realized what she was doing and stopped it.

T: How does this make you feel?

C: I can remember little spots—incidents—like when I moved in with my Dad when I was twelve or thirteen. It was hell. I attended a Methodist church. There was this one pastor and her daughter—love just *poured* out of them. Dad wouldn't let me go very often, but the few times I went there it was just kind of like . . . I could find little tidbits here and there but not for any extended time.

T: Have you talked to God about your anger toward your dad?

C: I thought I had. I've dealt more with that than I've dealt with my anger toward Mom. I just never realized I was angry toward Mom. I dealt a lot through inner-healing times with church people, praying and trying to cut down some of the anger—mostly at Dad because he was kind of a scapegoat. I was angry at him, and there was no question that I was angry at him.

T: What you've done is that you have excused your mother.

C: But I think I excused Mom because of her illness. I think, *but she was sick, she was raped as a child, she didn't know any better.* But now I don't even want her to touch me. I don't want to be seen in the car with her. I tighten up every time I'm with her. Her constant talking irritates me. I've gotten in touch with a dream I had the other night. I was so angry about her being sick, but other than that . . .

T: In your dream, you were angry with her being sick?

C: I dreamed that she was getting into the car and she was saying something. I said, "Stop! I'm so tired of taking care of you!" And that was the feeling of the dream.

T: You still take care of her?

C: Some. I try not to. And she doesn't ask me to take care of her, either. It's more subtle. For instance, I got a letter from her saying, "Wish you could call me every night"—and I think, *Go away!* I'm real sensitive. I can't listen to her talk about her being sick. She's on insulin . . . I can't listen to her talk about being sick at all. It's to the point that I'm even rude on the phone. I'll say, "I've got to go," and I'll hang up. I realize afterward what I've done. I haven't even let her finish her sentence. But I go to her and talk about *my* problems because I really respect her opinions. I say, "Hey, Mom, I'm thinking about going to school. How do you feel about this?" I really want her feedback, but when it goes to talking about *her* situation . . .

T: How does God feel about you?

C: *Disappointed* is the word that comes to mind.

T: Disappointed . . .

C: Not being all that I can be, holding back.

T: "All that you can be." Are you supposed to be in the army? [Both laugh] It's the army where you're supposed to "be all that you can be." So you're not a good soldier in God's army? You're not a productive one, not on the list when people get invitations—you're not a very high number.

C: I'm called in to cook.

T: That's what you feel, at least as much as you *can* feel. And that's because of these things you don't do right, your sins.

C: Or lack of passion for the Word—for lack of passion to serve.

T: You know there are about 1,050 commandments in the New Testament. How holy is God?

C: Very.

T: Absolutely. Sin is *any thought, word or deed which is against God's character*. That's the definition of it, right?

C: Kind of like the water glass with the sewer water in it?

T: I think you're close to really receiving help. I really do. And do you know why I think you're close? I think you're close to giving up. And when you give up, you *may* feel more of the pain you have expressed, but you can also experience *real* comfort, *true* love, kindness, and strength. God has a lot for you, Mary.

C: That's been "the word" this weekend. *Give it up!*

T: There will be a time in your life when you will see the truth and then you will see the light. You're seeing more of the truth. You're seeing more of your life and how much of it has been affected by that which is not true. Mary, many things that you believe are not true. In fact, most of your experience of life has not been based upon the truth. It's based on a deception—things that you think are truth that are not really truth. Intellectually, you hear it, process it, and feed it back.

You would like for God to come down and zap you so you wouldn't have to take a risk. Right? I think giving up means this . . .

Giving up means, *I am never going to be able to perform well enough for God.* Now that's the truth, right? Which means when he says he accepts me based on what Christ has done, if that's not true, I'll never make it. I can't take this by degrees or a little slice like this. I either have to take it, or I have to reject it. You have intellectual knowledge, but you don't have experiential knowledge. To have experiential knowledge is more risky because we have to be honest about our hurts and desires.

Mary, sometimes it is helpful to focus on the positive things God has done for us. That way, we can begin to see that he really does care about us. What could you praise God for?

C: Well, allowing me to come here was major. It's because of who he is. It's hard for me to identify a lot of things to praise God for.

T: The Scriptures tell us that the Lord is loving and kind. It says he is "near to the broken hearted." It also says he has made you his own beloved child—because of his grace, not because you were good enough to earn it. What would your life be like if you reflected on the fact that he loves you and accepts you in spite of your performance?

C: Scary.

T: You know what you're doing? You're using this condemnation to control yourself. Condemnation is very powerful. Maybe your mother, your father, and others used it to control your behavior—to get you to do and to be what they wanted. Maybe you learned from them to use condemnation on yourself.

C: To keep myself in line?

T: Yes, I mean you are really scared of yourself, aren't you? You may even fear you're going to end up like your mother.

C: Probably, yeah.

T: Did someone tell you that?

C: She did. She said, "This is biological and I can see that you and I have this same makeup. We have to struggle harder than everybody else does."

T: And you're going to end up just like her?

C: She didn't say that, but that's the fear.

T: So the way you deal with that fear is to control yourself as much as possible, knowing that if you don't comfort yourself once in awhile, no telling what might happen—no telling what you might do. If you didn't let a little of the pressure off every once in a awhile, maybe you couldn't control yourself. So maybe you're doing these things to keep from *really* sinning—or to keep from going crazy. It's almost like a balloon that's being blown up, and you're letting some of the air out to keep it from popping.

Mary, you seem to have a great fear of failure. Maybe you're afraid of failure because your parents demanded that you behave or else, and maybe you have assumed that God is like them: waiting for you to fail so he can *get* you.

C: Except that it's getting more and more constant.

T: That's because it doesn't work. We need to realize that God isn't like our parents—even the best of them. He is infinitely kind, even though he knows our most selfish thoughts. He is everywhere and he knows everything. He is strong for his children, but sometimes he doesn't seem to come through for us, does he? God didn't come through for your mother.

C: Uh, yes and no. I've always felt like somehow we've had to suffer more. The best example is how it took Mom a long time to get a car. And it just seems like she's always financially strapped. She prayed and prayed for a car, and she couldn't find one. I felt like, here we are again, and God's gypping us again. That's where some of the anger comes out.

T: You've never seen God come through . . . for you and your mother?

C: She's talked about feeling like God's around her—like God's hugged her—and I've seen her get off medication and attribute that to God; but generally I've seen Mom as real rebellious and not allowing God to work. But I have said that statement in the last couple of months—*why hasn't God come through?* It's been more of an attack toward material things.

T: I think that there are several things you can begin to do that will help you. First of all, I think you're going to have to give up. That means you will get fixated in a lot of this because of the fear. This fear leads you to believe that you have to control yourself. The way you control some of the hurt and anger inside you is to let some of the pressure out. A lot of this is just intellectual, and you feel like you're a fake because you're not experiencing it. You're going to have to let God be in charge of that outcome instead of you.

C: Does that mean just do whatever?

T: First of all, you have to understand that what you've done before hasn't worked. Change, then, makes more sense, doesn't it? Then, focus on God's forgiveness. Look at this passage, Mary. Colossians 2:13 says that he "forgave us all our sins," because Christ died on the cross to pay for our sins. In Colossians chapter 1, it says we have been reconciled to God:

> For God was pleased to have all his fullness dwell in him, and through him to reconcile to himself all things, whether things on earth or things in heaven, by making peace through his blood shed on the cross.
>
> Once you were alienated from God and were enemies in your minds because of your evil behavior. (vv. 19–21)

So we are forgiven and accepted by God because of Christ's death in our place. We couldn't earn all that. It was given to us by his grace! Our obedience then is not out of fear, but out of a desire to please the one who loves us so much. Some people don't feel that love, forgiveness, and acceptance, though. We feel fear instead. Do you fear anything else?

C: Rejecting God, not being committed like I should—that if I let myself, I'll go the other way, and I'll do my own thing [sexually].

T: Do you have sexual fears?

C: I think I do. I have this strong feeling inside of me. I haven't had sex since I was twenty, but I know masturbation is a real struggle. I feel a lot of that and I'm real sensitive to what I see on TV.

T: Do you have sexual cravings?

C: Yes, I think so.

T: How early in your life did you experience those?

C: I was very aware of them at my dad's, when I was eleven or twelve. That's when I first discovered masturbation. There was this incident with his other daughter—the two of us—and it was more of a stimulation type of thing, but I was the one who initiated it.

T: Do you recall your father's response?

C: The only thing that I'm aware of is that when his wife left, he became more affectionate toward me—but it was never anything inappropriate. He was just affectionate, but only when my mother left. You know, the wife runs off because she's ticked at him and, somehow, I became the wife. I would cook dinner and that kind of stuff. And there was an incident before I left when I asked him if I could smoke, and he said, "Sure." So I bought some cigarettes. One day he ran out of cigarettes and he said, "I sure wish I had a Marlboro." And I said, "Oh, I have one in my purse." Then we started talking and he gave me this whole lecture starting with cigarettes and ending with getting pregnant. He said that if I ever got pregnant before I was eighteen, he was going to see me in the bedroom and it wasn't going to be for a spanking. So my assumption at that point was that it would be sexual. His wife was free to tell me about their sexual relations and I was aware of him having *Playboys* in his drawer—I got that information from her. I had read some books and I was more open to some things that I had never before been exposed to.

When I was four, there were some boys in the back yard and we wanted to play on the swing. They wouldn't let us unless we pulled our pants down and let them touch us with their genitals. I was able to go and tell Mom about that. We talked about where babies come from. I don't remember a lot of sexual abuse. I remember being told a lot about things.

T: Even early?

C: Yeah, at four I was told about birth. Then when I was thirteen, Mom was raped—eleven or thirteen, can't remember—but Mom was raped and she told me about it. We'd have to run from the house because she thought this guy was going to come get us. So I've always been very sensitive to that and I've always been fearful of being raped—for a long time I thought that if I were raped, or if someone came in to rape me, God would do something. The Holy Spirit would make me bark like a dog or do anything to keep me safe. Then some incidents happened in the last three years where I didn't believe that anymore. I saw people get hurt—people I thought God should protect and He didn't.

T: So God let them down, too?

C: So there was no certainty that God was going to stop anything from happening. God would make whatever happened come to his good . . . you know, utilize it for his good.

T: God is inscrutable. He has his purposes and his ways. Sometimes they make sense to us, and sometimes they don't. But God is good and kind. No matter what happens, we can be sure he has our best interests at heart. Making us bark like a dog is not in our best interests. He not only uses circumstances for *his* good but for our good, too. What do you think would happen . . . ? Maybe you thought you would receive comfort if you were more sexual than you are now.

C: Yeah, I believe I would be more comforted. That's why I have a driving need to get married.

T: So you could feel comfort?

C: Yes, feel comfort.

T: So there's a real drive in you to feel comforted. Without comfort, there's a deadness inside of you. You've cut off the emotions because there wasn't anybody to comfort you. Pain is unbearable for many of us, but instead of finding a safe environment to work it out in a healthy way (for some of us no safe environment was available), we try to escape from it, deaden it, or control it in some way. If we don't experience comfort for our pain, we try to find a substitute for the comfort. Overeating can be a substitute.

C: It's also a protector because I won't have to deal with relationships. I desperately want one, but at the same point I don't have anybody chasing me down the street. When I was younger and I was real thin, there were guys all over the place. I had a tremendous amount of relationships. I'm much more comfortable with men than I am with women. All my friends, except for one, are men. I'm one of the guys.

T: But because of your weight, you're not perceived as a sexual object?

C: Right. When I think anybody's even interested, unless I'm very sure they're solid in God . . . and even then I think, *Whoa!*

T: You're sort of going both directions aren't you? You have anger toward God. You're not sure of his protection. You haven't experienced his comfort, but at the same time, you perceive yourself as having a need for a relationship with him. It's like if you left him you would end up like your mother. You know there are forces inside you that you're not capable of dealing with.

C: If I left God, I'd be dead—it's that simple.

T: On the one hand, our strengths become our weaknesses. You have a tremendous strong point here in being able to intellectually understand what we're talking about. There are a lot of folks who couldn't have this conversation because they wouldn't be able to process the information quickly enough. So this is a little bit different than how I could talk with someone else. But it's your greatest weakness because they're just words in some ways, too— until they become experiences. Your beliefs and feelings (or lack of feelings) and your view of life has been largely shaped by your relationships with your parents and a few others in your life. How you view yourself is based on those relationships and the shame, condemnation, and neglect you experienced there. It becomes easy to believe that God is like your parents.

But the Scriptures, through the Holy Spirit and the family of God can communicate God's love, forgiveness, and strength so that you can experience—really experience and know—the wonderful truth of what God is like. The differences between the truths of God and your perceptions is going to be an important distinction to see in the upcoming therapy sessions. The more you can know him and experience his comfort, the more you will be able to apply God's truths to everything else you know.

Until next time, I'd like you to work through the "Fear of Rejection" and "Reconciliation" sections of the workbook, and we'll discuss what you learn.

Let's close our time in prayer. Father, thank you that you've given us your salvation in which we can rejoice. Father, you are the God of all comfort, and so we claim your comfort. We ask your Holy Spirit to bring confirmation to all that we've talked about that is of your truth. We ask this in Jesus' name. Amen.

C: Thank you.

FOLLOW-UP

During the first few days in hospital, Mary was given psychiatric, physical, nursing, chemical dependency, psychosocial, dietary-nutritional, and spiritual assessments.

Readers may have special interest in the latter because it often is not part of standard psychiatric evaluations. According to the summary report, the patient went to church occasionally when she was in high school but near the end of her teen-age years she was "baptized in the Holy Spirit" and has been actively involved in the same charismatic church ever since. She stated that God plays a significant role in her life, although she feels a need to perform in order to get divine approval. Often she feels guilty because of her inability to act in ways that will bring divine approval. She mentioned that God seems unreachable at times, but she continues to be active in her church. Her friends, roommates, and co-workers were all from her congregation.

As a result of the different evaluations, a treatment plan was devised in an effort to uncover and treat the causes of both the depression and the eating disorder. The treatment plan was multifaceted and included the following.

Workbook assignments from *The Search for Significance*[1] were assigned to help identify Mary's distorted belief systems. The "Fear of Rejection" and "Reconciliation" assignments are examples of this. The book was also used to help Mary identify self-defeating beliefs and thinking that have led to a destructive self-concept. The process of identifying the destructive beliefs, rejecting those beliefs, and replacing them with biblical truths (concerning reconciliation, justification, and regeneration, for example), is known as the "trip-in." The process of rejecting and replacing the faulty thinking would be rehearsed throughout treatment so that Mary could learn to counter the self-condemnation and self-rejection she presented when she came to the hospital.

As the patient's awareness increased, the therapist would show how faulty thinking can also influence perceptions of one's family relation-ships. The workbook, *Your Parents and You*[2] could be used to help identify these issues. Sometimes this biblio-therapeutic approach is supplemented by more traditional techniques such as the Gestalt-based empty chair.

It was agreed that Mary should be assigned to a same-sex group for discussion of gender-specific issues, such as her compulsive masturbation, early memories of sexual trauma, and need for same-sex role models. Groups and individual therapy are both used in this approach. Both help Mary learn and practice "trip-in" techniques.

OUTCOME

Treatment goals were relatively well accomplished in terms of uncovering the etiology of Mary's depression and eating disorder. She was able to identify emotions underlying her depression and could identify specific false beliefs regarding her self-esteem and relationship to God. She obtained significant insight into her childhood issues that had led to her adult depression and the suppression of these feelings that had led to her eating disorder.

At discharge she returned to living with her roommates with medical follow-up to be by her usual physician. No medications were prescribed. Outpatient individual psychotherapy with a competent therapist was recommended, and Mary joined an Overeaters Anonymous support group. At discharge, her prognosis for continued recovery was good, and she was described as being non-suicidal, bright, and hopeful.

In treatment, she made good progress on all of her objectives, except those dealing with binging and hatred toward her mother. She was able to identify the four false beliefs and master the "trip-in" coping tool as a cognitive reconstruction. At discharge she was sleeping better and verbalizing hope. After-care recommendations included an emphasis on journaling to keep track of the emotions that precipitated binging behavior and to work through forgiveness toward her mother and significant others.

EDITOR'S COMMENTS

In reflecting on this chapter it is important to recognize that we are seeing a patient who had been in therapy for a long time, and had been in the hospital for four days before this interview began. To start the session, somewhat abruptly, with a prayer is appropriate when much is already known about the client, including her attitude toward prayer. Otherwise, this would be an awkward way to begin and might break rapport even before it is established.

Since the counselee was active in a church and sincerely interested in spiritual issues, the counselor could be free to use "God talk," even at the beginning. This often frees a counselor to discuss spiritual issues whenever this is appropriate. If the counselee is not a believer or if he or she resists spiritual things, then spiritual language must be used less often, at least until a better level of rapport has been reached.

In reading the interview, I felt the counselor had a tendency to talk too much, sometimes almost to the point of giving a lecture. It is true that the client was bright and at least somewhat sophisticated psychologically, but I wondered about phrases such as "God is inscrutable," "You have intellectual knowledge but you don't have experiential knowledge," or "How much do you intellectualize instead of feel?" Good therapy, like good writing, uses simple words. Simple is not the same as being simplistic.

The counseling literature has been dotted with bibliographic references—using books as an adjunct to counseling. This interview (and the Rapha approach) does this. If the counselee has the ability to concentrate, as Mary clearly did, then reading, completing a workbook, or discussing a book's contents can all be helpful. Sometimes the use of books replaces therapy. For some, that may be effective; but for a patient whose problems are severe enough to require hospitalization, it is important to assign reading with caution and discuss the reading after it has been completed, as the counselor notes near the end of the interview.

In his chapter, Robert McGee gives some insights into the Rapha treatment programs, but I suspect he would agree that there are individual differences within the organization that he heads. No one interview, therefore, should be considered typical of this or any other approach to treatment. As the chapter notes, patients like Mary have contact with a variety of professionals, most of whom were not mentioned in this chapter or are mentioned only in passing. Each of these people has a role to play in treatment.

More detailed information about Rapha is available on request.[3]

CHAPTER NINE
A CASE OF RITUALISTIC ABUSE

Lois Motz

Editor's note: *In the book of Ephesians, we are reminded that Christians are in a struggle, "not against flesh and blood, but against the rulers, against the authorities, against the powers of this dark world and against the spiritual forces of evil in the heavenly realms" (6:12). Many Christians seem to go through life oblivious to the battle, unaware of the enemy, and unprepared for any kind of spiritual warfare.*

It could be argued that all Christian counseling is, in one sense, a form of battle against the great deceiver and his forces. Rarely, however, does this become more apparent than in cases dealing with people whose lives have been scarred by involvement with ritualistic Satan worship. It appears that few counselors actively seek to work in this area but many find themselves drawn in because of the presenting symptoms of men like Richard, the counselee-subject of this chapter.

209

Lois Motz is both a counselor and nurse. After receiving an A.A. degree in nursing at Palomar College in San Marcos, California, she earned a B.A. in psychology from California State University at Los Angeles, and an M.A. in counseling from Wheaton College in Illinois. For several years she worked as head nurse on inpatient psychiatric units; currently she is involved with a private-practice group that offers counseling services in Villa Park, Illinois, a Chicago suburb.

THE FIRST TIME RICHARD CAME TO my office, I was somewhat surprised at the difference between the mental image I had formed of him while making his appointment and the young man sitting in front of me.

Several days before, I had received a call from this twenty-five-year-old man. He reported being disturbed by what seemed to be flashes of uncomfortable memories of himself with his father. At the time of our phone conversation, I envisioned a somewhat hesitant and fearful person of average height and weight. Yet here was someone who successfully ran his own business, presented himself as being confident and in control of his life, and who, in physical stature, could have been a football player.

Over the next two years, many memories would surface that would explain why Richard also had a fearful and hesitant side. Richard had been ritualistically abused by satanic cultists, some of whom were family members. These experiences were so terrifying that his only defense against them was to disassociate and place them far out of reach in his mind. Now, all these years later, the defenses that kept the events locked away beyond awareness began to break down.

At first, the memories came in fragments. There were times when he would have a single mental image, such as being naked from the waist down and being placed in a hole in the wall of a basement. Sometimes his body would give him physical sensations that had no reasonable explanations. One example of this was wanting to constantly rub his wrists because they felt sore, as though tied tightly with rope. At other times, Richard would be aware of nothing more than a generalized feeling of discomfort for which he could find no current source.

As time went by and therapy progressed, the past surfaced more rapidly and completely. He began to understand what, at times, triggered the memories. One day, as he was driving by an old white house in the neighborhood in which he used to live, he saw an old man going up the porch steps. Immediately he was aware that he had been in that house and had suffered abuse there. Some mornings Richard would wake up from what seemed to be a dream. But he was certain, after becoming alert, that it was a real event that had happened years before. He never knew when a memory would emerge. He could be sitting comfortably enjoying a television show when something said or visually presented on the screen would trigger a fragment or a more complete flashback.

Fortunately, there were periods of rest from the past. This gave Richard more energy to deal with the present and keep a sense of order in his life. However, what was even more amazing was this man's ability, as a child, to have done what seems to be a self-hypnosis that enabled him to immediately disassociate after an event took place. It seems that it was this remarkable ability that prevented Richard's ego from splitting and becoming a multiple personality, as so often occurs to ritualistic abuse victims.

Unless a therapist receives a specific referral dealing with ritual abuse, of which the client has already become aware, then these cases most often unfold in layers, with the more simple abuse being remembered first. That is not to say any abuse is simple, for it is certainly not. Perhaps it is more a sign of our times to differentiate between simple and complex abuse. All abuse takes its toll on the individual to different degrees and in a variety of ways. My belief is that God can bring healing to these individuals. Yet as with the rest of humanity, total healing and completeness will only come when those who have a personal relationship with Jesus Christ will enter into his presence (Rom. 8:18–23).

Early on in therapy I try to establish where the client is in his or her awareness and relationship with God. It does not matter if there are some theological differences between the client and me, and neither is it important to know which church, if any, the client attends. The foundation of Christianity is that Jesus Christ is God's only begotten Holy Son, who died on the cross willingly to pay the penalty for our sins. Truly, it is Jesus Christ plus nothing. If the client, in his or her knowledge of the truth, has already asked Christ to forgive sins, then this is the base of my integration of Christianity and psychology. If there is no knowledge or relationship, then I begin, as opportunities arise, to tell them of God's love.

In ritualistic abuse cases there is a purposeful[1] distortion of Christianity, especially of Jesus Christ. Not all of these types of clients are able, nor are they willing, to hear about God. It is very important that this attitude be respected. The love, gentleness, and sense of value that we offer will be our greatest representation of Christ. In time, as the clients respond to these qualities, they will also begin to question the reason for them.

Richard was blessed. He had an older sibling who would sneak him away into another room of the house and tell him that Jesus was the God in heaven and that he loved Richard. Many times as a child, Richard remembers asking Jesus, "the God up there," to forgive him. Through therapy, Richard began to grow and deepen in his understanding of and relationship with Jesus Christ.

As with any case where there are repressed memories, it is important to help the client feel safe and supported. Richard was assured of my availability by telephone or for extra appointments if there were any emergencies. He was also asked for permission to have a prayer group pray for him, while keeping confidentiality.

As the memories emerged, they were dealt with in several ways: first, on a feeling level (encouraging Richard to express and talk about his feelings); second, how what happened affected him at the time; and finally, how those experiences are affecting him now. An extensive family history was taken, from which a genogram[2] was developed. Diagrams and drawings were also used. As the satanic-abuse memories came to the surface, a trusted police officer was brought into the case as a consultant on the criminal aspects.

As therapy continued and a trust level was established, Richard began asking Jesus to walk through his memories with him. This proved to be a most valuable tool. Begun with prayer, this helped Richard feel safe in remembering so many horrifying experiences. I never *assumed* that prayer would be acceptable to Richard. After two years of therapy, even though he had never refused (and at times had even asked for) prayer, his permission was always sought before I prayed.

After the prayer, Richard would lie comfortably on the couch and go through a relaxation technique[3] of tensing his muscles from head to foot, one group of muscles at a time, keeping them tense for ten seconds or more, then slowly relaxing them in the opposite direction. When he felt his body was relaxed he would then go to the current fragment or partial memory and ask Jesus to stay beside him and help him feel safe so he could remember.

Of course, there is not the space to dialogue two years of therapy, nor does one chapter allow an indepth case study of a ritualistic abuse victim. If the client were a multiple personality, the space would be even more inadequate; therefore, the sessions will be presented by categories. The section titled Presenting Problems was taken from our first session (after some initial rapport had been built) and will be addressed first. The sections titled Beginning of Satanic Memories and Satanic Rituals are excerpted from sessions that occurred during the last eighteen months.

PRESENTING PROBLEMS

C: I've been feeling that I have needed help for some time but I have been afraid to get any.

T: Yes, it is often difficult to make the initial contact for therapy. Is there some reason you were finally able to come in?

C: Well, I'm going with this girl who has all the qualities that I want in a woman. I'm thinking of marrying her, but I'm not sure that I know how to feel love. And besides this, I am uncomfortable thinking of having her touch me [pause] down there.

T: It sounds as if you are unsure of how to feel emotional intimacy and feel uncomfortable with sexual intimacy as well.

C: Yes, I stayed away from dating in high school because I was afraid a girl might touch my [pause] genitals.

T: You still seem to be afraid of that. Is this a fear that you have all the time?

C: Well, with my girlfriend there are times that I get a really strong feeling that I'd like her to touch me and other times I want to yell at her to get away from me.

T: I imagine that it must be confusing to have those opposite feelings.

C: Yes, sometimes I'm not sure what's going on. What is even stranger is that I keep getting a sense of being in the corner of the basement, my father being over me, and my feeling like I have to go to the bathroom.

T: Are you able to tell me a little more about that?

C: [crying] Well, all I remember is that I'm little, maybe five years old, and my father is doing something to me and I have to go to the bathroom.

T: I can see that it hurts to tell me this. Is there more that you are feeling?

C: [still crying] I feel dirty and unloved.

T: As you feel that now, are you able to remember what your father was doing?

C: No, I think I'm too scared to remember.

T: Well, Richard, I can understand that. It sounds as if you have had a flashback and perhaps with time, as you feel safe with therapy, you will remember more. Do you mind if we talk a little about your father?

C: No, but there's not a whole lot I remember about him or even my childhood. He died seven years ago. I know I didn't feel sad when he died. What do you want to know?

T: Well, why don't you just tell me all the things that you can remember.

C: He yelled a lot and hit all of us. I never wanted him to touch me. If he ever drank milk out of my glass, I would throw out the rest and get a new glass. But I had to do it when he wasn't looking or he'd hit me. Everybody thought he was a wonderful man.

T: Do you think he was a wonderful man?

C: No [starting to cry], but I always thought there must be something wrong with me.

T: So instead of thinking other people didn't know him very well, you figured you were the person who was wrong?

[long silence]

C: It wasn't me, was it? They didn't know what he was really like, did they?

T: Well, I certainly wouldn't think that someone was very nice if they didn't treat their children well. And if I knew that the children were afraid of the parent, I would be even more suspicious.

[silence]

C: That was too hard for me to figure out before. I guess because Dad was never wrong. Everyone else was.

T: So you learned not to question him and tried to stay out of trouble?

214

C: Yes, but it didn't work. He always found something wrong.

T: Perhaps it's starting to be okay to remember, now that he is not here to tell you that you're wrong. If it is, then maybe this week you can allow yourself to think more about your childhood and your dad.

During the several sessions that followed, Richard became even more aware of the disparity between his father's public image and his actual behavior within the home. Insight was gained into how this had adversely affected Richard's confidence in his own judgment of not only people but situations as well.

In a later session Richard walked in with a heavy glass object in his hands, sat down and began to stare at it.

T: Richard, what do you have in your hand?

C: It's an ashtray. I was down in the basement cleaning and I found this. I suddenly remembered staring intently at it. I must have been about five years old at the time. I was lying down on top of the safe. It feels as if something is cutting me across my legs, right here [points to hip and lower abdomen area].

T: It sounds as if you are feeling that right now.

C: I am. I started to at home but I was too frightened and decided I should bring the ashtray here. I don't know why.

T: Perhaps you feel this is a safe place to remember.

C: Yes, I think so. I am surprised at how much I am remembering.

T: Can you look at the ashtray again and try to feel what you were describing a few moments ago?

C: I feel as if I have no pants on and my father is behind me. [long pause] I don't want to remember this.

T: Why don't you want to remember?

C: What my father did. Maybe I'm making this up.

T: It must be pretty painful if you've remembered something and then need to wonder if you are making it up. What reason would you have for making it up?

215

C: [crying] I don't know. Maybe it is because I hate my father.

T: You don't seem to be a person who would hate his father for no reason.

C: I hate him for what he did.

T: [pause] What did he do, Richard?

C: [crying] He pulled me against him and stuck his penis in me. It hurts.

T: Yes, I'm sure it did hurt. What your body is feeling now is the memory of what it felt then. It must have been very painful. You were just a little boy and he was a big man.

C: I feel so dirty. Why didn't I run away?

T: You are not dirty, Richard. You were just an innocent little boy feeling helpless with a powerful grownup. You did nothing wrong. It was your father who was responsible for what happened, not you. You must have known that if you had tried to run away, it would have done no good.

C: Why didn't God stop him?

T: I don't have those answers, Richard. I do know that it's not because God doesn't love you. He does. Your pain and tears mean something to him. Scripture tells us he keeps track of them all (Psalms 56:8). I also know that God speaks to men's hearts to get them to turn away from doing wrong. Obviously, your father didn't care and wasn't listening.

C: [long pause] Do you think this is why I feel so uncomfortable when I think of getting married and having sex?

T: Yes. Children are too little to understand that it is the older person's fault and that there is nothing wrong with them. They get a distorted view of physical closeness and retain a fear. I think it's going to be important for you to learn and feel the difference between this and sexual intimacy. A child has sensual feelings because God made the body with nerve endings that respond to touch. The adult has sexual feelings that go beyond just a physical sensation in the skin.

Over the next six months many more memories emerged, not only of abuse by the father, but of others who had various relationships with the father. As Richard was able to share these memories and the resulting feelings with his girlfriend, their relationship grew stronger. He began to feel and understand emotional intimacy and attain a more comfortable level of physical intimacy because he felt valued and loved. This also enabled him to more readily separate the past from the present. Richard and his girlfriend became engaged and set their wedding date. In a subsequent session, Richard reported a memory.

BEGINNING OF SATANIC MEMORIES

C: I had a dream last night; only when I woke up, I knew it wasn't a dream but a memory. I can only remember part of it. I woke up terrified.

T: Would you like to try to remember all of it?

C: Not really. This one was too scary, but I know that if I don't try, it will continue to frighten me. I'd rather know why I feel that way. Does that make sense?

T: Sure it does. When you're able to attach a meaning to your fear, you then have lost the part of fear that has to do with the unknown. Would you like to use imagery to help you remember?

C: Yes.

T: Would you mind if I prayed first?

C: I need you to pray. I'm scared.

T: Dear Lord, thank you that you are the power above all powers. Thank you that you love Richard beyond our comprehension. Thank you that nothing is hidden from you. Thank you that Richard is your precious child and your blood covers him, myself, and this session. Thank you that you will help him remember what he needs to remember and that you are in charge of his healing. May all the praise and glory go to you. In your holy and precious name, amen.

C: Amen. [proceeds to take off shoes, position himself comfortably on the couch and go through his relaxation technique]

T: Let me know when you are in the fragment of memory and when Jesus is beside you.

C: I'm there.

T: How do you feel?

C: Safe. Jesus is beside me.[4]

T: Tell me what you see.

C: I'm in our basement with Dad and [names three other men, including a priest]. It's dark except for some candles burning on the table. They're talking in a funny language and raising their hands and waving them around. I think they are worshiping the devil.

T: What makes you think they are worshiping the devil?

C: I don't know, they just are. [pause] Oh no!

T: What do you see?

C: There is a big animal's head being pushed at me. It looks like a wild boar, but it can't be. Someone is behind it. I'm falling backward. They are all laughing at me.

T: What are you feeling?

C: I'm scared. I think I've known for awhile that Dad worshiped the devil. I was just too scared to admit it.

T: Yes, it would be very scary to admit, especially if you were given the message as a child not to tell. What do you think you are afraid of?

C: That they will come and get me.

T: Who will come and get you?

C: The ones who worship the devil. But I guess they can't. Dad is dead and so are two of the others.

T: Richard, it's important to remember that there is safety in letting out the secret. When other people know, there is less of a chance that a cult can get away with something. Also, every day we can ask God to keep you safe.

C: [pause] You know, I think I know what happened to our animals that disappeared. Dad said they ran away, but I always knew he was lying.

T: What do you think happened?

C: I think they were sacrificed. [crying] Some were our pets.

T: That must have hurt to have lost your pets. It must have felt horrible if you thought they were sacrificed.

C: It did. [pause] This sure helps me understand why I thought that it was a waste of time to go to church. I never liked that priest. I wonder where he is now. I think I'm still scared of him.

T: Well, it's easy to see why you feel that way. He and others were trying very hard to frighten you.

This began the memories of satanic worship and involvement in the ritual abuse. Most came in fragments that took several sessions to piece together. We used imagery and the Lord being beside Richard as he remembered.

C: I think I'm remembering something that can't be true.

T: Does it feel like it's not true?

C: No, it seems like a memory. It is just very weird. I've been getting pieces of it every night when I lie down. I'd like to pray and go to the memory. This is too weird.

T: You sound like you're eager to put this puzzle together, but you are questioning how valid the memory will be.

C: Yes, but if it's true I shouldn't be here. But I am, so maybe there is more to it.

[After prayer and the relaxation technique, Richard begins.]

C: I'm lying in a box in the ground. Dad, the priest, and another man are standing over me talking in that stupid language. They are talking to the devil again. I'm scared. Jesus is standing there, too, and he is *very* angry with them. He doesn't want them to do this. I know I'm not to say anything or they will hurt me. Dad closed the lid on the box and I hear them shovel dirt over the top of me. I am very scared. [crying] I feel very unloved. I am afraid I'll never get out of the box. I'm going to die in here. The men are laughing. They leave. I feel calmer. I remember thinking I can't get out so I might as well go to sleep, and I did. Do you think that was God?

T: Well, it certainly could have been since most people would find that too scary to sleep through.

C: The next thing I remember was waking up and hearing my father's footsteps. I don't know how I knew they were his. Anyway, he shoveled off the dirt and opened the box so I could get out. I was so happy to see him even though he was angry with me.

T: Do you know why he was angry with you?

C: Yes. I wouldn't worship Satan at the meetings every week in our basement.

T: How did you feel about that?

C: I didn't care. I was just very glad to get out of the box. I went home, walked into the house, and forgot it. How could I do that?

T: How old were you in this memory?

C: I was about six or seven years old.

T: I imagine by that time you were very good at disassociating the terrors. That is what helped you survive. Richard, I think it is important that you allow yourself to feel now what you were not allowed to feel then.

C: But what if I stay in those feelings?

T: Well, it will help to remind yourself that your life is different now, that what happened was a long time ago, and that it is never going to happen again. You are safe now. A lot of people care about you and pray for you. Your fiancée helps you understand that your life is different now. I'm available to you. The police officer you've talked to is helping keep track of your case. You have broken contact with those people in your memories. You are making choices to make your life safe and different now.

Richard had made some healthy choices to improve his chances of being safe. He had moved out of the home in which he had been raised. He cut off family ties with those involved in his memories of satanic worship. He gave information to the police and allowed me to keep those lines of communication completely open.

SATANIC RITUALS

Survivors of satanic cults are not only the objects of ritual abuse but are forced to be participants in the abuse of other victims. With multiple-personality cases, there are often satanic alter egos programmed into the victim for the specific purpose of participating in the rituals. Richard's memories of forced involvement have been the latest and most painful to surface. For the sake of continuity, six sessions will be condensed into one dialogue section. By no means does this imply that six sessions healed the pain or eradicated the scars.

C: I'm sorry I forgot my last appointment. When you called I thought it was just because I was so busy that day.

T: Did you realize that there may have been another reason?

C: Not right away. It wasn't until things slowed down that I remembered my flashback from that morning.

T: Are you able to remember it now?

C: Sure, but it's not much. I'm about seven, in a robe in a basement. That's all. I don't feel afraid.

T: What do you feel?

C: Actually, I feel nothing. I guess that doesn't make sense. Every other time I've forgotten my appointment I've been aware I was afraid of what was coming up. This time I can't feel anything.

T: Would it be accurate to say you feel numb?

C: [pause] Yes, it's definitely numb. When you said that, I saw something else. There's a boy lying on a table. [pause] I'm losing this one.

T: Would you like to lie down and try to remember more?

C: Do I have to? Remember more, I mean?

T: No. It's up to you. Memories don't need to be forced. Sometimes they come too fast for your comfort, but we don't need to try to pull them out.

C: I'd like to say good, I'll go home then. [sigh] But I know I'll just keep getting pieces. So I might as well try to put it all together.

[We pray. Richard relaxes, then he begins.]

T: Where are you? And tell me in detail what you see around you.

C: I'm in a basement. I can tell because part of the floor is cement, part is dirt. There's a tiny window high up in the wall. That's also cement. There's black over the window. I'm wearing a robe.

[pause]

T: Can you tell me what's going on?

C: I started to think of some problems at work I need to take care of.

T: Perhaps it was hard remembering yourself in a robe.

C: I'm feeling numb again.

T: Where are you?

C: Back in the basement.

T: Can you see Jesus?

C: Yes, that helps, but I still feel numb.

T: Maybe you need the numbness in order to remember.

[pause]

C: There are candles all around. There's someone lying on a table. A boy, blond, maybe seventeen. He's gagged and tied. He looks at me. He's so scared. [Richard sits straight up and stares at the door.]

T: Can you tell me what's going on for you?

C: I wanted to run out of here.

T: Like you wanted to run out of that basement?

C: [sighing] Yes, but I knew they'd kill me if I tried. [Richard lies down again.]

T: My father and [names five other men]. Just like they were going to kill that boy.

T: Did you know the boy on the table?

C: No, they kidnapped him.

[pause]

T: Can you tell me what you see?

C: They have a knife. They're talking to Satan and waving their arms around.

T: What are you doing?

C: Staring at the floor. There's some dirt there.

T: It sounds as if you were trying very hard not to participate.

C: [sobbing] I didn't want to. I didn't want to. I didn't want to.

T: [allows sobbing to subside somewhat] What didn't you want to do, Richard?

C: Dad put a knife in my hand and made me stab him.

T: He made you stab him?

C: He kept his hands over mine because I tried to drop the knife and he made me stab him. [Richard is now sobbing.]

T: So you tried to drop the knife?

C: Yes, but Dad was very angry. My hands were hurting.

T: Are you hands hurting now?

C: [rubbing his hands] Yes, Dad's squeezing them hard. He wants to make sure I won't drop the knife. Now he's raising my arms. [yelling] Stop that! Stop that! [Richard begins sobbing.]

T: Did you tell your father to stop?

C: No, I couldn't. But I told him in my mind. I'm glad he's dead. I don't know what I'd do to him right now if he were alive.

T: You have a right to be angry with him. He was wrong. He had no right to take you to that basement. He had no right to force you to hold the knife. He was terribly, terribly wrong for forcing you to be there and to do that. He knew that you would be too frightened to resist. He knew that you would be afraid that you would also be killed. But Richard, do you realize that you did try to resist the best way any child could have in that situation?

C: I tried to drop the knife.

T: Yes, you tried to drop the knife and your father wouldn't let you. But there's another way you resisted. Are you able to recognize it?

[pause]

C: [crying] I didn't want to be there. I didn't want to do it. I didn't want that boy to die.

T: Yes, Richard, your father could make your hands move with the force and power of his hands, but he could never make you do it in your heart. He could never make any part of you want to do that. He didn't have the power and control over the inside of you. Richard, you stood up to him on the inside. You resisted with all of your might on the inside. You were just a little boy. It was impossible for you to overpower all those big men and save the boy on the table. Richard, even if you had been an adult, could you have rescued that boy?

C: No. I know I couldn't have, but maybe I should have tried and died, too.

T: It seems that you're feeling guilty for being alive.

C: Yes, but even as I said that I know it doesn't make sense, because I really couldn't have saved that boy. I still feel guilty, though.

T: Perhaps you're viewing the situation from your rational adult mind, and so you're very aware that nothing could have been done. But your feeling level is still back there at seven years old.

C: That makes sense. [pause] But what if I *am* guilty of not doing more or even of what I did do? How can God forgive me?

T: Scripture tells us in 1 John 1:9 that he will forgive all our unrighteousness if we only ask him. It doesn't say everything *but* and then list some things. It says *everything*. Richard, to me you did nothing wrong. You were powerless on the outside and on the inside you didn't participate, but I'm not you and I'm not God. If you feel you want or need to ask forgiveness, then that is the right thing for you to do.

C: I just don't want to be wrong and not ask God to forgive me.

T: I think that's very honorable, Richard. Then all you have to do is ask him. It doesn't matter if you pray silently or aloud or whether you're here in the office or alone, because Christ knows your heart and will answer your prayer.

C: I think I want to do it alone. I'm not sure why.

T: Maybe because it's personal between you and God and you're needing to preserve that intimacy.

C: My sister always taught me that the real Jesus loved me. Sometimes I can feel that and other times I have to remind myself.

T: Richard, most of all Jesus understands that. He knows what you've been through. He knows how much some people tried to confuse you about him. He even knows the part of you that feels you can't trust him because he didn't miraculously rescue you. That's okay because he loves you exactly as you are, no matter what.

Richard was slowly able to finish the details of this satanic sacrifice, even to the point of remembering how this young man was kidnapped. To graphically relate the additional experiences of this particular memory is not the main importance of this chapter. Richard's memories are consistent with those of other survivors. The emphasis here needs to be on the process of healing and the considerations that are necessary in order to assist in that healing.

Denial is a major defense that requires early attention with ritualistic abuse cases. Not only does the client find it difficult to believe the memories, but many times the therapist as well has a hard time hearing and understanding how these atrocities can take place. Denial gives an unreal sense to memories. This, coupled with the client's justifiable reluctance to remember, needs to be addressed. Assurance can be given that these feelings are common when memories are painful. An area to be explored is whether or not the client also has a sense that the memory is valid. This seems to emerge as the details of the experience surface. Working with denial is an ongoing process that is dealt with repeatedly. Richard has a great desire to be emotionally healthy. This enabled him to confront his denial and hesitation, move past it, and go on to full memories.

The affective level of the memories can be overwhelming for the client. While the therapist is to convey empathy, it is important that he or she is not, as well, overwhelmed. Conveying a sense of control and order is useful for the client in realizing that the memory is part of the past. This does not imply that the affect is to be discouraged or diminished. A commonality among these types of clients is that they were not allowed to express their emotions while the abuse was occurring. If they did, then often harsher abuse was incurred. Therefore, having the freedom to express their feelings in the secure environment of therapy is a very realistic need.

A level of safety in the client's life is, as well, required in order to allow the memories to be left in the past. Otherwise the client experiences a sense of ongoing calamity. The previously mentioned steps that Richard took were important and basic to meeting this need. I cannot assure him that he will ever feel completely safe from his past, but we can hope that his sense of safety will continue to increase.

Along with the memories comes an understanding of the origins of issues that formerly were a mystery. Richard had wondered for years why he had questioned whether or not he was a homosexual. He knew that he had never been attracted to males, nor had he ever wished attention from them. It was from his memories of abuse by his father and other men that he learned he was programmed to believe that he was a homosexual. With this knowledge he was then able to work with deprogramming and reprogramming. First he had to recognize that he had been led to believe lies. A child thinks in the concrete mode and believes what he or she is told, especially by authority figures. Reprogramming came with the repetitive reminders, from both myself and himself, that his thoughts and behaviors were entirely heterosexual.

In remembering the past and identifying issues that resulted from the abuse, Richard was then able to relate how these outcomes impacted his present life and situations. Many times his growth was dependent on doing the opposite of his programming. Talking about his memories with myself and his girlfriend was frightening. He had been warned that awful things (such as he had experienced and seen) would happen again if he did this. Yet it was in taking this risk that he was able to begin to develop a trust level and sense of safety. Bad things didn't happen, and the information was not used against him in any way.

Although similar situations may be reported to the therapist by different clients, each person needs to be treated uniquely. We cannot assume that all ritualistically abused clients have the same issues in exactly the same way. They still remain individuals with specific results of their abuse. Some, like Richard, are very active in their own healing. Others do not have this capacity and the process is more difficult for both the client and therapist.

With these types of cases it is easy for the therapist to be inundated not only by the pain that is expressed, but also by the criminal content of what is being remembered. Therefore it is vital that steps be taken to ensure that the therapist maintains a clear perspective. This can be achieved in several ways. The first way is to become as educated as possible through reading books and papers written on the subject, attending seminars and conferences, or obtaining tapes from reputable sources. The Cult Awareness Network can often give direction to sources for this type of information. Another step for the therapist to take is attending a support group with others who deal with ritualistic abuse cases. If none is available, then meet with trusted colleagues to do case studies.

Not only is it wise to keep thorough records, but also to make copies of them and put them in various safe places. At some point a decision may need to be reached about contacting the authorities about the criminal aspects of the memories. This seems especially true if the cult is local. However, then another complication may be added, as in Richard's case, where some police officers were remembered as perpetrators.

There are some people who believe that ritualistic abuse is totally fabricated. On the other end of the spectrum are those who see it everywhere. It is important to maintain a balance. Although it is not everywhere, it certainly does exist. Several years ago in Chicago at the annual International Conference on Multiple Personality and Disassociative Disorders, I was amazed at the hundreds of therapists from around the United States and other countries who were reporting very similar types of cases involving ritual abuse. I wondered how many of those therapists were Christians and were able to rely on God in working with these difficult cases. Personally, knowing that people are praying for my clients and myself brings a sense of peace. Teaching these victims about a true and loving God is done by being an example of Christ, telling truths given us in Scripture and at times showing them where specific verses are found. No one could possibly have all the answers for these people, nor can we truly understand why these things are allowed to happen. Yet God is able to bring a level of healing that is amazing.

Richard is now married and experiencing the usual ups and downs of newly married life. He continues to struggle with trust and other issues. Occasionally a new memory surfaces, but now he has new resources with which to deal with them. He knows his memories can be felt and dealt with, then left in the past. He has a loving wife with whom he is certain he wants to spend the rest of his life. Most of all, he has a relationship with Jesus Christ. Richard is one of the fortunate ones. He will make it. Not all ritualistic abuse victims do.

EDITOR'S COMMENTS

When she submitted the manuscript for this chapter, Lois Motz enclosed a cover letter that contains her own commentary on the case. "I can't say I'm happy with the chapter," she wrote with refreshing honesty. "There are so many more things that need to be covered. Other areas are mentioned only briefly. I chose a fairly simple case because it wouldn't be possible to deal with the multiplicity of ritualistic abuse in one chapter." Fortunately for her readers, writing this chapter has helped stimulate the author to begin a book on this important and relevant topic.

Until that book appears, we have in these pages a fascinating and personally unsettling case of a young man whose brain was hiding memories of sexual abuse, beatings, psychological torture, and even involvement with a murder. The case raises a number of issues that are not discussed elsewhere in this book.

First, Richard's dreams appeared to be significant. Of course, dream interpretation has been part of psychotherapy at least since the time of Freud, but critics have wondered if counselee dreams really mean what some counselors claim. Ms. Motz tends to avoid these controversies by not offering her own interpretations. Like many counselors, however, she recognizes that dreams sometimes reveal hidden memories. The counselor asked about the dream content, and this triggered memories from the past—memories that had long been buried.

Second, notice this emphasis on memories. Victims of trauma often protect themselves by hiding the hurts, but like overripe bananas that are pushed to the back of a cupboard, hidden memories send out foul odors that can make life miserable and rob the victim of peace or joy. Ms. Motz recognizes the importance of providing a safe, supportive environment where these memories can be exposed to conscious awareness, one at a time, like layers being peeled from an onion.

Third, the author apparently uses a couch to help the counselee relax. The use of a couch is rare among counselors today, but in this case the counselee is given some relaxation exercises that enable him to reduce his body tension so he can deal more effectively with the highly traumatic material that is being uncovered. The couch helps him relax.

Fourth, Lois Motz uses some techniques that have been criticized by writers in the anti-psychology movement. For example, the author writes that "Richard began asking Jesus to walk through his memories with him." This proved to be a valuable tool. Usually this was preceded by prayer to help Richard "feel safe in remembering so many horrifying experiences." In passing, you might note that the counselor always asked Richard's permission before she prayed. This shows respect for the counselee, but it also shows the counselor's perspective on the power and importance of prayer.

Some of those who criticize "healing of memories" are concerned lest we are trying to bring Jesus back into our presence, like Saul attempted to make contact with Samuel through the witch at Endor (1 Sam. 28). Saul was condemned for such activities. God had clearly forbidden any contact with mediums, spiritists, or others who attempt to "bring up" the dead or engage in similar practices.

This, however, is not the intent of what the counselor does in this case. As he thinks about his past, the counselee finds comfort and encouragement in recognizing that Jesus is with him as he faces the past traumas of life. Most believers have gone through difficult situations comforted by the knowledge that we have a friend who sticks closer than a brother. Often we are especially aware of his presence in times of need. This in no way implies that we are trying to conjure up his presence in some mystical or manipulative way.

One small, but significant point might be added. "Jesus" is a common name in some parts of the world. We know that demons have names (Mark 5:9), and it is conceivable that Jesus could be one of these names. That kind of Jesus will be of no help to a person who is plagued with memories of demonic activity and Satan worship. It is well to remind ourselves and our clients that we are not simply talking about Jesus. We are considering Jesus Christ, the Son of God who alone is Lord. He alone is the one who brings comfort, freedom from anxiety, and healing as we deal with past traumas.

Fifth, one ethical issue is mentioned almost in passing. Ms. Motz writes: "As the satanic-abuse memories came to the surface, a trusted police officer was brought into the case as a consultant on the criminal aspects." If Richard's memories are accurate, he was present when a murder was committed. In most states, counselors are not granted the privilege of withholding homicide information from authorities. The police officer's involvement can protect both the counselor and the counselee as this sensitive information is uncovered.

Finally, notice the potential relevance of missed appointments and clients who show up late. Freud assumed that all behavior was meaningful and that missed appointments indicated resistance. We could debate about whether or not this is always true, but Richard recognized that he was more inclined to miss appointments or come late when he didn't want to deal with a painful memory from his past.

This case is likely to stir your thinking. It is a good reminder of how past events can have present impact, and how our skills as Christian counselors must be guided by the wisdom, insight, and spiritual protections that come from the Holy Spirit.

CHAPTER TEN

COUNSELING FOR PANIC DISORDER WITH AGORAPHOBIA

Timothy E. Clinton

Editor's note: *What does one do with a massive, 350-pound man who has panic attacks and is afraid to leave the house? This was the case that Timothy Clinton encountered when Bill, the subject of this chapter, came for counseling several years ago.*

Once again, as we have seen before, the counselor expressed difficulty summarizing large and complex amounts of data into a few pages. To help with our understanding, the author presents his case by discussing several categories of treatment instead of giving a sequential account from beginning to end. As you go through the chapter, you will see another variation of cognitive-behavioral therapy but with a strong emphasis on biblical and theological input.

Timothy E. Clinton was born in Pennsylvania and earned a B.S. degree in pastoral ministries and an M.A. in counseling, both from

Liberty University. His Ed.S. and Ed.D. degrees in counseling are from The College of William and Mary in Williamsburg, Virginia. Currently he is president of Light Counseling Associates in Lynchburg, Virginia, associate professor and chairperson of the Counseling and Psychology Departments at Liberty University, and associate dean of the Liberty School of Lifelong Learning. He is a licensed professional counselor and is certified by the National Board of Certified Counselors.

WHEN YOU ARE six-feet nine-inches tall and weigh 350 pounds, you are supposed to be a starting lineman in the National Football League. Most would assume that you are controlling, stable, and certainly not afraid of anything or anybody. If you have ever been around such a large person, it can be very intimidating to say the least. Across from me sat such a man. He was large in size, but broken and virtually paralyzed with fear and anxiety. He reminded me of the Cowardly Lion in *The Wizard of Oz.*

In the sections that follow, the identifying information was changed to protect the client. The chapter includes an introduction to the case with a preliminary diagnosis, an overview of my theoretical orientation, followed by dialogue and discussion. Since I worked with the client for an extended period of time, the case presentation will highlight the most salient therapeutic issues, interaction, and treatment.

Before the initial session, I usually have the client fill out a short nonstandardized Life History questionnaire and/or a Biographical Information Blank. I have found these personal data inventories to be invaluable data collection tools and useful for starting "talk," building rapport, and identifying potential areas of concern. The data is straightforward, including descriptives of family history, health, spiritual life, career, interpersonal relationships, and some personal and general information. It also asks for a short description by the clients as to why they came for counseling and includes statements regarding my commitment to confidentiality, the therapeutic relationship, and to them as clients.

What follows is a brief synopsis of the initially collected identifying information for this case study.

BIOGRAPHICAL AND PERSONAL SOCIAL HISTORY DATA

Bill was a thirty-nine-year-old Caucasian male. He and his wife had been married for just over twenty years. Together, they had one child, a daughter aged nineteen. His wife was previously married and brought to their marriage two daughters (now ages twenty-five and twenty-one). All three children lived outside the home.

The client was born in Washington, D.C., and was raised in a southeastern mid-sized city. He was the fourth of five children in his family, and he is an only son.

His father, who quit school in the ninth grade, was a fairly successful building contractor. His mother graduated from high school and worked at home.

Bill described his early childhood and teen-age years as "normal—just like any family." However, he dropped out of high school at age fifteen. He related this to an accident in which he seriously injured his right foot. Later, he managed to finish his GED in 1975 and earn a certificate in electronics in 1977 from a local community college.

Between his late teen-age years and his early twenties, the client concluded that his father was "alcoholic, financially unstable, mean, and depressed." In April 1975, a tragedy occurred. His father, frustrated and unhappy with life, committed suicide. In the suicide note, the father wrote that he was "sorry" and encouraged his son to seek a country-music singing career. Bill had been playing and singing since his teen-age years.

Bill avidly followed this country-music career. After his father's suicide, he pressed hard and ultimately made his way to Nashville. Unfortunately, financial mismanagement and other poor decisions led to the demise of his young career. This collapse led to complete financial ruin and put a tremendous amount of pressure on his family. So, with nowhere else to go, he moved back home.

He then started a TV/VCR electronic-repair business which he maintains to this day. He describes this type of work as challenging and what he studied for, but lacking creativity. He is also somewhat discontent because he works alone and is "constantly pushed by customers and the impending need for money to go on." Some of his hobbies and interests include music, reading, and television. Interestingly, he does view himself as social and enjoys others who are friendly and honest. He gets angry and frustrated with those who tend to be quiet and manipulative. A lack of structure, states of anxiety, and depression make him feel very uncomfortable. Additionally, he stressed that he hates the thought of being alone or without family.

Bill and his wife are members of a small, local Baptist church and attend regularly. He describes his relationship to God as "fair" and claims that he is a Christian and prays daily.

Relevant Medical History

At the onset of counseling, the client described his health condition as "fair." Bill did identify that he had some back problems and had received chiropractic care. Further, he claimed to be troubled by "nervousness" (i.e., trouble sleeping, upset stomach, jittery feelings, heart racing at times, and some shortness of breath). He had not received any medical treatment, nor was he taking any medication. No other physical concerns were initially identified by the client.

PRESENTING PROBLEM

Bill came for counseling because he was experiencing extreme periods of fear and anxiety in his daily life. At times, this became so intense that he felt he was having severe "panic attacks."

Describing these attacks he wrote, "At times I feel as if I am going to pass out or die." During the three months prior to counseling, these sudden attacks would get so severe that he was afraid to leave home without his wife. It even got to the point that he would not permit her to leave him alone at home. As he later realized, this was causing serious marital strain, was hindering his business, and left him feeling like a failure. At times he felt very guilty and was extremely frustrated because he could not deal with the stress. On the form he wrote, "Please help me ease my mind, relax, and bring some stability to my personal life, job, and family."

Based on the personal data inventories, I attempt to establish issues that I think are necessary to pursue during the initial sessions. I identified the following issues specific to this case:

- Severity and frequency of the panic attacks
- Father's suicide

- Thought life
- Beliefs about himself and life
- Spiritual depth
- Weight and health issues
- Business/finances

DIAGNOSIS

While I am not fond of diagnostic classification, I do practice this for several reasons: communicating with other professionals, reviewing related literature concerning the diagnosis, considering issues for planning treatment, and of course, meeting reimbursement requirements for third-party payments.

After it was established that an organic factor did not initiate and maintain the disorder, the following preliminary diagnosis was made:

DSM-III-R[1]
Axis I –   300.21 Panic disorder with agoraphobia (severe)
Axis II –   V71.09 No diagnosis
Axis III –   Allergies, chronic back pain
Axis IV –   Psychosocial stressors: financial, marital strain with loss of
             contact with friends; career change
Axis V –   Current GAF: 51
             Highest GAF past year: 65

COUNSELOR ORIENTATION

I believe one's theoretical perspective determines what is looked for and what is seen in therapy. It also determines the focus and course of therapy. My primary approach to counseling is cognitive-behavioral. Much of this is due to the fact that I view therapy as a learning experience. However, over the last few years, I have developed a more systematic, eclectic approach to counseling as exemplified by theorists such as A. Lazarus in his book, *The Practice of Multimodal Therapy* and Allen Ivey's *Developmental Therapy*.[2]

I believe there are a multiplicity of factors like health, family, and culture that can contribute to the etiology, continuation, and treatment of a problem issue or disorder. Therefore, my selection of techniques, while primarily cognitive-behavioral, are drawn from a number of theoretical orientations that appear to be case related and appropriate. However, I do believe all principles and techniques should be consistent with Scripture.

As a therapist, I continually attempt to give attention to each influencing factor as it is related to the counseling relationship. However, I view personal accountability and responsibility ultimately at the heart of each matter. Hence, my intent is twofold: to move the client to a place where he or she makes sound, informed, responsible decisions, and to help the client learn more appropriate and Christ-honoring thoughts, feelings, and actions. To clarify this, let me provide a quick scenario. An adult who was sexually abused by his or her father as a child is not to blame for what has happened, even though the consequences often are quite tragic. However, if that past experience continues to cause personal distress and disability, the client then owns the responsibility to work through it.

Most important, I believe that Christian counselors who claim to be offering professional *Christian* therapy should practice what they claim to believe. If we believe that the greatest need of human beings is restoration of a relationship with God through Christ, and that God is sovereign, if we believe in the truths and promises of Scripture and in the power and guidance of the Holy Spirit, then these and similar beliefs should be the foundation and catalyst of the therapeutic effort. If we really believe these issues and offer a Christian-counseling service to clients then our beliefs should influence what we do!

I certainly do not view this as an issue of imposition. This is, rather, a reasoned and professional presentation of God's message of hope, meaning, and truth and probably what the client expects when he or she solicits our professional Christian services.

Of course, we cannot own the ultimate responsibility for client change. But we do own the responsibility for providing the opportunity for change. What a resource God can be in this process!

Some may be thinking, *He must pound his clients with Scripture, and be really imposing in his therapy. He must not be given to the application of therapeutic knowledge and skill.* That is not my style or intent at all. Rather, I believe every therapist has a theoretical orientation that drives the course and focus of therapy. Hence, every therapist must deal with the issues of truth, the nature of man, and pathology.

I am committed to a foundation of biblical truth that undergirds and infiltrates my holistic perspective for understanding the nature of human beings. Additionally, I agree that neglecting or not giving attention to all the influencing factors of a disorder and the means to help resolve these compounding issues is to do a complete disservice to the client. If I believe that persons, situations, and disorders are unique to each client, family, or group, then I must tailor treatment to these specific needs. As a result, I am also very reliant on sound empirical investigation of populations, situations, disorders, treatment methodologies, and other related therapeutic issues. In my view, if I have my foundation of truth, then empirical investigation is not going to undermine my position and efforts, but rather these will help clarify and facilitate the therapeutic effort.

I believe in the professional counseling context, I am there for and with my client. I am to hear before I speak. Such hearing demands extensive training in listening skills, and other means and measures for information gathering. This, in addition to further therapeutic knowledge and skill leads to problem clarification, goal development, and effective treatment strategies culminating (hopefully) in problem resolution. Once again, this effort is rooted in the authority of Scripture and in my beliefs, knowledge, and understanding regarding the multifaceted factors that influence human behavior. I think D. Johns Lee articulated this well. He stated, "The change process and the counselor's role in a theory is rooted in anthropological assumptions. Beliefs about a person's capabilities, motivating forces, or the etiology of their condition (affect, thought and behavior) necessarily precede mechanisms and parameters of change."[3]

CASE PRESENTATION AND DISCUSSION

During the initial three sessions, I devote a lot of my energy to the assessment process. I believe that it is important to work toward a clear knowledge and understanding of a person's thoughts and beliefs surrounding the problem issue and life in general. This, in essence, drives my counseling. However, in this effort, as stated before, I also attempt to be cognizant of contributing or linking factors to the problem issue. I believe a problem rarely is caused by only one contributing factor. Hence, it is not likely that a single, focused treatment program will work.

The following excerpts are drawn primarily from the first three sessions with Bill. We agreed to meet for ten hourly sessions to accomplish our goals. At the completion of the ten sessions, we also agreed to set aside some time for review and evaluation of our progress.

As I begin, let me stress that I believe a positive, client-centered climate is an important element of the counseling relationship.

The following four areas of concern will be presented: neuro-physiological factors, cognitive issues, family relations, and the issues of suicide, financial/business concerns, and faith and practice.

Neuro-Physiological Factors

Bill's characteristics can often be the result of or resemble a physiological problem such as hyper-thyroidism or caffeine intoxication. Hence, there was an obvious need to consider neuro-physiological factors.

T: Bill, I'm concerned about those panic attacks you wrote about and briefly mentioned. Tell me a little more about what exactly is happening when you are having one.

C: Well, they are very difficult for me to describe. I don't know—something just comes over me and I begin to totally lose it.

T: Okay—help me this way. Sit back for a moment and I want you to sort of walk me through what's happening to you physically. For example, you wrote that you had "shortness of breath." If it gets difficult, let me know.

C: [sits back and takes a breath] When it really comes on, I have trouble breathing. I just can't seem to get air. I start feeling like I'm choking. I sort of feel numb all over, and my chest gets tight. Sometimes I really feel like I'm going to faint. At times, I get the shakes. I almost feel paralyzed.

Let me tell ya, I was scared to death to come here for fear I would have one on the way or while I was in session.

T: Are you feeling okay now?

C: Yes.

T: How did you get here?

C: My wife brought me. She is waiting in the car. She didn't want to come in.

T: Let her know she is more than welcome to come in and stay in the lobby. Bill, how often are you having the chest pains and discomfort?

C: Not too often. It usually comes and goes with the attacks.

T: Okay. How frequently do you have these attacks? I hate to keep hitting you with questions, but I'm just trying to understand what's going on a little better.

C: That's no problem. Well, when they first started [about four months prior] it was maybe once every two weeks—but now I have one almost every day. I really hate this stuff—can you believe I'm this big and I'm virtually overwhelmed by everything?

T: Bill, that's why we're here together.

[some additional small talk]

T: Bill, who is your physician?

C: Dr. Sarkis

T: Good, he has an excellent reputation, and I have found him to be an excellent physician. Bill, when was the last time you had a physical, a complete physical exam?

T: I guess a few years ago.

T: Did he give you a clean bill of health?

C: Basically he did—but I guess it really wasn't too extensive a physical. I just went in to see him for some stomach trouble.

T: Okay, I'd really like for you to get an appointment to see him. This way we both can know for sure as much as possible about how you're doing physically and maybe a little more about these panic attacks. . . . Any number of things can contribute to the anxiety, and I want us to know for sure what we're up against.

C: I think you're right. I've been wanting to do it, so I guess I will.

T: Great, I want you to be sure and describe how and what you are feeling physically, especially when you are having these panic attacks.

Again, my primary reason for sending him to the physician was because anxiety disorders can resemble other physiological problems.

Bill went to the physician for a physical within a week. The results indicated a variety of previously unknown allergies. These included ingredients in some of the foods he was eating and being allergic to dust. Interestingly, he was working out of his basement, which was quite dirty. One of the exercises I had him and his wife do was to clean his work environment and arrange it into a business place. The doctor also helped educate Bill on how to control these allergies and put him on a special program for weight loss and control.

The doctor prescribed a mild dose of Valium for the client to take, especially when he felt overwhelmed with fear and anxiety. While I am at times skeptical of the use of drugs in therapy, I do value carefully monitored psychopharmocological intervention for the treatment of various disorders as an aid in therapy. The attacks were quite frequent and severe, and Bill needed relief. I was encouraged by the client's position on taking medication. He was very reluctant to take the medication, but decided he would do so until he was able to manage the anxiety. The Valium did seem to help him.

The doctor's visit was relieving to Bill. He later told me that he was quite fearful something was wrong with him physically and that his mind was just racing about it. The medical report helped him to know a little about what was going on.

COGNITIVE ISSUES

As we continued, it became quite apparent that Bill had developed several cognitive distortions that were influencing his behavior. Much of his current fear, anxiety, and subsequent panic attacks revolved around thoughts of being a failure in his life pursuits.

C: Tim, I just seem to be a failure at everything I touch . . . Probably if you really knew me and what goes on in my mind you would . . . [with a nervous, fearful look in his eye—afraid he might say something stupid or that I may think he was crazy or something, I commented.]

T: Bill, I know that sitting there and having to become vulnerable is difficult . . . Let me say I am pleased and impressed with what you've done so far. A lot of people don't have the courage to go out and try to do something about the problems they struggle with. You have, and I believe you have done the right thing. We'll go through this together.

C: Yeah—you're right, I'm glad I'm here. Tim, I have always worked so hard.

We went on to discuss his country-music career, financial situation, family, friends, and weight. His theme was: "You see, I really have blown it and I'm probably going to wind up like my father." Some key statements he gave were:

- I almost made it to the big time and just blew it—lost it all.
- I can't meet the bills anymore . . . at times I get into arguments with customers. The pressure is terrible.
- My wife and I are at each other's throats every day. I know I'm putting too much pressure on her.
- I don't spend time with my friends anymore. Since I became a Christian, I dropped a lot of them and stopped playing my guitar. I was told that it [playing] wasn't pleasing to the Lord.
- My weight is out of control. I need to lose some—a lot. You won't believe it, but I used to be lean and trim. I hate being like this.

Bill and I spent time working through his thoughts and beliefs. Persons who are agoraphobic tend to have more of an irrational and sinful belief system than those with more generalized anxiety. Some of the lies Bill was telling himself included:

- I'm okay if I succeed.
- Being a failure is a result of failing.
- Things are supposed to go the way I want.
- I must have everyone's love and approval.
- If I avoid my problems they will go away.
- God's love is conditional.
- God's love can be earned.
- God could never use me.
- God hates sin and the sinner.

During the remaining sessions, we spent time challenging and disputing each of these lies. I also had him reading and processing related material. Some material he found especially helpful included *Telling Yourself the Truth* by W. Backus, *The Search for Significance* by Robert McGee, and *More Help for Your Nerves* by Clara Weeks.[4] This bibliotherapy was very helpful and really challenged his thought life. We also spent time on the "flow" of the anxiety.

C: I guess usually what happens when I feel it come on is that I am feeling pressured by something or start thinking how out of control everything is. The next thing you know, I see myself getting into all kinds of crazy situations and doing dumb things. My mind really goes on me.

T: What do you see yourself doing?

C: I don't know, just dumb stuff like *I want to smash the TV in front of me,* to *Everyone else is crazy and they're plotting against me,* or *I'm going to be just like my dad.* It's just so crazy.

T: What do you think you are telling yourself when you are struggling with this?

C: I don't understand what you mean.

T: Describe how or what you are thinking about, Bill, when you are going through this.

C: That maybe I really am crazy, a real failure, and that one day I will snap and go off.

T: Do you think it will happen?

C: No—I hope not. And that's why I am here. I really want to get through this. I care about my future and family.

T: Okay. Finish telling what is happening in this "flow."

C: After my mind gets going, I start feeling funny. That's when my chest starts getting tight, I have problems breathing, my stomach gets messed up. You know what I told you; that stuff scares me to death. It's the worst feeling in all the world.

T: Bill, have you ever noticed any particular times, issues, or persons that sort of bring panic attacks?

C: Lately it's just about anything.

T: Bill, try to sit back and think about some of the times you started having some anxiety and it led to a panic attack. Can you think of any issues around that time? I'm just looking for a few.

Some of the situations that he brought up were:

- Rent due with no money to pay it
- Fights with wife and family
- Frustration with repairs
- Time alone and wondering why everything has happened to him

C: One of the problems I now face is that I am becoming overwhelmed with the fear of having another panic attack.

T: Bill, in working with others who have experienced what you do, I know that the attacks are real and difficult to handle. Let me share two things with you that I have learned about panic attacks. First, having a panic attack is not going to kill you. I think you know that.

C: Yeah, I do.

T: Also, Bill, you can learn to have control over these panic attacks. It will take some work and I need for you to give it your all—but you can overcome these.

T: Let's work on a few things that I think will be of help to you. When you feel like you are getting real anxious or you are going to have an attack, I want you to try the following:

1. Get yourself to a "safe place." Try to lie down if you can and get your breathing under control.

2. Change your focus—I want you to go to your "safe place." [Some imagery work that I explained—an example included lying in bed reading.] Or meditate on some comforting Scripture.

3. Remind yourself that you will be okay, God is in control, that he cares for you and how you are making progress.

4. Relax! Laugh a little. Growl like the lion of the jungle if you want—but maybe not in public, you might scare someone. [He laughed but he did not forget it.]

5. Go back and challenge those thoughts and remind yourself of those new thoughts we practiced to deal with those lies like . . . (sort of a "stress inoculation" process).

- I do a good job in TV repairs.
- I'm not a total failure, even when I blow it.
- God loves me.
- God forgives.
- I must focus on what I do, not how I feel.

Together we also developed a daily schedule that included time for prayer, devotions, work, family, and time for *worry*. This helped take away the continuous negative thought life and exposed how the anxiety and negative thought life was consuming him. The time for worry really helped demystify the anxiety process. Further, we worked on sensible self-talk in light of God's Word and his love for each of us. I also used some thought-stopping, guided imagery, and relaxation techniques to aid the therapy and target the flow of the anxiety.

We spent time practicing and role-playing how to control the panic attacks in the office. Bill started using the techniques at home. This experience helped him understand what was happening. From this, we transitioned to having half of our session in the car going to mutually agreed-upon areas and back. This move from the office and back into the real world took some effort, but we managed. Over the next six months he continued to make gradual progress and began taking carefully planned steps on his own. When we terminated therapy, he was spending time with friends in restaurants, going out speaking, playing his guitar, and singing.

I appreciate the Adlerian emphasis on purposeful and goal-oriented behavior. The client's behavior was designed to meet specific needs in his life. He was closing himself off from external events, situations, and pressures, and demanding the presence of his wife for security, safety, and significance. Furthermore, as he faced threatening stimuli, he would sequentially develop distorted perceptions, which usually led to negative imagery, to negative bodily sensations, and ultimately into intense fear, anxiety, and then the panic attack. Thus, threatening stimuli became associated with the reaction (fear, anxiety) which led to further withdrawal and a stronger felt need for security, safety, and significance. In time, this type of disorder begins to feed on itself.

Between attacks the client was nervous and apprehensive. This condition was the result of his continuous preoccupation with his irrational beliefs and thoughts about himself and his consuming fear of the panic attacks.

In summary, his irrational beliefs and thoughts led to distorted perceptions which in turn resulted in the fear, anxiety panic attacks, and agoraphobia. As a result, he had become insecure, frustrated, guilt-ridden, and powerless to function autonomously interpersonally. As a counselor, I believe that self-understanding is essential for the development of individual autonomy and interpersonal functioning. Throughout the therapy, time was spent on understanding a simplified version of Ellis's A–B–C theory[5] concerning the lies he believed about God, himself, and life. Also, some self-instructional training[6] was used to replace irrational, self-defeating thoughts with challenging and comforting Scripture, and realistic self-statements in light of his personal qualities, abilities, and God's never-ending love, strength, and presence. Further, the client and I spent time "tracking" what was happening, a multimodal therapy exercise. As presented earlier, this helped me "tune in" to the behavioral flow that often led to the panic attacks and I was able to use appropriate interventions to deter these attacks.

I also had Bill start a journal that gave specific attention to his job, marriage, and spiritual life. This permitted him to track the times and issues that precipitated anxiety. In turn this helped him see what was happening each day and enabled him to build a schedule into his life.

FAMILY RELATIONS AND THE ISSUE OF SUICIDE

Although it was not a presenting problem, the issue of suicide became an immediate concern for me in light of the client's present functioning and past history, primarily his father's suicide.

During the first session, shortly after he described the problem and what was happening physically, I moved our focus toward his family background. During this phase of information gathering, I usually start the construction of a genogram. This helps me to systematically and graphically review family history and present functioning. The genogram also helps me understand issues like familial patterns of relationships, values, or medical history, and can be instrumental for identifying critical incidents in the client's life.

T: Bill, I read a little about your family from the intake form. Sounds like you really have a close relationship with your sister, Mary, and your mother.

C: I really appreciate them. They have meant a lot to me during difficult times. Other than my wife and children, they are about the only ones I talk to.

Bill went on to describe them both and their relationship to his wife and grown children. One issue of concern was his mother, who has problems with angina and has Parkinson's disease.

T: Has she been to a doctor for help?

C: Oh, yes. They are watching her closely and she is taking medication for different things. But she really has had some tough days.

T: How is she holding up?

C: She's just a strong woman. She has a lot of faith in God and handles life sort of a day at a time. [Bill went on to describe his relationship with his mother.] That's not to say she doesn't have bad days or doesn't get down. She has her bad times.

T: It sounds like you all are doing everything you can—that's what's important.

I always try to find an area where the client is of value to someone else. Their giving or altruism says something about them as persons. From this we shifted to dialogue about his father.

T: Bill, I read the comments about your dad. That must have been a really difficult thing to go through . . . How did the family handle it?

C: That was pure hell for everyone. [Silence for about a minute] My uncle found him. He shot himself. I spent seventeen of the longest, most difficult hours of my life in a hospital beside him before he died. It was terrible.

T: Were you able to talk to him?

C: No, but he left a note. He said it wasn't any of our faults. . . . He also told me to go on with my country-music career. He must have really been frustrated and miserable with life. I still don't really understand it all. But I guess, who can?

We went on and discussed his father and their relationship at length.

T: With all your pressure and the panic attacks, Bill, have you ever thought about suicide?

[silence]

C: Yes, at times I have thought about it. [silence for about thirty seconds] But I experienced first-hand what happened [to us] as a result of my dad's suicide and will not let that happen to my family and loved ones. I just wouldn't do such a terrible thing to them. But, you know how your mind races and sometimes my mind gets going crazy-like.

T: Have you ever gone as far as developing any plans for suicide?

C: No, I haven't. But sometimes I do wonder if I am going to wind up just like the old man. At least I have thirteen years to go before I reach his age [when he committed suicide].

His external support from and communication with his family, his presence, and desire in initial sessions helped alleviate my concerns about suicide. We did contract that if he ever thought about suicide, he would immediately call me or let someone know. As we continued in therapy, it really wasn't an issue. The last statement by Bill, however, was very significant. It was closely tied to his negative thoughts and feelings about himself. While Bill verbally and nonverbally revealed his thoughts and feelings about his father and the suicide, it was obvious that his father had a powerful influence over him. Their relationship, estranged by his father's alcohol, anger, and depression, was fused and conflictual. It became evident that Bill was partially driven for success because he felt he was supposed to do this for his dad.

Hence, he was telling himself that personal value and worth are based on performance and what others think of you. This concern in particular was carefully challenged throughout the cognitive work.

FINANCIAL/BUSINESS CONCERNS

Financial burdens can be heavy burdens. While I won't present dialogue here, it was necessary to give attention to this area. Because of the increasing anxiety, Bill stopped going out and generating business and he slowed in his regular productivity. This lowered his income substantially. The bills never stopped.

I had Bill and his wife work on a budget. They tightened up some extraneous expenditures and worked hard at keeping the bills paid. It was difficult because he had gotten himself into debt. Each week I also held him accountable for giving attention to his business.

They managed to bring it under some control. To ignore this area would have been a grave mistake. The ability to provide for his family was very important and to let it fail would have reinforced his belief that "I am a failure."

FAITH AND PRACTICE

Clients who have sought a Christian professional and desire a commitment to their faith in counseling deserve to get this. I do not believe that therapy is no more than Scripture reading and prayer. But, on the other hand, Christian resources and techniques such as these should be a part of therapy at least periodically. Religious and spiritual issues should not be passed over, and pastoral/Christian techniques should be used as clinically appropriate.

A major area of concern for this client was his relationship to God. He did not come into therapy shouting this out, but as we progressed, it became increasingly apparent. Bill had accepted Christ as Savior and wanted to live for the Lord. However, he didn't think he could, nor did he think he was good enough.

As a practice, I pray for each client and his or her problem issue in therapy. I have never had a client get upset over this practice. I believe it says something to the client about what I believe. Also, I have found Scripture to be challenging, direct, energizing, and comforting, to say the least. I use God's Word in counseling. I have had situations where a client wanted to challenge or triangle me in the therapeutic relationship, but I don't think the counseling relationship should be a theological battleground. I do believe that Christian resources and techniques like prayer, Scripture, and reliance on the Holy Spirit have a prominent place in Christians counseling.

As we worked through the insecurity, meaninglessness, and rejection Bill faced, it was exciting to see how God moved in his life.

> **T:** Bill, let's quickly go through Psalm 46 and then discuss your assignment. [I had assigned him Psalm 46 and a chapter on anxiety

out of Chuck Swindoll's book, *Three Steps Forward—Two Steps Back.*[7]]

C: That was good. I really enjoyed the homework. What a powerful passage of Scripture.

T: Bill, what did you learn from this passage?

C: I guess most importantly that God is in control and that I can really give myself over to him. He is a *present* help in the time of need!

[We spent some time going over the earlier verses.]

T: Bill, I really like verse 10, where it says, "Be still." In other words, slow down! Relax! Too often, Bill, we try so hard to control everything, we want it to just go our way, we sin. And the truth is that sometimes things don't work out the way we plan, or we blow it, we make mistakes, we sin. But the beauty is that when we give it over to the Lord and when we have to walk face in the wind, when it's difficult, lonely, troublesome, God is still there. He has promised to never leave us or forsake us. He sticks closer than a brother. He forgives us. Remember what we discussed before, regarding Paul saying to Timothy that "God hath not given us the Spirit of fear. . . .

C: "But of love, and power, and of a sound mind." It's tough at times not to have doubt or to really believe Scripture, but I'm learning. I do know that I put God in a box at times. I limit him. And I need to stop. I know I've been wrong and I have asked him for forgiveness and strength. He has been good to me.

T: That's why I want *you* to stay with your homework—I want you to learn to taste his goodness, develop new self-talk, and understand who you are, Bill, and what it really means to be alive in Christ.

We spent a lot of time working through Bill's relationship with God. He stated that while he believed in and loved the Lord, he did not feel close to him. Much of his view here was founded on a lack of confidence in God's love for him and the lack of emphasis Bill put on relating to God. This revealed a God concept very similar to the image he had of his father. Such a concept created a "performance to please" to gain

God's approval. This was contrary to his stated belief system (God is holy and full of love, mercy, grace, forgiveness, and is faithful). He was challenged repeatedly to align his thoughts, feelings, and actions with his belief system and to monitor his actual beliefs and practices.

This type of anxiety is not readily understood in Christian circles. Sometimes persons are told to just "give it over to God," or given some other cliché.

While there may be times to be outrightly confrontive, usually this confrontation only intensifies the feelings of guilt and hopelessness, and thoughts and feelings of worthlessness. It also can signify another personal failure and the doom of God's rejection. Carefully working through this can help a person bring the fear and anxiety back into a proper perspective, work for resolve, get rid of sin, and become more dependent on the Lord.

OUTCOME AND PROGNOSIS

Bill made some significant gains in therapy. However, it was hard work. We did evaluate our efforts and continued in therapy about six months beyond the initial ten sessions. During this time he learned how to control the panic attacks, challenge his self-defeating thoughts, grow spiritually, and stabilize his business. He worked on his family and marital relationships, going out alone, losing weight, and going off the Valium. He and his family began getting involved in an evangelistic and music ministry. Since I last saw him, they have completed two new albums. Today, they travel regularly. Bill really felt called to begin a ministry-preparation program, and he was ordained by his local church recently. Of course he still wrestles with issues in his life, but he feels that God has really ministered to him.

Two years after therapy, Bill sent me a letter:

I don't wish to sum this up by making you think I have arrived to some great plateau. I'm still struggling some. However, Philippians 3:13–14 says, "Brothers, I do not consider myself yet to have taken hold of it. But one thing I do: Forgetting what is behind and straining toward what is ahead. I press on toward the goal to win the prize for which God has called me heavenward in Christ Jesus."

I am reminded of Paul when on three different occasions he asked God to remove the thorn from his flesh. God showed that his light shines more brightly through people when they are at their weakest. God simply said no to Paul's request but added that his grace is sufficient for us.

Maybe my fear and nervous illness was a way for God to get my attention and keep me humble; I don't know. But I do know that through God's Word applied in caring, Christian counseling, plus that aid of good self-help books, I've been able to face up to poor self-talk (most of which were lies from Satan) and an overwhelming fear that I otherwise would not have overcome.

For some people, fear and psychological instability may be a thorn in the flesh that allows God to get their attention and to work through them in special ways. For others, these symptoms are painful realities that often can be alleviated through God's Word, applied in Christian counseling, frequently accompanied by standard methods of therapy. The words of 2 Timothy 1:7 are still relevant. "For God did not give us a spirit of timidity, but a spirit of power, of love and of self-discipline." The old King James Bible says it well. We do not have a "spirit of fear; but of power, and of love, and of a sound mind."

EDITOR'S COMMENTS

While he was working on this chapter, Dr. Clinton and I talked one day and he expressed the opinion that it is unethical for a therapist to label himself or herself as a "Christian counselor" but then to never mention the name of Christ unless the client raises religious issues. This was a challenging thought to me, expressed most clearly in the "counselor orientation" section of this chapter.

Many of us, it seems, claim to be Christian counselors and even advertise that we are Christian, but our counseling differs little from the work of our secular colleagues. Firmly held Christian values and beliefs are likely to influence all that we Christians do, including our counseling, but this case shows that there are times when "religious and spiritual issues should not be passed over." Instead, "pastoral/Christian techniques should be used as clinically appropriate." I wish the author had given a clearer indication of what he means by "pastoral/Christian techniques" (he does mention prayer and homework assignments involving the use of Scripture), and I wish he had indicated how one can tell when something is "clinically appropriate."

Every counselor knows, however, that some aspects of therapy cannot be done in an orchestrated or stereotypical way. Making interventions that are "clinically appropriate" often depends on the therapist's judgment which, in turn, is based on experience. To use an old cliché, some methods might be caught rather than taught. The chapter mentions the Holy Spirit only briefly, but undoubtedly Dr. Clinton would agree that the Spirit's guidance, working through a committed servant of Christ, often is the major determinant of *what* is appropriate and *when* spiritual interventions are best introduced.

This conclusion in no way rules out sound clinical practice and utilization of scientific psychological methods. The author writes that he is "very reliant on sound empirical investigation." My thinking was stimulated by his view that if the Christian has a foundation in biblically based truth, "then empirical investigation is not going to undermine my position and efforts but rather these will help clarify and facilitate the therapeutic effort." Some Christian counselors and their non-Christian colleagues seem to assume that professional excellence and Christian counseling are in opposition to each other. This conflict need not characterize good Christian therapy. When our beliefs and behaviors are rooted in the authority of Scripture, we are free to draw on diverse techniques and to consider "multifaceted factors" provided that these do not violate biblical truth.

In reading this case, I was impressed with the counselor's sensitivity to the anxiety-producing nature of counseling. Bill was prone to anxiety attacks, and near the beginning he mentioned that the thought of counseling made him feel nervous. Had the counselor confronted the client in a threatening way, or had there been no awareness of Bill's nervousness, he surely would have dropped out of therapy after one of the early sessions. As they talked about significant issues, Dr. Clinton kept assuring Bill that he was doing okay. In this way, anxiety-reduction techniques were not only being discussed, they were being introduced and applied as part of the counseling.

Some readers will have noticed the counselor's suggestion that Bill should plan time for worry into his busy schedule. This would seem to be a wise suggestion. As the chapter notes, time for worry takes away the continuous negative thinking and helps to demystify the anxiety process.

If Bill had been told not to worry at all, or if he had been instructed to memorize and start applying Philippians 4:6 ("Do not be anxious about anything. . . ."), he would have been set up for more failure. To tell an anxious person not to worry is likely to have little impact, except, perhaps, to create guilt and more anxiety when the worry reappears. To plan a time for worry gives the client permission to be anxious, at least periodically instead of continually, and creates the mindset that he can get on with other things and leave his anxieties for the worry times.

This is the second case in the book to mention a genogram. For those who are unfamiliar with this tool, you might think of drawing a detailed family tree that can then be discussed with the counselee. This is a procedure that can be interesting for the counselee and most informative for the counselor.

One concluding observation is worth noting. Obesity and anxiety are among the conditions that have a strong physical component. The counselor insisted that Bill get a complete physical examination. This could have led to the detection of any physiological basis for the psychological problems. In this case it helped indirectly with Bill's anxiety because the physician was able to give an assurance that the basic problem was not the result of disease or other biological malfunctioning.

When should a medical consultation be encouraged? Once again, we can raise a cliché that is good guidance for all of Christian counseling: When there's doubt, check it out!

EPILOGUE

Gary R. Collins

The Monday-morning newspaper in our community, and probably in yours, usually has a large sports section. In addition to all the news about weekend athletic events, several columnists add their colorful commentaries on the events, personalities, and emotions connected with the world of sports. These columnists, like many of their readers, can be very good at analyzing what happened in the various games or meets and what the athletic participants should have done differently.

"Monday-morning quarterbacks" are like historians, economists, political candidates, or others who look back on past events, decry the mistakes that were made, and proclaim that *we* would have done better. Hindsight is always clearer than foresight. It is easier to look back and spot mistakes than to avoid similar errors in the midst of a tense and demanding situation.

In reading the preceding chapters, undoubtedly you have seen examples of poor counseling techniques, inappropriate comments, failure to pick up some emotion or important point in an interview, or insensitivity to the counselee's feelings. If we had included an example of your counseling, others would have seen mistakes, as well. No person is immune from error in the midst of a battle. That is true whether the battle is in a war, on a playing field, at a political meeting, or in the quiet of a counseling room. Dedicated people do the best they can, learn from their mistakes, and go on to do better next time. That is what learning and growing are all about.

Hopefully, the preceding chapters have taught us all some lessons about what to do and what not to do in counseling. The authors, brave enough to expose their work to public scrutiny, have shown us the counseling diversity that I mentioned in chapter 1. Some critics will complain because the Bible was used too much in some cases—or not enough. Some may have expected prayer to be more prominent, or less. Perhaps there were methods or interventions with which you disagreed; others may have fit your image of what Christian counseling really should be like.

Christian counseling is not a movement of robots, all doing the same thing in the same way. Counselors and counselees are individuals, with different personalities, different perspectives, and different procedures. We who counsel are not rescuers, saviors, messiahs, or judges. We are not always right, wise, patient, aware of what to do, all-knowing, sinless, or available.

We are, instead, redeemed followers of Jesus Christ, servants of the God of the universe, imperfect men and women who seek to be faithful and to use our divinely given skills to serve and honor the Lord. Committed believers are people of prayer who worship regularly, read the Scriptures consistently, seek to be guided by the Holy Spirit, and are open to correction and help that comes from our colleagues. We strive for counseling excellence and are dedicated to therapeutic competence, even though at times we fail. We learn from Scriptures and at times from one another. When there are differences, we try to resolve these in love and in the spirit of Matthew 18:15–19, instead of resorting to gossip or to a self-righteous condemnation of others.

In the years ahead, we can hope that there will be other books like this one—only better, in part because our techniques will have improved and our understanding will be better. Soon, perhaps, some person will produce another book like this, but a book that is accompanied by video-taped transcripts of what transpires in Christian counseling.

Christian counseling is a growing field, filled with challenges and dis-appointments. As this field continues to grow, let us all be grateful for the opportunity to be people-helpers, consistent in our commitment to counseling excellence, and dedicated believers who serve God by coun-seling others.

BIBLIOGRAPHY

In addition to the works cited in the Notes, some of the chapter authors recommend these books and articles for further reading.

Chapter 3 Cognitive Therapy with a Depressed Client *Mark R. McMinn*

Beck, A. T. 1976. *Cognitive Therapy and the Emotional Disorders*. New York: International Universities Press.
_____ 1988. *Love Is Never Enough*. New York: Harper & Row.
Beck, A. T., G. Emery. 1985. *Anxiety Disorders and Phobias: A Cognitive Perspective*. New York: Basic Books.
Beck, A. T., A. J. Rush, B. F. Shaw, G. Emery. 1979. *Cognitive Therapy of Depression*. New York: Guilford Press.
Burns, D. D. 1980. *Feeling Good*. New York: William Morrow and Company.
McMinn, M. R. *Cognitive Therapy Techniques in Christian Counseling*. 1991. Dallas: Word.
McMinn, M. R., C. J. Lebold. 1989. Collaborative efforts in cognitive therapy with religious clients. *Journal of Psychology and Theology*, 17:101–9.
Meichenbaum, D. 1977. *Cognitive-Behavior Modification: An Integrative Approach*. New York: Plenum Press.

Tan, S. -Y. 1987. Cognitive-behavior therapy: A biblical approach and critique. *Journal of Psychology and Theology,* 15:103–12.

Chapter 9 A Case of Ritualistic Abuse *Lois Motz*

Raschke, Carl. A. *Painted Black.* San Francisco: Harper and Row, 1990.
Johnston, Jerry. *The Edge of Evil.* Dallas: Word, 1989.
Larson, Bob. *Satanism: The Seduction of America's Youth.* Nashville: Thomas Nelson Publishers, 1989.

Other Resources:

Cult Awareness Network
2421 West Pratt Boulevard
Suite 1173
Chicago, Illinois 60645
312–267–7777

Detective Robert Simandl, police consultant
6427 West Irving Park Road
Suite 145
Chicago, Illinois 60634
312–237–5458

Center for Childhood Trauma
555 Wilson Lane
Des Plaines, Illinois 60016
708–635–4100, ext. 118

Chapter 10 Counseling for Panic Disorder with Agoraphobia *Timothy E. Clinton*

Hart, A. *Overcoming Anxiety.* Dallas: Word Publishing, 1986.
Norcross, J. C., ed. *Handbook of Eclectic Psycho Therapy.* New York: Brummer/Mazel, 1986.

Epilogue *Gary R. Collins*

Benner, David G. *Psychotherapy and the Spiritual Quest.* Grand Rapids: Baker, 1988.

Collins, Gary R. *Christian Counseling: A Comprehensive Guide*, rev. ed. Dallas: Word, 1988.

Crabb, Larry. *Inside Out*. Colorado Springs: NavPress, 1988.

Jones, Stanton and Richard Butman. *Modern Psychotherapies: A Comprehensive Christian Appraisal*. Downers Grove, Ill.: InterVarsity, 1991.

Rodiger, Georgiana G. *The Miracle of Therapy: A Layperson's Guide to the Mysteries of Christian Psychology*. Dallas: Word, 1989.

Seamands, David A. *Healing Grace*. Wheaton, Ill.: Victor Books, 1988.

Smith, Darrell. *Integrative Therapy*. Grand Rapids: Baker, 1990.

Tan, Siang-Yang. *Lay Counseling: Equipping Christians for a Helping Ministry*. Grand Rapids: Zondervan, 1991.

Worthington, Everett L., Jr. *Marriage Counseling: A Christian Approach to Counseling Couples*. Downers Grove: InterVarsity, 1989.

NOTES

Chapter 1 What Is Christian Counseling? *Gary R. Collins*

1. In an earlier book, *Helping People Grow* (Santa Ana, Calif.: Vision House, 1980), I attempted to summarize some of the different Christian approaches to counseling and included invited chapters written by Jay Adams, Lawrence Crabb, Howard Clinebell, and others who have contributed to the development of Christian counseling approaches. Since it is now out of print, I have drawn from portions of that book's chapter 17, "The Distinctives of Christian Counseling" in the following paragraphs.

2. William P. Wilson, "A New Structure for Psychiatry," *CMS Journal* 19 (1988): 22.

3. Some professionals make a distinction between counseling and therapy or psychotherapy. Counseling is assumed to be for normally functioning individuals who need help in coping with life problems; therapy is for more seriously disturbed people who require in-depth, often long-term help with their psychological disturbances. In this chapter and in my other writings I do not make this distinction; counseling and therapy are used interchangeably. Others who write chapters in this book may hold different views; but I agree with Patterson, who concluded that "there are no essential differences between counseling and psychotherapy in the nature of the relationship, in the process, in the methods or techniques, in goals or outcomes (broadly conceived), or even in the kinds of clients involved" (C. H. Patterson, *Theories of*

Counseling and Psychotherapy, 4th ed., New York: Harper & Row, 1986, *xix.*)

4. Professional organizations include the Christian Association for Psychological Studies and the American Association of Christian Counselors; training programs include master's level courses at numerous institutions and doctoral level education at Fuller Graduate School of Psychology and Rosemead School of Psychology. Publications include the *Journal of Psychology and Theology* and the *Journal of Psychology and Christianity.* For information about one group of residential treatment facilities write Rapha, 8876 Gulf Freeway, Suite 340, Houston, Texas 77017. Congresses have been held in the United States, Germany, and Australia. A Southeast Asia congress is in preparation. The next North American congress is Atlanta '92, to be held in Atlanta, Georgia, 12–15 November 1992.

5. Ray S. Anderson, *Christians Who Counsel* (Grand Rapids, Mich.: Zondervan, 1990); David G. Benner, *Psychotherapy and the Spiritual Quest* (Grand Rapids, Mich.: Baker, 1988); Roger F. Hurding, *The Tree of Healing: Psychological and Biblical Foundations for Counseling and Pastoral Care* (Grand Rapids, Mich.: Zondervan, 1985); Georgiana G. Rodiger, *The Miracle of Therapy: A Layperson's Guide to the Mysteries of Christian Psychology* (Dallas: Word, 1989); Darrell Smith, *Integrative Therapy* (Grand Rapids: Baker, 1990); Samuel Southard, *Theology and Therapy: The Wisdom of God in a Context of Friendship* (Dallas: Word 1989); and Everett L. Worthington, Jr., *Marriage Counseling: A Christian Approach to Counseling Couples* (Downers Grove, Ill.: InterVarsity, 1989). Perhaps I should also mention my book, *Christian Counseling: A Comprehensive Guide,* rev. ed. (Dallas: Word, 1988).

6. Alan A. Nelson, "What is Christian Psychiatry?" *CMS Journal* 19 (1988): 8.

7. From the concluding paragraph in Benner's article on "Christian Counseling and Psychotherapy," in David G. Benner, ed., *Baker Encyclopedia of Psychology* (Grand Rapids, Mich.: Baker, 1985), 158–64.

8. William A. Clebsch and Charles R. Jaekle, *Pastoral Care in Historical Perspective* (Englewood Cliffs, N.J.: Prentice-Hall, 1964), 4. Emphasis is in the original.

9. Once again in the following paragraphs, I will draw heavily on the previously mentioned chapter from *Helping People Grow.* The following could be viewed as an expansion and update of the earlier work. I also discussed this briefly on pages 18 and 19 of my book *Christian Counseling: A Comprehensive Guide,* rev. ed. (Dallas: Word, 1988).

10. This view is stated succinctly in an excellent and thought-provoking chapter titled "Values and the Helping Relationship," in Gerald Corey, Marianne Schneider Corey, and Patrick Callanan, *Issues and Ethics in the Helping Professions*, 3rd ed. (Pacific Grove, Calif.: Brooks/Cole, 1988). See also A. C. Tjelt-veit, "The Ethics of Value Conversion in Psychotherapy: Appropriate and Inappropriate Therapist Influence on Client Values," in *Clinical Psychology Review* 6 (9186): 515–37; and A. Keller and S. R. Heyman, eds., *Innovations in Clinical Practice: A Source Book* 8 (1989): 405–15.

11. In a recent study using college students, researchers discovered that most people assume that therapists will be competent. Apart from "very religious clients," most don't care one way or another whether the counselor is Christian. See Steven C. Wyatt and Ray W. Johnson, "The Influence of Counselors' Religious Values on Clients' Perceptions of the Counselor," *Journal of Psychology and Theology* 18 (1990): 158–65. This article also gives a brief history of the debate surrounding the place of values in counseling. See also E. L. Worthington, Jr., "Understanding the Values of Religious Clients: A Model and Its Application to Counseling," *Journal of Counseling Psychology* 35 (1988): 166–74.

12. William P. Wilson, "A New Structure for Psychiatry," *CMS Journal* 19 (1988): 22–25.

13. Gary R. Collins, *The Rebuilding of Psychology* (Wheaton, Ill.: Tyndale, 1977).

14. Smith, *Integrative Therapy*, 46.

15. Ibid., 47.

16. Jay Adams, *Competent to Counsel* (Grand Rapids, Mich.: Baker, 1970), 70.

17. For the reader who is interested in understanding the diversities of theology, see Clark H. Pinnock, *Tracking the Maze: Finding Our Way Through Modern Theology from an Evangelical Perspective* (San Francisco: Harper & Row, 1990).

18. Carl R. Rogers, "The Necessary and Sufficient Conditions of Therapeutic Personality Change," *Journal of Consulting Psychology* 21 (1957): 95–103.

19. Jay E. Adams, *How to Help People Change* (Grand Rapids, Mich.: Zondervan, 1986), vii.

20. Linda Seligman, *Selecting Effective Treatments: A Comprehensive, Systematic Guide to Treating Adult Mental Disorders* (San Francisco: Jossey-Bass, 1990), 49. For a more complete review of research on

counselor characteristics, see Sol L. Garfield and Allen E. Bergin, eds., *Handbook of Psychotherapy and Behavior Change: An Empirical Analysis,* 3d ed. (New York: Wiley, 1986). See also Harvey R. Freeman, "Influence of Client and Counselor Characteristics on Satisfaction with Counseling Services," *Journal of Mental Health Counseling* 11 (1989): 375–83.

21. Anderson, *Christians Who Counsel,* 17. The following paragraphs on competence are adapted from pages 20–22.

22. See, for example, *The Family Therapy Networker* 15, no. 5 (September-October 1990). The theme of the issue is "Psychotherapy and Spirituality: Rethinking Age Old Questions." A more balanced treatment is presented in *The Counseling Psychologist* 17, no. 4 (October 1989), with the theme "Religious Faith Across the Life Span."

23. Nelson, "What Is Christian Psychiatry?" 10.

24. See, for example, M. L. Smith and G. V. Glass, "Metaanalysis of Psychotherapy Outcome Studies," *American Psychologist* 32 (1977): 752–60.

25. In fairness, it should be noted that many non-Christians would abide by similar guidelines. In a survey of 465 professional psychologists, for example, 61.9 percent agreed that the use of sexual surrogates was unethical; 87.5 percent never or almost never have used such a practice. See Kenneth S. Pope, Barbara G. Tabachnick, and Patricia Keith-Spiegel, "The Beliefs and Behaviors of Psychologists as Therapists," *American Psychologist* 42 (1987): 993–1006.

26. To get an overview of the criticisms and to consider answers to some of the issues, see Gary R. Collins, *Can You Trust Psychology?* (Downers Grove, Ill.: InterVarsity, 1988) or Mark McMinn and James Foster, *Christians in the Crossfire* (Newberg, Ore.: Barclay, 1990).

27. James M. Siwy and Carol E. Smith, "Christian Group Therapy: Sitting with Job," *Journal of Psychology and Theology* 16 (1988): 318–21.

28. This is controversial and there appear to be many extremes and evidences of incompetence in the healing of memories/inner-healing field. For the best discussion, see the works of David Seamands, including *Healing of Memories* (Wheaton, Ill.: Victor, 1985).

29. Everett L. Worthington, Jr., "Religious Faith Across the Life Span: Implications for Counseling and Research," *The Counseling Psychologist* 17 (1989): 555–612.

30. Despite the difficulties, researchers have investigated some of these topics. For example, a literature review of research found that prayer could facilitate ego development and be effective as a therapeutic intervention. See John R. Finney and H. Newton Malony, Jr., "Empirical Studies

of Christian Prayer: A Review of the Literature," *Journal of Psychology and Theology* 13 (1985): 104–15.

31. This was found to be true in a study by E. L. Worthington, Jr., P. S. Dupont, J. T. Berry, and L. A. Duncan, "Christian Therapists' and Clients' Perceptions of Religious Psychotherapy in Private and Agency Settings," *Journal of Psychology and Theology* 16 (1988): 281–293. For a further discussion of religious issues in counseling, see F. J. White, "Spiritual and Religious Issues in Therapy," in David G. Benner, ed., *Baker Encyclopedia of Psychology* (Grand Rapids, Mich.: Baker, 1985), 1110–14.

32. Corey, Corey, and Callanan, *Issues and Ethics*, 67.

Chapter 2 A Case of Sexual Obsessions *Stanton L. Jones*

1. T. Oden, "What Psychologists Can Learn from the Historic Pastoral Care Tradition," a paper presented at the Rech Conference on Christian Graduate Training in Psychology, Lisle, Ill., 27 October 1990.

2. This soliloquy and all others in this chapter are reconstructions from detailed session notes rather than verbatim transcripts. In the transcripts that follow, many details are omitted, and the time frame in which issues were examined is probably compressed. Perhaps most importantly, such reconstructions give ample leeway for me to flatter myself as appearing much more insightful, articulate, and generally wiser than I was then or am now. The reconstructed "transcripts" are offered not to show specific verbal or behavioral techniques, but to communicate the general flow of a portion of the session and the general way in which I tried to handle certain issues.

3. See S. Jones and R. Butman, *Modern Psychotherapies: A Comprehensive Christian Appraisal* (Downers Grove, Ill.: InterVarsity, 1991), chapter 1.

4. See Jones and Butman, *Modern Psychotherapies: A Comprehensive Christian Appraisal*, chapter 15, for a discussion of different approaches to eclecticism.

5. Ibid., chapters 6–8.

6. J. Adams, *More Than Redemption: A Theology of Christian Counseling* (Phillipsburg, N.J.: Presbyterian and Reformed, 1979).

7. E. Sturgis, "Obsessional and Compulsive Disorders," in H. Adams and P. Sutker, eds., *Comprehensive Handbook of Psychopathology* (New York: Plenum, 1984), 251–78; and E. Sturgis and V. Meyer, "Obsessive-Compulsive Disorder," in S. Turner, K. Calhoun, and H. Adams, eds., *Handbook of Clinical Behavior Therapy* (New York: Wiley, 1980), 143–75.

8. W. Masters and V. Johnson, *Human Sexual Inadequacy* (Boston: Little, Brown, 1970).

9. E. Wheat, *Intended for Pleasure* (Old Tappan, N.J.: Revell, 1981).

10. Clifford Penner and Joyce Penner, *The Gift of Sex* (Dallas: Word, 1990).

11. I. Marks, *Cure and Care of Neuroses: Theory and Practice of Behavioral Psychotherapy* (New York: John Wiley & Sons, 1981).

12. D. Barlow, *Anxiety and Its Disorders: The Nature and Treatment of Anxiety and Panic* (New York: Guilford, 1988).

13. Marks, *Cure and Care of Neuroses*.

14. D. Wegner, *White Bears and Other Unwanted Thoughts: Suppression, Obsession, and the Psychology of Mental Control* (New York: Viking, 1990).

15. Penner and Penner, *The Gift of Sex;* and S. Jones, "Sexuality," in D. Benner, ed., *Baker Encyclopedia of Psychology* (Grand Rapids, Mich.: Baker, 1985), 1064–72.

16. See Penner and Penner, *The Gift of Sex,* for a full description of these exercises.

17. For a very readable and edifying presentation of Kierkegaard's psychological thought, see C. Evans, *Søren Kierkegaard's Christian Psychology* (Grand Rapids, Mich.: Zondervan, 1990).

18. Jones and Butman, *Modern Psychotherapies: A Comprehensive Christian Appraisal*.

19. Evans, *Søren Kierkegaard's Christian Psychology*.

Chapter 4 Marriage Counseling with Christian Couples
Everett L. Worthington, Jr.

1. E. L. Worthington, Jr., *Marriage Counseling: A Christian Approach to Counseling Couples* (Downers Grove, Ill.: InterVarsity Press, 1989).

2. M. T. Schaefer and D. H. Olson, "Assessing Intimacy: The PAIR Inventory," *Journal of Marital and Family Therapy* 7 (1981): 47–60.

3. R. B. Stuart and B. Jacobson, *Couples Pre-counseling Inventory,* rev. ed. (Champaign, Ill.: Research Press, 1987).

4. S. R. H. Beach, E. E. Sandeen, and K. D. O'Leary, *Depression in Marriage: A Model for Etiology and Treatment* (New York: Guilford, 1990).

5. My thanks to Mary Graham, William Hoyt, Susan Nicholson, Jeanne Possenti, Melissa Rose, Eric Walter, and Paris Williams, who

helped make the videotape from which the transcript is taken. The videotape, complete transcripts, and supplementary materials are available from Box 2018, 800 West Franklin Street, Richmond, Va. 23284–2018 for a small fee to cover expenses.

6. *Diagnostic and Statistical Manual of Mental Disorders,* 3d. ed., rev. (Washington, D.C.: American Psychiatric Association, 1987), 309.28.

7. R. Fisher and W. Ury, *Getting to Yes: Negotiating Agreement Without Giving In* (New York: Penguin, 1981).

8. For a fuller description of forgiveness within marriage, see Worthington, E. L., Jr., and F. A. DiBlasio, "Promoting Mutual Forgiveness within the Fractured Relationship," *Psychotherapy* 27 (1990): 219–23.

Chapter 5 Counseling Another Counselor *David E. Carlson*

1. For a fuller description and illustration of these questions, see David E. Carlson, *Counseling and Self-Esteem* (Dallas: Word, 1988), 56–61.

2. For a definition and description of the sensory process, see Carlson, *Counseling and Self-Esteem,* 95–125.

3. Erik H. Erikson, *Childhood and Society* (New York: Norton, 1986); and Erik H. Erikson, *Identity and the Life Cycle* (New York: Norton, 1968).

4. Carlson, 155–6, 185–86. See also Jean Illsley Clarke, *Self-Esteem: A Family Affair* (Minneapolis: Winston, 1978) for additional permission statements.

5. For a popular description of Winnicott, see Harville Hendrix, *Getting the Love You Want* (New York: Henry Holt, 1988). See also Alice Miller, *Prisoners of Childhood: The Drama of the Gifted Child and the Search for the True Self* (New York: Basic Books, Inc., 1981); and D. W. Winnicott, *Home Is Where We Start From* (New York: Norton, 1986).

6. Hendrix, *Getting the Love You Want.*

7. Rokelle Lerner, *Boundaries for Codependents* (Center City, Minn.: Hazelden, 1988).

8. Carlson, *Counseling and Self-Esteem,* 171–2.

9. Hendrix, *Getting the Love You Want,* 19–28.

10. David E. Carlson, "Jesus Style of Relating: The Search for a Biblical View of Counseling," *Journal of Psychology and Theology* 4 (1976): 181–92. See also David E. Carlson, "Relationship Counseling," in Gary Collins, ed., *Helping People Grow* (Santa Ana, Calif.: Vision House, 1980).

Chapter 6 The Use of Hypnotherapy in Counseling a Christian
Robert R. King, Jr.

1. D. Elman, *Hypnotherapy,* originally published as *Findings in Hypnosis* (Los Angeles: Westwood Publishing Co., 1964).
2. Ibid.
3. L. Wallas, *Stories for the Third Ear* (New York: W. W. Norton & Co., 1985), chapter 13.
4. Ibid.
5. Jay Adams, *Competent to Counsel* (Philipsburg, N.J.: Presbyterian and Reformed, 1970).
6. David Hunt and T. A. McMahon, *The Seduction of Christianity* (Eugene, Ore.: Harvest House, 1985).
7. Martin Bobgan and Deidre Bobgan, *Psychoheresy: The Psychological Seduction of Christianity* (Santa Barbara, Calif.: East Gate Publishers, 1987).
8. Martin Bobgan and Deidre Bobgan, *Hypnosis and the Christian* (Minneapolis: Bethany House Publishers, 1984).
9. W. F. English, "An Integrationist's Critique of and a Challenge to the Bobgans' View of Counseling and Psychotherapy," *Journal of Psychology and Theology* 18 (1990): 228–36.

Chapter 8 An Inpatient Assessment with a Severely Depressed Hospitalized Patient *Robert S. McGee*

1. Robert S. McGee, *The Search for Significance,* 2d. ed. (Houston: Rapha Publishing, 1990).
2. Robert S. McGee, Pat Springle, and Jim Craddock, *Your Parents and You,* rev. ed. (Houston: Rapha Publishing, 1990).
3. Write to Rapha Treatment Centers, 8876 Gulf Freeway, Suite 340, Houston, Texas 77017. The inclusion of this case is not intended to "push" Rapha to the exclusion of other inpatient treatment programs. In preparing for this book, representatives of other Christian inpatient treatment programs were contacted, but none was able to participate.

Chapter 9 A Case of Ritualistic Abuse *Lois Motz*

1. Common reports from survivors include Scripture being quoted while abuse is taking place, and sexual molestation by a man with long hair wearing a long robe who is reported to be Jesus Christ.

2. The genograms in these cases go beyond the general use of names, ages, and offspring. They are modified to include the extended family (as far back as can be remembered); adoption; cause of deaths; years of birth, marriage, divorce, death; line of work; religion and church attended; and substance abuse.

3. The importance is not which relaxation techniques to use, but to assist the client to a state of relaxation to allow full concentration on the memory.

4. Guided imagery is when the therapist suggests the images to the client. This can be details of entire scenarios or singular images. With these clients, I do not set any scenes, nor give a description of Christ. I do this so their memory can remain clear and not be the result of suggestion. I simply ask if they can see Jesus beside them.

Chapter 10 Counseling for Panic Disorder with Agoraphobia
Timothy E. Clinton

1. *Diagnostic and Statistical Manual of Mental Disorders,* 3d. ed., rev. (Washington, D.C.: American Psychiatric Association, 1987).

2. A. A. Lazarus, *The Practice of Multimodal Therapy* (Baltimore: Johns Hopkins University Press, 1989); and A. Ivey, *Developmental Therapy* (San Francisco: Jossey-Bass, 1986).

3. D. Johns Lee, "Philosophy and Counseling: A Metatheoretical Analysis," *Personnel and Guidance Journal* 61 (1983): 523–526.

4. W. Backus and Marie Chapian, *Telling Yourself the Truth* (Minneapolis: Bethany House, 1980); Robert S. McGee, *The Search for Significance* (Houston: Rapha Publishing, 1990); and Clara Weeks, *More Help for Your Nerves* (New York: Bantam Books, 1984).

5. A. Ellis, "Rational-Emotive Therapy," in R. J. Corsini and D. Wedding, eds., *Current Psychotherapies,* 4th ed. (Itasca, Ill.: F. E. Peacock, 1989), 197–238.

6. D. B. Meichenbaum, *Cognitive Behavior Modification: An Integrative Approach* (New York: Plenum, 1977).

7. Charles Swindoll, *Three Steps Forward—Two Steps Back* (New York: Bantam Books, 1980).

INDEX

Abandonment, 34, 47, 101,
  113, 115, 120, 166, 187, 193,
  197
A-B-C therapy, 245
Absalom, 181
Abuse, ritualistic, 209–230
Acceptance, 30, 36, 38, 40,
  42–43
Adams, Jay, 8, 158
Adjustment disorder, 79
Afraid: *See* Fear.
Agoraphobia, 28–29, 231–253
AIDS, counseling and, 164–185
Alcoholism, 77, 168
Allergies, 240
Anderson, Ray, 9
Anger, 12, 29–30, 34, 57, 79,
  86, 95, 101, 112–114, 117,
  122, 148–150, 166, 171–173,
  178, 188, 190–198, 201
Anorexia, 125, 132, 154
Anxiety, 24, 26-28, 39–41, 56–
  57, 67, 69–70, 79, 166–167,

187, 234, 239–240, 244–245,
  252–253 (*See also* Fear)
Assessment, 75–79, 98–99, 166;
  with severely depressed hospitalized patient, 186–208
Automatic thoughts, 48–49, 67–69
Avoidance, 27, 28, 109

B.A.T., 104
Backus, W., 241
Biofeedback, 166, 167
Bobgan, Martin and Deidre, 158
Boundaries for Co-dependents,
  110

Carlson, David, 18, 100–101, 122–
  123
Christ, Jesus, 5, 8, 10–12, 14–16,
  20, 35, 42–43, 65, 96–97, 105–
  106, 116, 121–123, 125, 137,
  155, 157, 160, 167, 170, 183,
  188, 211–212, 217, 222, 228–
  230, 249–250, 255

Clinton, Timothy, E., 18, 230–232, 251–253
Cognitive reframing, 173, 183, 185
Cognitive therapy, 46–71, 74
Cognitive-behavioral therapy, 21–42, 188–189, 235
Commitment, marital, 74, 76–77, 79
Communication, 14, 76, 79–80, 86–87, 179; sexual, 29
Conflict management, 79–87
Core beliefs, 48–49, 68–70
Counseling, Christian: another counselor, 100–123; attributes of, 10, 235–237; compared with secular counseling, 6–8, 96–98; defined, 3–5, 116–117, 123, 156–157; diversity in, 16–17; persons in, 8–10, 17–18; presuppositions of, 5–8; procedures of, 10–14; purpose of, 14–16; techniques of, 10–14,
Counseling and Self-esteem, 112
Counselor: characteristics of, 9–10; feelings of, 8–9, 33, 43–44, 106, 118–121, 154
Couples Pre-counseling Inventory, 75, 79
Cult Awareness Network, 227

Death, 30, 38, 43, 175, 183
Denial, 225–226
Depression, 46, 47, 70, 77, 79, 130–131, 154, 186–209
Desertion: (*See* Abandonment)

Developmental Therapy, 235
Distance, using as emotional metaphor, 87–91, 99
Dream interpretation, 228

Eating disorder, 124–163, 187–188, 190, 204, 206
Effectiveness: of cognitive therapy, 68–69; of counselor, 9, 11; of lifestyle, 9
Ellis, Albert, 16, 245
Elman, David, 136
Empathy, 87–91, 128, 154, 156, 226
Erikson, Eric, 104
Exorcism, 13
Experiential counseling, 105

Faith, 21, 116–117, 248–250
Family therapy, 74, 77
Fear, 20–21, 27–28, 30–31, 33–34, 39, 47, 106, 107, 114, 130, 189, 200–202, 210, 213 (*See also* Anxiety)
Financial burdens, 247–248
Forgiveness, 74, 77, 92–95, 189, 202, 211, 225, 249
Frankl, Victor, 129–130
Freud, Sigmund, 5

Genogram, 212, 245, 253
Getting the Love You Want, 108
Getting to Yes, 80
Grace, 165, 168, 183–184, 185
Great Commission, 6

Healing, 13, 42, 128, 159, 166, 180, 227–229
Hendrix, Harville, 108

Homosexuality, 20, 24, 26, 34,
168–185, 226
Hunt, David, 158
Hypervigilance, 25, 38
Hypnosis: (*See* Hypnotherapy)
Hypnotherapy: 12, 124–163;
and storytelling, 137–139,
141–153, 154–155, 160

Imagery, 12
Insecurity, 21
Insight therapy, 102–106
Interruptions, 98–99
Intimacy, 78–79, 87–91,
216–217
Ivey, Allen, 235

Jones, Stanton, 18, 19–20,
42–44
Joshua intervention, 95–96, 99

Kierkegaard, Søren, 40, 43
King, Robert R., 18, 124–125,
159–160

Lazarus, A., 235
Lee, D. Johns, 237
Lerner, Rokelle, 110
Love: God's, 9, 41, 42, 46, 49,
64, 69, 70, 117, 143, 184,
185, 189, 200, 205, 216, 241,
244–245
Luther, Martin, 165

Marriage counseling, 72–99
Masters and Johnson, 28, 29,
McGee, Robert, 18, 186–187,
207–208, 241
McMinn, Mark R., 18, 45–46,
70–71

Metaphor, 87–91, 152, 155–156
Minnesota Multiphasic Personality Inventory, 166
More Help for Your Nerves, 241
Motz, Lois, 18, 209, 228–229
Multimodal therapy, 127–155,
245
Multiple personality, 211, 227

Obesity, 187–188, 253
Obsessive-compulsive disorder,
28–29, 165

Panic disorder, 28; with agoraphobia, 231–253
Pathology, 7–8
Perception, 98, 167, 244–245
Permission statements, 105
Personal Assessment of Intimacy
in Relationships, 75
Post-traumatic stress disorder, 28
Powell, James L., 18, 164–165,
184–185
Practice of Multimodal Therapy,
235
Prayer, 13, 44, 55, 152–153, 156,
167, 176, 188, 190, 201, 206,
217, 227–228, 228, 252, 255
Procrastination, 101, 109

Rapha treatment, 188–189, 208
Relaxation technique, 212
Rejection, 33–36, 47, 51, 52, 54,
63–64, 68–69, 107–108, 166,
187
Rogers, Carl, 8

Satanic cults, 210, 221
Satanic rituals, 209–229

Search for Significance, 206,
241
Self-control, 20, 25–26, 155,
156
Self-talk, 12, 52, 61–62, 70, 188
Self-worth, 30, 40, 158
Sexual abuse, 197
Shame, 107, 111, 112, 114, 126,
128, 189, 195, 205
Spirituality, 9–10
Storytelling, 137–139, 141–153,
154–155, 159 (See also
Hypotherapy)
Suicide, 234, 247
Swindoll, Chuck, 249

Telling Yourself the Truth, 241
Therapist. See Counselor

Three Steps Forward—Two Steps
Back, 249
Tournier, Paul, 8, 98

Ury and Fisher, 80, 86

Valium, 240, 250
Visualization, 12

Weeks, Clara, 241
Wesley, John, 165
Winnicott's four selves, 105–106
Workaholism, 77
Worthington, Everett, 14, 18, 72–
73, 98–99

Your Parents and You, 207